Publish and be Damned!

The astonishing story of the Daily Mirror

by

Hugh Cudlipp

Revel Barker
Publishing

First published by Andrew Dakers Ltd, September 1953.

This revised edition published by Revel Barker Publishing, November 2009

072 CUD

ISBN: 978-0-9558238-9-3
Revel Barker Publishing 66 Florence Road Brighton BN2 6DJ
United Kingdom
revelbarker@gmail.com

So now the Mirror of the day,
The gift most lavish, and the last,
Lies waiting, Woman, in your way,
To show your face, to hold the past,
To catch each ray the time outpours
And flash it back. The glass is yours.

— ADRIAN ROSS
Dedication in the first issue of
Northcliffe's daily newspaper for
gentlewomen

CONTENTS

FOREWORD: Brought to book, by Revel Barker   9

INTRODUCTION: The Cudlipp classic, by Geoffrey Goodman   13

STOP PRESS: by Hugh Cudlipp   16

1. CAN A WOMAN HATCH EGGS?   18
'Cock-a-doodle-do' – The Mirror *tackles the problem of Higher Production – Elephant Sees editor, drops dead – The Colorado beetle racket – How to assassinate your readers' pets and blow up their houses*

2. NORTHCLIFFE DROPS A BRICK   23
The gentlewomen of England disappoint Alfred Harmsworth – How to make consommé aux nids d'hirondelles *and lose £100,000 – 'So mad a frolic...' – Sacking the women was 'like drowning kittens'*

3. WHEN THE *MIRROR* WAS BORN   28
Life was grim... gay... passionate – Mr Arkas Sapt has a bright idea - then hides himself in a railway cloakroom – The romance of 'The Two Tumpties'

4. THE HURRYING YEARS   33
A shock for an erring mistress – The first Flying Saucers – A scoop at the Royal deathbed – Hannen Swaffer hears a secret in a pub – Bernard Shaw says ' Worth a shilling'

5. ROTHERMERE – FINANCIER   36
1,210,354 readers for £100,000 – Why the Evening Mirror *did not appear – Rothermere's ace of spades – How to build financial empires – The public offer £40,000,000 – His provincial Waterloo – Armistice with the Berrys*

6. ROTHERMERE – JOURNALIST   45
The frugalities of a millionaire – 'Squandermania'- and anti-Socialism – Lord 'Wibbly-Wob's' truce with Fleet Street's other Wicked Uncle – Baldwin the Great and Baldwin the Incompetent – Was the Mirror *guilty?*

7. YOU CAN'T SHOOT THE PROPRIETOR   53
A study in decline – Gentility and reaction – How to ruin a newspaper – The decade when Fleet Street went mad – 'Give 'em a grand piano'

8. THE BART REVOLUTION   58
The metamorphosis of a practical man – How a genius grows up – Breaking the record from Paris to Calais – The 'Bart Legend' – The invention that brought him fame – Rothermere sells his controlling shares

9. BARTHOLOMEW THE BOSS   65
The man who walked alone – Fleet Street's enfant terrible *– 'He won't like that!' – Informal dress for Abdication night – The cult of secrecy – A hush-hush paper for the submariners – The rebirth of* Reveille *– 'Publish and be damned!'*

10. SHOCKING 'EM AND SOCKING 'EM   71
The birth of the sledge-hammer headline – 2,000 readers besiege a cruel man's house – Candour about the Birthday Honours List – A rector's son becomes a tabloid editor – One soft answer from the short-tempered Suffern

11. JANE GIVES ALL!   78
Pip, Squeak and Wilfred pioneer for Jane and Garth – Churchill's gaffe – Secrets of the Mirror *strips – How the cartoonists work – Man, 35, artisan class, wants body like Garth's*

12. AIN'T LOVE GLAND?   89
Brief and punchy, barbed and bright – 'Bossy wife gets husband's goat - he wants a vamp at 40' – Basil D Nicholson passes by – 'Knock, knock. Who's there? It's the younger generation ...' – The ideas that made Britain sit up and Fleet Street take notice

13. THE ABDICATION: SHOULD A NEWSPAPER TELL?   101
The Duke of Windsor gets his facts wrong – Beaverbrook acts for the King in Fleet Street – How the Mirror *broke the conspiracy of silence – The first picture of Mrs Simpson – editor Thomas attacks the 'niminy-piminy press'*

14. THE NEW CRUSADERS   111
The conscience of a popular newspaper – What the Mirror *said about appeasement and* The Times *– Applause for Mr Churchill – 'Seven Souls in Search of Sanctuary'*

15. THE FABULOUS GODFREY WINN   116
The stock-in-trade of a successful young man – 250,000 honeyed words in twelve months – How to make friends with women and influence editors – Winn at work – What he saw in Rio makes his readers blush

16. CLEAN AND CLEVER   121
The unpopularity of success – The Express *scents battle and the* Daily Sketch *swoons – Lord Kemsley's tut-tut campaign boosts the* Mirror *– What happened to Barbara Ann Scott's briefs – The tale of a bull*

17. BEHOLD – THE READER!   126
The customers under a microscope – Their sex, age and income – Their fads and fancies – Do women read politics? – The mother who studies 'Live Letters' while feeding baby

18. THE MAN HITLER CHANGED   129
He didn't like noise – then made the loudest – The curious transformation of Richard Jennings – Exposing the 'upper-crust riff-raff' who loved a pale spy – The Mirror *and Munich*

19. WHAT MAKES CASSANDRA CLANG   134
Clues for psychiatrists – The fugitive from advertising – TNT meets forked lightning – Why he distrusts underdogs – The tale of a night out with Godfrey Winn

20. ENTER SIR WINSTON   140
Voice of the People – 'Aren't we a very old team?' – Churchill's misconceptions –
Jennings and Cassandra go to war – The anti-Chamberlain crusade

21. THE *MIRROR* IS WARNED   145
Churchill and 'the hammerblow of circumstance' – The end of the Churchill-
Mirror *honeymoon – Cassandra fights the British Army – Heated exchanges at*
No. 10 Downing Street – Secrets from a diary

22. LETTERS FROM DOWNING STREET   159
Churchill accuses Cassandra of malevolence – 'Some hatred might be kept for the
enemy' – How I would conduct a Fifth Column movement - by the Premier –
Winston recalls 'our past friendly relations' and talks of vitriol throwing

23. SECONDS OUT – FINAL ROUND!   166
How Bartholomew answered the threat – Cassandra makes new enemies and
crosses swords with Mr Morrison – Speeches Churchill had forgotten

24. A MAN ON A BICYCLE   169
A piece of cardboard makes history – Philip Zee, and the crisis that came to a
man with a conscience – Patriotic - or subversive? – The facts about the petrol
cartoon

25. SUMMONS TO WESTMINSTER   174
Why the Generals saw red – Whitehall's quest for hidden hands and evil motives –
Churchill demands action and Morrison delivers a message – Our 'Erb and the
editor – A verdict ten years after

26. SILENCE – OR SUPPRESSION   179
The Cabinet selects its weapon – Five men speak out for freedom – Crime,
punishment and the words that were missing from the evidence – Blackening the
record

27. ALARM AND DESPONDENCY   183
Black ties – for a funeral – The Express *weeps – The* Telegraph *comforts the*
suppressors – What the public thought – Cassandra tries harder than ever to
please

28. IN THE STOCKS   186
Thumb-screws for the Mirror *– Heat in the Commons, ice in the Lords – Strip-*
tease – and political principles – 'Damned disgusting', says APH – A shock for
Mr Morrison – Benevolent mastiff nips ill-bred cur – Cassandra is warned of 'a
sticky end'

29. A FISHING STORY   192
What happened when Churchill took time off in Quebec – A journey to La Lac de
Neige in seventeen cars and nine Army trucks – The 20-inch trout and the secret
the Premier did not know

30. HITLER BOMBS THE *MIRROR* 194
The Cabinet orders the Press to 'print on' – 50lb base of landmine lands on office roof – Fifteen fires surround the Mirror *on Incendiary Night – How the newspapers carried on in the war and never missed a single day's issue*

31. VD DAY 200
Another 'shocking' campaign – The curious story of the Government advertisement which Fleet Street censored – More lively controversies – Captain Henry Longhurst MP makes a public fool of himself

32. DEATH – FOR A HEADLINE 204
How two war correspondents lost their lives – Healy escapes from France - to be bombed in London – Adventures of David Walker – the man the Gestapo 'moved on', the Serbs wanted to shoot, and the Italians imprisoned

33. FORWARD WITH THE PEOPLE 207
The Mirror *becomes a power in the land – How the war educated the masses – 'Victory - then reconstruction' – Labour forewarned to prepare for power – Challenging the* Express *and dwarfing the* Herald

34. HOW POWERFUL IS THE PRESS? 212
Lord Beaverbrook concedes a failure – Do newspapers form or control mass opinion? – Campaigns that flopped – When the reader knows best – The Russians, the Press, and the Public – 'Funny people, the British'

35. VOTE FOR HIM! 217
What did the Mirror *say in 1945? – The story of two newspapers and an historic election – The* Express - *by Mr Attlee – The* Mirror - *by Mr Morrison – Stunts versus subtleties – How to conduct a successful campaign*

36. WHY THE *MIRROR* WAS RIGHT 224
A 'decisive influence' in the election – Express *misinterprets the mood of the electorate – Who made the* Mirror *turn Left? – The facts Churchill forgot - and the advice he rejected – 1945 vindicates a newspaper's policy*

37. TALKING DOGS, FALSIES, AND QUINS 230
Good fortune comes to Mr Whitcomb – A Nightie at the Opera – The chivalrous Aga Khan – Love-starved wives and roving husbands – How much padding and how much girl? – 'The note of gentle madness'

38. SENSATIONALISM 236
'Nothing to beat a good meaty crime', said Mr Jones – Cecil Thomas advocates revealing all – Bolam promises to be 'sensational to the best of our ability' – Economics for the millions – An editor goes to Brixton Gaol

39. *MIRROR* VERSUS *EXPRESS* 242
Behind the scenes in the battle for the World's Greatest Sale – Factors that worried the Express *– Five rounds of a heavyweight contest – The paper Bartholomew did not read – Why the* Mirror's *sale suddenly leapt up one million*

40. CHURCHILL SUES FOR LIBEL 247
Which way would the Mirror jump in the new election? – Brickbats for Attlee over

Labour's failures – The campaigns of 1950 and 1951 – Can a strip-cartoon canvass votes? – 'Whose finger on the trigger?'

41. LIVE LETTERS, ALIVE O!   251
The girl who loved a strangler – The things that worry Mirror *readers – Wrong bed, wrong husband – How a newspaper makes friends - and keeps them – Why the Archbishop said 'Thank you' and the war bride cried 'Halt'*

42. WHO OWNS THE *MIRROR*   256
Lord Camrose, Lord Beaverbrook and The Enigma – Rumours about a syndicate – The financial facts – Rothermere and Cowley exchange letters – The deal of 1947 – How many stockholders?

43. YOUNGER MEN   261
The end of The Bart Legend – A nephew of Northcliffe takes command – The Bartholomew-Cecil King collaboration – When a genius erupts – The paper's policy – Character of the new chairman

ILLUSTRATIONS

Lord Northcliffe	27
A Newspaper is Born	31
Alexander Kenealy	32
The Dead King Edward VII	34
Lord Rothermere	42
Harry Guy Bartholomew	60
A Negro is Lynched	73
Cecil Thomas	75
The Work of W K Haselden	80
Jane	82
Characters from the Strips	86
John Cowley	91
The Abdication	110
Cassandra	137
'Wanted for Murder'	139
Philip Zee	171
The Price of Petrol	173
Clearing up the Mess	197
Fleet Street Scene	199
'Don't Lose It Again'	216
Silvester Bolam	241
Up – Up – Up!	245
Cecil Harmsworth King	263
Coronation	269

Brought to book

FOREWORD

By Revel Barker

'Oh that my enemy would publish a book,' said Gilbert Beyfus QC, as he hammered the final nail into the coffin of the *Daily Mirror* and William Connor (Cassandra) in a libel case brought against them by the pianist Liberace.

Brandishing a copy of the first edition of *Publish and be Damned!* and gesturing towards its author, who was sitting in the well of the court, he said he thought 'somebody had once said that'. He was right, sort of, for he was slightly misquoting the *Book of Job* (chapter 31, verse 35).

Beyfus continued: 'Well, any prayer to that effect has been abundantly answered in this case.'

The beginning of June, 1959, had been good for sales of the six-year-old book, with copies provided for the judge and jury, for leading counsel and for some of the witnesses. It was referred to and quoted from almost every day for a week and reported in newspapers all round the world. This may have been beneficial for retailing and subsequent royalties but it was no help to the defendants. For the plaintiff *Publish and be Damned!* was largely the tool Beyfus relied on to suggest to the jury that Cudlipp's friend and colleague Bill Connor was being less than honest in his testimony.

Three years earlier Connor had described Liberace in his column as:

> ... this deadly, winking, sniggering, snuggling, chromium-plated, scent-impregnated, luminous, quivering, giggling, fruit-flavoured, mincing, ice-covered heap of mother-love... He reeks with emetic language that can only make grown men long for a quiet corner, an aspidistra, a handkerchief and the old heave-ho... Without doubt he is the biggest sentimental vomit of all time.

And Beyfus – the leading libel man of the day – had retaliated by describing the columnist as: 'a literary assassin who dips his pen in vitriol, hired by this sensational newspaper to murder reputations and hand out sensational articles on which its circulation is built'... 'as vicious and violent a writer as has ever been in the profession of journalism in this city of London.'

He had put it straight to Connor:

'Do you think it would be wrong to call you a violent and vitriolic writer?'

Connor: 'It would indeed.'

Beyfus went on:

Would it be right to say that the *Daily Mirror* is a sensational newspaper? – A: No. It is quite wrong.

–You are on oath, are you not? – A: I know I am on oath.

–Are you a comparatively close friend of Mr Hugh Cudlipp... Did you both join the *Daily Mirror* together in about 1935... Is he now the head both of the *Daily Mirror* and the *Sunday Pictorial*? – A: That is right.

–You have been intimately associated with Mr Cudlipp for 24 years... And are not only constantly with him in Geraldine House but constantly with him socially... Drinking together in bars in Fleet Street. – A: 'Associating' is the word I would like.

–You have not in the last few years in any way fallen out with Mr Hugh Cudlipp. – A: Mr Hugh Cudlipp and I quarrel so violently almost every day that you would never believe it.

–Is that a fair indication of your character, then, that you quarrel violently nearly every day with one of your closest friends? – A: That is quite true.

–In 1953 Mr Hugh Cudlipp wrote a book which is a history of the *Daily Mirror*, did he not... With some assistance from you, which he greatly acknowledges in the preface? – A: That is so.

–You wrote in the *Daily Mirror* of Monday September 7 1953 a review of that book... In which you did not complain or suggest that any part of it was untrue. – A: I did not; not in the review.

–That is all I am saying; not in the review. You did make one reference to what Mr Cudlipp said about you. You said this: 'The book sparkles and flashes... It has everything – even the damned impudence to include disrespectful and distasteful details in the worst possible taste about myself.' – A: That is true.

Later...

–You have sworn that in your opinion the *Daily Mirror* is not a sensational newspaper. Would you look at this book you reviewed (without suggesting it was inaccurate)? This is Mr Cudlipp. What was he at that time, 1953, when he wrote the book, editor? – A: No, I think that he was editorial director, but I am not sure.

–Time and experience, and the trials of the conflict, had tempered its
brashness. It remained and still remains a popular sensational newspaper,
but its sense of purpose became highly developed; it regarded itself as a
paper with a mission and it was accepted as such.

...You see there it is being described by the editorial director as a
popular sensational newspaper; do you regard that as wrong? – A: I regard
it as wrong. One of the strengths of the friendship with Mr Cudlipp is we
have disagreed continually. I draw a line between sensation, which means
exploiting something for commercial matters, and forthright and strong
opinions well held.

Connor stubbornly, and fairly sullenly, denied most things that opposing
counsel put to him.

It became a childish war of words, the top writer on the top newspaper in
Fleet Street versus the top advocate in the High Court.

But in denying that the *Daily Mirror* could be described as sensational he
was out on a limb. Beyfus had all the references in *Publish and be
Damned!* – about 30 in total – marked for him and he reeled them off.
What he missed – suggesting that perhaps he read the highlighted
paragraphs but didn't actually read the book – was that there was even a
chapter entitled 'Sensationalism'. Connor, as both a contributor and a
reviewer, must have been aware of that. Indeed, the subtitle of the book
could justifiably have been The *Sensational* Story Of The *Daily Mirror*.

As to whether Cassandra had a reputation for being a 'vitriolic' writer,
that was covered in the book, too. In a letter sent in 1941 to Winston
Churchill, then Prime Minister, Cecil H King, a *Mirror* director who by
the time of the trial had become chairman, had written: 'Cassandra is a
hard-hitting journalist with a vitriolic style.'

Cudlipp gamely went to his friend's aid, explaining from the witness box
that sensationalism didn't mean what the QC was claiming it meant –
publishing anything at all calculated to increase circulation... even to the
point of possibly implying that the world's most successful entertainer was
homosexual (a criminal offence, in those days).

Sensationalism had many meanings, said the author. He preferred the one
he had quoted from Silvester Bolam, a former editor:

> Sensationalism does not mean distorting the truth. It means the vivid
> and dramatic presentation of events so as to give them a forceful impact
> on the mind of the reader. It means big headlines, vigorous writing,
> simplification into familiar everyday language, and the wide use of
> illustration by cartoon and photograph.

Cudlipp had never had any doubt that the Cassandra column was defamatory. He hadn't believed that it would come to trial for he thought Liberace would have been advised that the case would be laughed out of court. As editorial director he could have settled it with an apology when the writ landed, and had another opportunity towards the closing stages of the case, when the *Mirror*'s own QC confided that he thought they were losing.

But his view was that to do so would be to let his friend down – and the newspaper, and the readers, who were enjoying the hearing.

The trial cost the *Daily Mirror* £35,000 – about half a million pounds in modern (2009) terms. But Cudlipp's verdict was that it had been money well spent.

The newspaper emerged from court poorer financially but with its reputation for sensational (vivid and vigorous, forthright, strongly opinioned) journalism intact and its already world-beating circulation continuing to increase.

And they'd had fun, even if the witness box experience of the *Mirror* team had been at times frustrating, and some of the argument seemingly perverse.

And the readers shared in the fun.

And, as the book explained, more than anything, the people at the *Mirror* had fun and supplied fun inside a spectacularly caring and campaigning newspaper, sometimes against seemingly insurmountable opposition.

It was what they did best.

Revel Barker spent 27 years, from reporter to managing editor, with the Mirror group of newspapers. He now publishes – and republishes – classic books about newspapers and journalists and is the author of *Crying All The Way To The Bank: Liberace v Cassandra and the Daily Mirror* (2009).

The Cudlipp classic

INTRODUCTION

By Geoffrey Goodman

There are moments, nowadays, when I fantasise about what would happen if by some ultra-super supernatural force it might be possible to re-instate Hugh Cudlipp onto the 9th floor of the old *Daily Mirror* building in Holborn Circus. Of course one huge snag is that the building no longer exists; true to the times we live in it is now the headquarters of supermarket emperors J Sainsbury plc. The old *Mirror* castle was razed to the ground to be rebuilt for Sainsbury's.

'Symbolic, my boy,' I feel sure Cudlipp would adjudicate were he still around to update his superb classic on old Fleet Street – which , in my view, remains one of the finest books ever written on our capricious trade and which is now finally republished.

Along with this 'Symbolic, my boy' gruffly-edged Cudlippian retort would come a huge guffaw of laughter as he began to lay out the dummy for his 21st century *Daily Mirror*. Journalism always meant fun as much as anything else for Hugh Cudlipp.

OK then: fantasy.

The conventional wisdom would have us believe that Cudlipp's popular journalistic genius has had its day. That we now live in a different era, a different ethos of popular culture and, to be sure, an almost entirely different mantra of journalistic values. I am far from persuaded. Especially after re-reading this remarkable book which first fascinated me more than fifty years ago as a young reporter on the *News Chronicle*.

The book is strictly about what its sub-title says: the astonishing story of the *Daily Mirror*. But of course it is far more than the history of a single national newspaper.

It is as much concerned with the social, political and cultural development of a nation and its people from early in the 20th century [the *Mirror* was launched on November 2 1903], through two world wars, poverty , wealth, power, mass unemployment of the twenties and thirties plus the rise of Hitler and European fascism. Across this canvas of history Cudlipp's book describes the power struggle of newspaper moguls from Northcliffe onwards as this single newspaper, the *Daily Mirror,* began to emerge from a mish-mash of experiment and failure climbing to astonishing success as an international journalistic phenomenon.

In the fourth Cudlipp Memorial lecture at the London Press Club [circa 2001] I described Hugh Cudlipp as the greatest popular journalist of 20th century British journalism; I do not withdraw a single word of that. Yet Cudlipp himself would have brushed it aside – not from modesty, which was not one of his chosen virtues – but because he was selflessly objective about the *Mirror's* origins and success.

The paper was founded by the visionary Alfred Harmsworth [Lord Northcliffe] as a daily paper for 'gentlewomen'. It was then almost sunk by his brother Harold [the first Lord Rothermere] who disregarded its potential while he concentrated on building the financial power of the *Daily Mail* group, which then owned the *Daily Mirror.* Finally the *Mail* group sold out and the paper was rescued by Harry Guy Bartholomew – 'Bart' – who prompted the title of the book with a quote borrowed from the Duke of Wellington.

Cudlipp describes Bartholomew as 'brilliant, truculent, mercurial' with an exceptional instinct for understanding 'the pulse of the masses'. Cudlipp always insisted that the foundation of the *Mirror's* success came from Bart, who was a Northcliffe protégé. Maybe. But it was Cudlipp himself who picked it up from a cantankerous, fractious and failing Bart to turn the *Mirror* into the 'biggest daily sale on earth'. All this, and far more, is contained in this extraordinary classic on the Fleet Street we recognised.

Far more of what?

Brilliant profiles on Beaverbrook, Cecil Harmsworth King, Bill [Cassandra] Connor, as well as the Rothermere family: a riveting account of how the *Daily Mirror* was twice almost banned by Churchill's war-time Government for its insolent criticism of the great war leader's style in conducting his war-time Government. Winston objected to Cassandra's column and the carpingly critical editorials written by Richard Jennings. Despite the paper's fundamental support for Churchill's own war leadership qualities the *Mirror* constantly challenged the early military strategy.

Then came a second threat to stop the paper – this time via Herbert Morrison, Home Secretary in Churchill's war cabinet and a former *Mirror* contributor. In March 1942 Philip Zec, the paper's famed cartoonist, produced a cartoon which is still argued over between politicians and journalists: it showed a torpedoed sailor adrift on a raft in a black, angry ocean with this caption; 'The Price of Petrol has been increased by One Penny (official)'. It was Zec's – and the paper's – response to stories of a wartime black market in petrol. The cartoon raised thunderous protest from Government – 'treasonable propaganda', some called it – though it won glowing support from many *Mirror* readers. Zec and the *Mirror* had accurately tested the popular pulse, always its supreme secret until recent years.

The whole account as told in this book [including wartime correspondence between Churchill and the paper] remains riveting history. And these are but epic snatches from a dramatic, colourful and uniquely historic journey.

So how much is relevant to modern journalism? There are, of course, some inescapable time-induced flaws in the book: but frankly these are minor compared with its overall commanding relevance to anyone entering, or who is already in, contemporary journalism.

Without hesitation I reckon Cudlipp's book rates around 200-plus per cent relevance – not least his descriptions of what makes great newspaper journalism tick. They alone should be MUST texts for all media schools and their professorial experts as they emerge from web sites. It is a pleasure for me to see *Publish and be Damned!* re-issued as a paperback after too many years out of print.

Geoffrey Goodman is a former industrial editor, columnist and assistant editor of the *Daily Mirror*. He previously reported for the *Daily Herald*, the Odhams *Sun*, the *News Chronicle* and the *Manchester Guardian*, and was founding editor of the *British Journalism Review*, where he remains the emeritus chairman and where a version of this critique originally appeared. He was awarded the CBE in 1998 for his services to journalism and is the author of *From Bevan to Blair* (2003), a memoir of 50 years of political reporting.

STOP PRESS

This book is the story of the newspaper with the world's greatest daily circulation – London's *Daily Mirror,* fifty years old this year.

Millions cherish that tabloid journal, swear by it, regard it as their daily Bible; others loathe it, curse it, reject its news and views as the modern works of Satan. It has been threatened with suppression by Parliament, attacked by other newspapers, denounced by prelates, and one of its editors was obliged to sew mailbags for three months in Brixton Prison for contempt of court. It has also done a great deal of good, exerted much influence and bedevilled its rivals.

It has always been a spirited and controversial newspaper, and no one would accuse it of cant or moral cowardice; correct, too, to say that some of the politicians who have flayed it in public have enjoyed, or sought in private, its approbation.

That is the newspaper this book dissects: it delves behind the scenes of the most popular of the Popular Press.

A word about the author. He joined the *Mirror* in 1935, was its features editor until 1937, and then became editor of its companion journal the *Sunday Pictorial.* His close-up association with the subject and the personalities involved therefore extends over a period of eighteen years.

Others might have written this story differently; there is more than one book in a newspaper and there is no law yet against writing books. They might have omitted names here prominently mentioned or dealt in affectionate or affected detail with careers here dismissed in a sentence.

But this is the exciting story as one man has seen it, told so far as he is aware without prejudice or rancour, and above all he hopes without humbug.

Before we go to press he desires to place on record his gratitude

to Sir Winston Churchill for permission to publish for the first time confidential correspondence in which as Prime Minister he expounded his distaste for the newspaper's wartime policy;

to Cecil Harmsworth King for access to war-time diaries recording heated exchanges at No 10 Downing Street;

to collaborator Len Jackson for the opportunity to draw without inhibition upon his 120,000-word chronicle of the *Mirror* and its staff, particularly in Chapters 2, 3, 4, 7 and 38;

to William Connor, Philip Zee, James G Lovell, Sydney Jacobson, Fred Redman, John Walters and others for assistance from the archives of their memories.

For the finished work, its opinions, its profiles – critical or laudatory – the author holds entire responsibility.

Hugh Cudlipp
September, 1953

1
CAN A WOMAN HATCH EGGS?

On March 29 1939, six months before Adolf Schickelgruber inveigled the human race into a second global war, an announcement was published in the editorial columns of a London national newspaper:

> BORED IN BED?
> We want to get hold of somebody who's bed-ridden, or likely to be for the next month or so, preferably in or around London.
> We don't want anybody really ill, or suffering from a serious disease.
> We arc thinking of somebody fairly young, who doesn't mind a little publicity, and who would co-operate with us in a little sporting idea we are toying with.
> People in hospitals are NOT ELIGIBLE.

That is how it all began; now read on. William Connor and Bill Herbert, the journalists who had conceived this experiment, were at the material time joint editors of a readers' letters page known as 'Live Letter Box'. They had considered it 'a good idea' to evolve a technique whereby a lady could hatch chickens from a clutch of eggs.

Hundreds replied to the invitation, not knowing they were the potential mothers of chicks. A girl in Battersea was selected from the clucking brood, and on May 22 'Live Letter Box' announced her results under the headline:

THE EGGS THAT FAILED

Here was their report to millions of solicitous readers:

> Something snapped in his brain. On March 29 one of the Editors of L.L.B. flung his absinthe aside with a muttered curse and said fiercely: 'I don't believe it. If a mere hen can hatch an egg, so can a human being!'
> So we got hold of Peggy.
> Peggy hurt her leg and broke a bone in her knee. She had been in bed for seven weeks when we found her, and her right leg was still in plaster.

18

She said she was willing, so we procured a clutch of fertile eggs, wrapped them in cottonwool and put them in bed alongside her.

Our pals in the egg-hatching world (you'd be surprised whom we know) told us that a steady temperature of 104 degrees was required. To make sure we bought an electric heating pad with a variable temperature control, and fixed the whole apparatus up in a way that would have won a friendly smile from the most pernickety hen.

Peggy settled comfortably back on the nest.

Smirking intolerantly and clucking quietly to ourselves, we went about our business. Now and again we'd send one of our eggy pals down to see Peggy.

Days passed. Weeks passed. And as we approached the dreadful hour when the young brood would burst from their shells into the glare of waiting arcs and the clicking of innumerable cameras, the tension grew unbearable. We threw away our ham sandwiches and pecked lightly at a little corn.

On the twenty-firs! day, with the mighty presses waiting and with messenger boys straining at the leash, we stood by.

Hours passed. Not a sign. Not a drum was heard, not a funeral note. The second day passed. Silence. No word from the eggy tomb. Peggy, grim and serious, sat steadily on.

'Chicken—where art thou?'

Were the editors of 'Live Letter Box' depressed by the negative result? Not they. 'It takes more than sterile hen-fruit to beat the mad monomaniacs of the L.L.B.,' they informed their public. 'Rhode Island Red for ever. Cock-a-doodle-do!'

But Miss Peggy and her parents were crestfallen. What had begun as a dubious stunt had taken on serious proportions. Family friends and neighbours visited the bedroom every night, half Battersea keenly followed the experiment, and when the eggs failed to hatch and the nest was taken away they were left with a highly agitated girl on their hands.

Peggy felt she had let the paper down.

Harry Guy Bartholomew, newspaper chairman, called a conference to figure out how he could assist the Government in solving a major post-war problem, Higher Production. His journal had advocated the ascension of Labour to power; now it would help the Cabinet to do its job.

There he sat at his office desk, thrashing the matter out with his executives and a covey of economists. Agreement was reached that the solution to Higher Production was harder work all round, fewer restrictive practices, production councils lie factories. Executives and economists agreed. The policy was crystal clear. Work. Work. Work.

Their deliberations were then interrupted by the din of hammering from constructional engineers at work upstairs.

Bartholomew grabbed the telephone and hollered at the operator: 'Get somebody up to the floor above me at once and stop that bloody noise!'

An inspired editorial chump bought three baby elephants, Jimbo, Jumbo and Babs, which paraded at charity fetes and raised money for a Christmas pudding fund for children. When the high-spirited art staff led Babs – cost, £300; uninsured – into the editor's room, Babs shivered, sneezed, and dropped dead. Human beings have since failed to make their views so dramatically clear.

John Mather is a skilled journalist, now pride of the *Daily Express* sub-editors' table.

Earlier in his career, in 1937, he was engaged by another newspaper to write a column called 'Secrets', specifically designed to make Walter Winchell's essays in acidity read like an anaemic schoolgirl's love letter. He set about his task with the verve expected of him; the column sizzled when he wrote it, crackled when it was being set on the linotypes, and exploded when it was delivered at the breakfast table. It was not his fault – far from it: but the column had to stop.

Late at night, after scouring the West End for the latest news and gossip, John Mather burst into the office with this announcement: 'Boy, I know every secret in town to-night.'

'John,' I said, 'here's one secret you don't know.'

'Rubbish,' said Mather. 'Impossible.'

I whispered in his ear: 'The column won't be appearing tomorrow. You're fired.'

When I handed Mather the handsome pay-off cheque his eyes glistened. He fingered the present, read the amount aloud, and studied the signatures to ensure there was no risk of forgery.

'I've never had one of these. What do you do with them?' he asked.

'Can't say,' I replied. 'I've never had one either.'

'You will,' said Mather.

Vintage journalists occasionally ask themselves this question: When a newspaper disinterestedly resolves to concern itself with the fortunes of society as a whole, is it really worth while? Does the Christian spirit reap its own reward, or are there unsuspected pitfalls awaiting the pure in heart?

The Ministry of Agriculture was fearful of the ravages of the Colorado beetle and was gratified when Britain's most popular paper came to its aid. The beetle was photographed, sketched and described in monosyllables so that all who spotted it at work in the potato crops could capture it, pop it into a matchbox and post it in. A prize of £10 was offered for each sample received.

The Ministry of Agriculture was jubilant at this unusual example of Fleet Street largesse until it was discovered that enterprising London barrow-boys arranged with the continental spivs' cartel to import Colorados from France so diat they could filch all the prizes.

The offer was withdrawn, with no explanation to respectable readers.

Herewith two intelligence tests for would-be executive newspapermen. Time to answer: 15 seconds.

1. You arrive at the office at nine o'clock one morning to find the Dog Expert, pale and distraught, awaiting you on the doorstep. In his right hand he is waving a copy of the current issue.

'My God,' he exclaims. 'In my column to-day I give a prescription for puppies with a cold in the nose. It includes a poison which is perfectly safe when mixed with water, and I mean lots of water. Some idiot has deleted my reference to the water. This means that hundreds of our readers' pets are being bumped off at this very moment.'

The question is: what does one do?

2. The telephone rings at eleven o'clock one morning and you answer it. The voice on the phone says:

'I am Professor A M Low. I have just been reading some advice given by one of your readers this morning in the column called Women's Parliament. She describes a method of saving fuel. Her idea is that you wrap a wet newspaper around a few handfuls of powdered coal, then wrap another wet newspaper around that, placing the result upon the fire. I thought you might care to know that any reader who follows her advice is likely to blow up her husband's house. Good morning.'

The question is: what does one do?

These events, and many others as gay or as disconcerting, occurred on the London *Daily Mirror*, the newspaper which in 1914 achieved the world's largest daily sale, nearly died on its feet in 1934, then suddenly emerged from a coma and achieved the largest sale for the second time.

In 1934 its circulation had dropped well below a million. Within five years the figure had doubled. When wartime newsprint restrictions were taken off for the first time for five years in September 1946 it leapt up a million to 3,279,441 and held its audience with ease until the dollar shortage again imposed a halt. Eighteen months later, with the second go-ahead from Whitehall, the total reached four millions and went on rising until at 4,187,403 it set up the record. The *Daily Express,* which proudly proclaimed itself as 'the world's greatest newspaper,' had been outstripped. It remained outstripped, for the *Mirror* now sells more than 4,500,000 copies daily; more than 7,000,000 people bought its Coronation issue a few months ago.

What makes the *Mirror* tick? What are the secrets of its astonishing success? Who owns it? Who are the men who have increased its stature and its influence? Who reads it?

It has advocated unpopular though noble causes; no doubt of that. Could it, indeed, have expanded without sincerity of purpose? When *The Times* was smugly extolling Neville Chamberlain's policy of appeasement the *Mirror* was exposing his vanity and gullibility. When the *Express* was declaring there would be no Hitler war the *Mirror* and its associate newspaper were prophesying the date when war would begin. When the rest of the British Press were telling their customers that Churchill would remain the nation's chosen post-war leader, the *Mirror* was daily proving that this would not be so. It has never lulled its followers with a false sense of security: over the years, more than any other widely-read journal, it has hammered home the harsh reality of Britain's position in the cabinet of nations in language that all could understand. There are those, outside the paper itself, who hold that without the advocacy of the *Mirror* the Party which swept the polls in 1945 would not have gained power.

This book answers the questions and probes the legends, and in so doing discloses what went on inside the curious wedding-cake building known as Geraldine House – named after Northcliffe's mother – where the newspaper is written, produced and published in Fetter Lane, Fleet Street, London, EC4.

The story begins in 1903.

2

NORTHCLIFFE DROPS A BRICK

The *Daily Mirror* was a bad idea.

Northcliffe's.

'Failure,' he had written, 'is not in our vocabulary'; then, when time healed punctured pride, the failure was conceded.

'No newspaper,' said Northcliffe, 'was ever started with such a boom. I advertised it everywhere. If there was anyone in the United Kingdom not aware that the *Daily Mirror* was to be started he must have been deaf, dumb, blind, or all three.' The birth took place in the *Daily Mail* offices in Carmelite Street, London on a November Sunday night; six days before – in the land of the deaf, the dumb, and the blind – the readers of *Punch* were warned in an advertisement that the; first daily newspaper for gentlewomen was about to burst upon the waiting world.

Alfred Harmsworth had to this date known only success. George Newnes and Arthur Pearson were licking their wounds after a three-cornered heavyweight contest with no holds barred in the magazine ring; the *Evening News,* bought for £25,000 in 1894, was making money; *the Daily Mail,* which he had created, was expanding its profits and had achieved the world's largest sale. The future Lord Northcliffe was powerful, assured: about to make a major miscalculation.

The idea was simple: a daily newspaper produced by ladies of breeding from the high-class weeklies for ladies with the desire to ape new fashions, the leisure to hunt and travel, and the means to squander a thousand pounds a year on luxury. In Northcliffe's philosophy of life there were vices worse than snobbery; the lower middle-classes, he felt, owed him a living. Was this not the formula, and were these not the people, who had already brought him wealth and influence?

Though later he acknowledged how wrong he had been in launching 'so mad a frolic as a paper for ladies', it was with pride and confidence that he sounded the fanfare in the first hopeful issue:

> All that experience can do in shaping it has already been done. The last feather of its wings is adjusted, so that I have now only to open the door of the cage and ask your good wishes for the flight.

This newspaper was to be different. Cookery and fashion were to be taught in new ways. The *Daily Mirror* was going to be entertaining without being frivolous, serious without being dull – and it would deal with everything from the stitching of a flounce to changes in Imperial defence.

'The hideous fashion plate will find no place in the *Mirror,*' said Sir George Sutton, favoured man in the Harmsworth empire. 'Our pictures will be studies from life, showing the dress actually being worn. Every recipe will be tested by expert chefs. We shall study the requirements of the girl bachelor; the use of the chafing dish – or cookery above stairs, as it is sometimes called – will be fully dealt with. Information on society functions will be provided by the people concerned, not merely professional reporters.'

The ladies, the expert chefs, the society informants, and the writer of the leaderette in French failed, and statistics cruelly etch the detail of their disaster. The first issue of the paper for gentlewomen broke records with a circulation of 265,217 copies, and the founder boasted that with enough printing presses he could have sold several million. The second issue 'exceeded 143,000', the seventh fell short of 100,000, and within three months the elegant customers had dwindled to a garden party of 24,000.

There were not enough gentlewomen. Or if there were, they were not interested in what the gentlewomen who wrote the *Mirror* had to tell them.

Alfred Harmsworth had surrounded himself with people who did not consider it their first duty to expose his misjudgments, but here was an error which the originator was obliged to perceive for himself. The baby was dying in its father's arms.

He had invited the British public to a diet of *consomme aux nids d'hirondelles,* followed by sole in white wine with mushrooms and truffles; the readers were told how to make these lavish delicacies. Also recorded in the first issue, but only briefly, was an inquest on a fourteen-year-old orphan girl of Oswaldtwistle who lost one eye and went blind in the other. She had been sacked from the mill and had committed suicide during temporary insanity, for the child had no prospect of earning her living again. The paper for gentlewomen made no comment.

The *Mirror,* which was to deprive its founder of £100,000, was rubbish and the readers knew it. Harold, the future first Lord Rothermere, drew his

24

brother's attention to the sorry tale recorded in the ledgers: a melancholic duty he chose to forget twenty-one years later when he referred to the paper's foundation as 'a stroke of inspiration'.

The imperturbable Mrs Mary Howarth, who had been taken from the *Mail* to edit the new paper at fifty pounds a month[12], returned to her former work. Northcliffe sent for Hamilton Fyfe and told him that he had learnt two things, 'that women can't write and don't want to read'.

The situation called for a newspaper doctor. Fyfe became editor, and Kennedy Jones, also called in, decided that 'the monstrous regiment of women' must go.

'You can't imagine the things I had to blue-pencil,' he told his friends. 'Two people acting at Drury Lane got married and went on acting as usual – they didn't go away for a honeymoon. The paragraph about this ended: The usual performance took place in the evening.' When a letter about French affairs was sent daily from Paris the original headline, written by a lady, was set up in type but did not appear: it was changed to 'Yesterday in Paris'. Women journalists, as Hamilton Fyfe remarked long afterwards, are not so ingenuous now.

There was a further delaying factor in production: the anxiety of compositors to make-up a page, and re-make up a page, under the appraising eye of elegant women in low-cut evening gowns who had just returned from the theatre to supervise the assembling of their works of art in the mechanical department.

Fyfe wrote most of the leaders and the brilliant Alexander Kenealy joined him to organise the news, stunts and 'talking points', succeeding Fyfe as editor in 1907. The despondent Northcliffe, losing £500 with every issue until this new combination started work, now saw the fortunes of his offspring change for the better.

To Fyfe fell the distasteful task of sacking the women, and the rape of the Sabines wasn't in it. 'They begged to be allowed to stay,' he recalled. 'They left little presents on my desk. They waylaid me tearfully in the corridors. It was a horrid experience, like drowning kittens.'

1

[2] Extract from a 1952 speech by Cecil Harmsworth King, Northcliffe's nephew, now chairman of the Daily Mirror and Sunday Pictorial: '... the editor of a national newspaper [today] looks for something near the remuneration of the Prime Minister.'

The *Mirror* was born in 1903. Where, during that first tremulous year, were the three men who were to become entangled in its adventures over the coming half century?

Winston Spencer Churchill, who was to write for its companion paper after his departure from the Admiralty in the first world war, who was to use the *Mirror* as his platform in 1939, chafe at its criticisms of his Cabinet in 1942, and sue it for libel in 1951, was twenty-nine years old. He had left the 4th Hussars to embark upon a political career in the Oldham constituency.

Herbert Morrison, who was to write for the *Mirror* in 1939, threaten its suppression in 1942, and subsequently seek its political aid, was a perky fifteen-year-old with an unruly quiff which would not consent to be combed into position. He was still under the influence of his parents, a Tory-minded policeman and a former housemaid, at 240, Ferndale Road, Brixton. He had left the Lingham Street Church of England School the year before, had worked as an errand boy and shop assistant, and was looking forward to his new job as a telephonist at Whitbread's Brewery.

Harry Guy Bartholomew, the paper's leading spirit in later turbulent years, was about to become assistant art editor.

The Napoleon of the Press

'N' meant Napoleon. So that he could also sign his letters 'N', Alfred Harmsworth became Lord Northcliffe. He was delighted, at Fontainebleau, to find that the Emperor's hat was too small for him.

3
WHEN THE *MIRROR* WAS BORN

Mr Arkas Sapt was a resourceful technician and the editor of one of Northcliffe's minor publications: he was also the midwife who revived the puny *Mirror* by turning it upside down, holding it up by the feet, and slapping it heartily on the back.

Arkas Sapt was a visionary. 'I can fill a daily newspaper with photographs printed on high-speed rotary presses,' he told Northcliffe. The *Daily Graphic* was already publishing occasional half-tones, but by a cumbersome method and at the depressing rate of 10,000 an hour. 'I can double or treble that speed,' said Sapt, 'and print on an ordinary Hoe press.'

Hannen Swaffer, the first art editor, says that Northcliffe never understood pictures and loathed the day when the *Mirror's* sale passed his cherished *Mail*. But at this stage the paper was faced with the probability of having to close down to cut its losses; something had to be done and the moment was propitious for experiment.

On January 25 1904 the new product appeared, *The Daily Illustrated Mirror,* 'a paper for men and women, the first halfpenny daily illustrated publication in the history of journalism , printing picture pages at 24,000 copies an hour. Its circulation trebled to 71,690, and reached 140,000 within a month.

Britain was a country of boisterous contrast in those days when the *Mirror* set out to record its affairs in photographs, pen-and-ink sketches and words. The paper's own pages tell the story:

LIFE WAS JINGOISTIC: Colonel Younghusband was marching to Lhasa to convince the Tibetans that they must not show disrespect to the British Raj. At one stage it was recorded that 'the only offensive operations so far are the flogging of various porters who refused to march further; this was accomplished with so much success that order was immediately restored and the march continued unchecked.'

In the Aden hinterland Captain Lloyd-Jones and sixty men were surrounded by a thousand tribesmen and eight Britons were killed. Troops were fighting in Nigeria, and a desert force was busy cornering the Mullah in Somaliland.

Said a *Mirror* leader:

> That England is always at war shows an amount of energy and superabundant spirits that go a long way to demonstrate that we are not a decaying race. Three little wars going on, and the prospect of a large one looming before us, we take quite as a matter of course.

A month earlier there died in poverty the man who gave the word 'jingo' to the language, Mr G W Hunt. When the Russians had threatened our Middle East interests in 1877, he had written: 'We don't want to fight, but, by jingo, if we do...'

LIFE WAS GRIM: There were processions of unemployed; children worked long hours for a few pence a week – up at dawn delivering milk and out after dark delivering beer. Babies of four helped their mothers turn out matchboxes at twopence-halfpenny a gross. Women worked seventeen hours a day making artificial flowers for eight shillings a week; some men laboured twelve hours on the railways for tenpence.

A one-night winter census of the homeless in central London found 1,800 people, fifty children among them, tramping the streets. A reporter saw East End women giving their infants gin and beer 'to make them sleep'. A coroner's jury found that a child of nine died of alcoholic poisoning. The only man with a bath in a huge South London parish of 13,000 souls was Canon Horsley.

When a London coroner recorded a verdict of 'natural death' on a seven-year-old child who had died of starvation, editor Hamilton Fyfe let himself go:

> In the capital of the greatest Empire in the world death from starvation is natural death. If this is natural, let us give up talking about the benefits of civilisation. Let us speak of the curse of civilisation, the Devil's mockery of progress, the hell upon earth created for hundreds of thousands by social conditions such as those which prevail in England to-day.
>
> Is there no leading man in Britain who will come forward as the champion of the poor? Is there no one who can point a way and induce the nation to follow, no way of saving the next generation from the same plight?
>
> If there be such a man, in God's name let him come forward.

Robert Blatchford noticed Fyfe's words. 'It is so seldom one feels the warm pulse of human passion in a British newspaper,' he wrote. George Bernard Shaw contributed this cynical comment: 'You want a leader of men to come forward to champion the cause of the poor. What will happen if he does come forward? How many votes will he get? Our statesmanship destroys the character of the people and so we go on helplessly in a vicious circle, made cowardly and narrow-minded by poverty, and kept poor by our cowardice and narrow-mindedness.'

LIFE WAS GAY: At the other end of the scale was a world of opulence, sables, orchids and folly. When two men were fined £500 for keeping a gaming house in Belgravia the police found letters which showed that a leader of fashion had lost £1,500 in a single night at the tables. The game card was published when Lord James of Hereford went shooting with his friends in Hampshire: it showed 4,000 corpses, including 1,324 pheasants. Alfred Beit, the richest man in England, died; he had controlled businesses worth £100,000,000.

The young Marquis of Anglesey spent one million pounds in three years after inheriting his estates. A poet, two valets, a secretary and a hairdresser accompanied him on his travels, and his overcoat cost one thousand pounds.

Hamilton Fyfe asked in an editorial: 'How long can this butterfly-dance continue, this frivolity and pleasure-seeking of Society?'

AND PASSION BURNED: It was the age of Royalty and Debrett, impoverished English earls and American heiresses, breach of promise cases, Gaiety Girls and Stage Door Johnnies.

Fyfe condemned the 'butterfly dance', but when the Gaiety chorus was decimated by the high rate of marriage into the aristocracy, his paper gallantly offered to find a fresh covey of beauties for George Edwardes' show. Hundreds of girls with 'grace of manner, a singing voice, and personal charm' sent in their photographs.

Marion, from Daly's, sued Heinrich, the son of a German steelmaster, and until the case was withdrawn readers enjoyed *The Tale of the Two Tumpties.* The couple had given each other pet names, Heinrich being Tumpty Number One and Marion Tumpty Number Two. Their letters were read in court and the public followed the course of their love affair in numerals. For when passion was fleeting the lady reduced herself to Tumpty One-and-a-half. And when finally forlorn she tearfully wrote as Tumpty Number 0.

This was the world into which the *Mirror* was re-born.

What happened to its unpredictable, eccentric midwife Mr Arkas Sapt, the man whose vision made it possible for the paper to sell nearly 290,000 illustrated copies by the date of its first birthday? He was a lavish spender, irked by creditors. Duns cornered him in Cannon Street railway station, where, labelling himself like a piece of luggage, he concealed himself in the lost property office and sent the ticket to the *Mirror* by District Messenger with a note saying:

'Come and get me out.'

The office sent him the money.

Sapt's working agreement was on a commission basis – the higher the sales, the higher his pay. When he left he surrendered his financial interest for a comparatively small sum and thereby lost a fortune.

PUNCH, OR THE LONDON CHARIVARI.—October 28, 1903. iii

No. 1 of

THE DAILY MIRROR

The First Daily Newspaper for Gentlewomen,

Will be issued on

MONDAY MORNING,
NOVEMBER 2.

Those who desire Copies should give immediate Orders
to their Newsvendors.

ONE PENNY.
MONDAY, NOVEMBER 2nd.

ALEXANDER KENEALY

Not only that rare bird, the Inspired Editor, but in his time a bar-room gladiator of note.

4
THE HURRYING YEARS

In the hurrying years the *Mirror* began to reach out and take up strange handfuls from the brantub of life.

A headline proclaimed:

SAVED BY STRONG CORSETS

Three revolver shots had been fired at a lady who refused to return to her lover; her armour of whalebone and steel saved her life.

Introduction of mixed bathing at the seaside was celebrated by an offer to female readers of an elegant up-to-the-minute pattern for a combination skirt needing five-and-a-half yards of serge. Photographs disclosed a rear view of bathing belles glancing coyly over the left shoulder. Winning styles in a bathing dress contest were displayed on dolls.

The Times pioneered in hastening news, the *Mirror* in hastening pictures. Enterprising, courageous young cameramen like the Three Brothers Grant, Frank Magee, Armand Console, David McLellan, Graham Healey and Alexander Muirhead photographed wars and revolutions, earthquakes and shipwrecks, kings and murderers, and travelled by Zeppelin, submarine, rickshaw, and camel.

They scooped the Italian atrocities at Tripoli in 1911, ascended Mont Blanc in winter, descended into the crater of the erupting Vesuvius and crossed the Alps in a balloon!

Why? So that their paper could say:

FIRST PICTURES, EXCLUSIVE.

Mr Justice Ridley appeared on the front page, black cap on his head, sentencing to death a young clerk who had shot his sweetheart.

An unemployed man wrote to the editor: 'Thousands are starving like me. I want to be fed for certain and have a bit to give my wife and four youngsters. Give me just a chance – you can buy me as a slave if you like.'

Flying Saucers – the joke of 1952 and 1953 – are not new. Forty-three years ago the headlines were asking: ARE AIRSHIPS HOVERING OVER BRITAIN AT NIGHT? From seven districts came reports of 'a mysterious cigar-shaped object hanging above the earth and emitting whirring noises.'

Intrusion into grief? The *Mirror* made history by publishing a double-page picture of King Edward VII at rest, eyes closed, hands folded, and at his elbow a spray of white roses placed there by his Queen. Two million of the monarch's subjects bought the memorial number, and years later Hannen Swaffer told how the photograph was obtained. The scene moves to a public house:

> In the Falstaff, the Friday after the monarch's death, I heard Sir Percival Phillips (famous as a war correspondent) telling another *Express* man that such a picture had been taken. They knew – but didn't go and get it! Next morning I sent Ivor Castle down to old man Downey, the Court photographer – I guessed he might be the man chosen to take it – to offer him £100 if he would go and ask Queen Alexandra if we could use it. 'It can only go in one paper, the *Mirror,*' said Alexandra, 'because that is my favourite'. So the finest news photograph the world has ever seen occupied the two centre pages of the *Daily Mirror.*

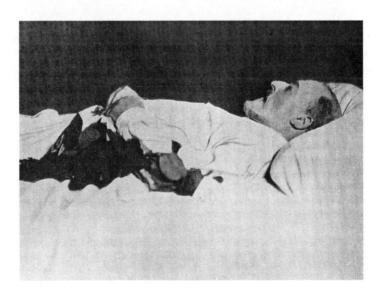

David McLellan caused a hullabaloo with his magnesium flash-powder when he tried to take the first night picture of Piccadilly Circus from Swan and Edgar's balcony. The powder was wrongly mixed, and a terrific explosion tore off a corner of the balcony and blew in fifty-two windows. Other newspapers next morning were speculating about 'anarchist bombs in the heart of London'.

New Year's Day was greeted with the perky banner-line:

HULLO –HAPPY DAYS.

The year was 1914.

£5,000 was offered for war pictures by amateurs. First prize of £1,000 went to a survivor of the *Falaba,* torpedoed off Ireland. He took his pictures, wrapped his camera in an oilskin tobacco pouch, crammed it into his mackintosh pocket, and leapt into the sea. He was picked up an hour later. When the camera was opened in the office the outer films were sodden, but an inner film carried a magnificent close-up of ten men clinging to an upturned lifeboat beside the sinking ship. It filled the front page.

The price of the paper went up to a penny in 1917, never to come down again. George Bernard Shaw wrote: 'Why not make it a shilling?'

To cover the midnight funeral of Emperor Mutsuhito, maker of modern Japan, Tom Grant got himself appointed hon. assistant with top hat and evening dress to the official court photographer, and had to be in his place twelve hours before the obsequies began. An explosion of vapour lamps during experiments to provide sufficient lighting killed two men and injured several others, but the *Mirror* had its pictures.

When an apiarist claimed that bees could live and thrive in a crowded city, two colonies of the insects – making fifty thousand in all – were installed on the office roof. They were lightly powdered with flour so that the public could spot them in gardens and squares within a two-mile radius.

The *Mirror* offered a thousand pounds for ideas to improve the paper, and two hundred readers received a fiver each – for useless suggestions. One chump wanted to perfume the newspaper with the fragrance of a different flower each day.

5
ROTHERMERE – FINANCIER

Harold Harmsworth, first Lord Rothermere, and brother of Northcliffe, died in 1940. It is time his association with the *Mirror* was assessed in true perspective. There are two parallel narratives to be told; one of financial success, the other of editorial failure.

In 1914, when he became chief proprietor, the average daily net sale was 1,210,354; public interest in the declaration of war stimulated newspaper sales. In 1931 when he sold the last of his *Mirror* shares on the Stock Exchange the average daily net sale had sorrowfully slumped to 987,080, with a one day 'low' of 829,704. The result of seventeen years of editorial activity failed even to maintain the *status quo*.

Yet the *Mirror-Pictorial* companies under his direction handled millions of pounds, and investments became more important and lucrative than the paper itself. Publication could have been abandoned with the company still flourishing on the income from its subsidiary operations. How all this came to pass is one of the newspaper industry's fascinating sagas.

In 1904, the year after the paper was born, the copyright was acquired from the *Daily Mail* Publishing Company Limited by Pictorial Newspaper Company Limited.

This company was liquidated in 1910, when Pictorial Newspaper Company (1910) Limited was formed with the same directors.

The public applied for nearly a million shares, more than twice the number offered: such was the magic of its founder's name.

In January, 1914 it was announced that the impetuous Northcliffe was 'anxious to concentrate his energies and limit his activities', and that he had sold the *Mirror* to his brother. The price, said Bernard Falk, who knew both men well, was £100,000 – the sum the founder had lost in the early hapless days.

Rothermere as chief proprietor held command for seventeen years. A financier was at the helm. There is no doubt that he inherited a popular newspaper, and that its conduct on skilful lines would have ensured an expanding future with the public; he also inherited a problem in accountancy.

Newspapermen, politicians and shareholders were puzzled to know why Northcliffe had sold out, for they did not know then the facts known now. There was much speculation.

At a time when the *Mirror* had no real national appeal Northcliffe had decided to print it in Manchester as well as in London. The move was a blunder and the loss of £600 a week had to be cut. Did the genius who said that failure was not in his vocabulary loathe the prospect of public retreat?

A second explanation was advanced by Roy Lewis. 'The paper had scooped death-bed scenes of King Edward VII, incidents connected with the *Titanic,* the funeral of the Emperor of Japan,' he wrote. 'It had photographed the interior of Vesuvius, been delivered in Bath by air, inspired the founding rival *Daily Sketch,* and published a Boy Scouts' number. Northcliffe felt there was no more real fun to be got out of it.'

A third theory has gained credence since the recent appearance of the final volume of *The History of The Times.*

Northcliffe ['When I want a peerage I will buy one, like an honest man'] had become chief proprietor of that journal in 1908, and the publication of his correspondence shows that in 1913 he evolved his plan to remould the paper the following year into an instrument of his personal ambition. He was attacking 'the dullards' and urging that the 'muddlers' must go. He was consumed with his desire to bend *The Times* to his will, was ridiculing its traditions and the 'priggish slackness' of its staff, persecuting the editor, boasting of his 'spies' and 'ferrets', throwing overboard those whose presence was inconvenient to him, keel-hauling executives whose pride he wished to prick, deriding strong men as weaklings and extolling sycophants as strong men.

Northcliffe was nearing the peak of his influence when in Churchill's words 'the sun of newspaper power began to glow with unprecedented heat'. Already the self-styled Ogre of Printing House Square, he was soon to rejoice in the title of Napoleon of Fleet Street, trying on the Emperor's hat during a visit to Fontainebleau and finding it too small for him. He was signing his communications 'Lord Vigour and Venom.'

The Mail and *The Times* were now closer to his heart and purpose. *The Mirror* was no longer the instrument for the megalomaniac who was to make wartime Cabinets and threaten to 'break' Lloyd George.

He would therefore 'concentrate his energies and limit his activities.'

The theories are plausible, and these factors may have played their part. But the specific decision to hand over the *Mirror* to his younger brother in 1914 sprang from a mundane personal consideration.

Irascibility and conflicting interests between Alfred and Harold Harmsworth had reached the stage of breach. Complete collaboration was no longer possible. The time had come, just as it came years later to the brothers Camrose and Kemsley, to divide the empire and go their separate ways.

Rothermere took over, to make the *Mirror* and its associated properties the most potent financial combination in the newspaper industry. He studied the accounts and resolved that withdrawal from Manchester was urgent and imperative. The experiment launched with strident publicity was peremptorily concluded in a stage whisper inaudible to readers.

Little could be done with the paper in a business sense during the war which began eight months after the new proprietor's enthronement, but there was one direction in which Rothermere could and did exhibit enterprise. On March 14 1915 he launched the *Sunday Pictorial*, the first Sunday picture paper; it was conceived in a rush, deliberately planned to forestall a new Hulton publication due to appear a fortnight later. The first number sold over a million, and its immediate and continued success established the firm's financial strength.

The end of the war brought the chance for further expansion which Rothermere awaited. Bertram Lima, his personal representative on the firm and later chairman, was entrusted with plans for a new London evening paper. A tiny token issue of the *Evening Mirror* was, and still is, printed daily to preserve the copyright of the title.

Rothermere named as his editorial executives for the new publication the two men who had created the *Pictorial*, F R Sanderson the editor and Alexander Campbell his assistant. Staff were engaged. Then in 1919 came Lima's sudden death at thirty-five; a victim of the influenza epidemic.

The decision over the *Evening Mirror* now rested with John Cowley, the new chairman, a gentleman whom recent experience had taught to be cautious. The Harmsworths had bought Cowley when they took over the London *Evening News:* he went 'with the business', and when the brothers launched the *Daily Mail* his name appeared on the imprint as manager and director.

An estrangement, not uncommon in the newspaper industry, parted Cowley from the Northcliffe stable. It led him into the perils of proprietorship on his own account and into a double disaster which sadly depleted his personal fortune. A racing paper he ran with his two life-long friends Edgar Wallace and Bernard Falk failed, mainly (says Falk) owing to 'Our inability to control Wallace'. The London *Evening Times* also bit the dust.

It was not surprising that John Cowley, reconciled with the Harmsworths during the First World War, doubted whether the new evening paper project would succeed; the blue-print was shelved and stayed shelved.

A new company was formed. The Daily Mirror Newspapers, incorporated in 1920, had an issued capital of 350,000 eight per cent cumulative preference shares and 700,000 ordinary shares, each of £1[3]. Directors included Wallace D Roome, John Cowley (both of whom remained with the company until their death), H G Bartholomew and Alexander Campbell.

The Rothermere financial empire began to take shape when in 1922 the *Mirror* and *Pictorial* guaranteed £650,000 debentures of the Empire Paper Mills at Greenhithe, Kent, and nearly £15,000,000 was subscribed in the few minutes the list was open.

In the twenties and thirties newspaper finance became news, activities of Rothermere more often than not making the headlines. The industry was entering upon a period of ruthless conflict, with free gift schemes and big money prizes as the corrupting influence in an unedifying scramble for new readers. Yet, to the *Mirror,* there came comforting enrichment.

Just as Northcliffe was known to the public as a genius of journalism, so Rothermere's reputation grew as a financial colossus. His ambition was unbridled, but it was not until Northcliffe died in 1922 that his supreme moment came. He sensed, astutely, that the industry lay at his feet.

A manoeuvre to dominate *The Times* failed, but he took control of Associated Newspapers, formed the Daily Mail Trust from this foundation, and offered to the public £1,600,000 guaranteed debenture stock. The security was 400,000 deferred shares in Associated Newspapers, owning the *Daily Mail, Evening News* and *Sunday Dispatch,* and the principal and interest were guaranteed by the *Mirror* and *Pictorial.*

The unhappy role of the two 'picture paper' companies in the Rothermere empire was now ordained. They generally shouldered two-thirds of the responsibility in any fresh development for they held a seventy per cent interest in the Daily Mail Trust. They were Rothermere's financial ace of spades.

---

[3] Subsequently the ordinary shares were converted into 5s. units and in 1941 the preference and ordinary shares were converted into stock.

A newspaper must make a healthy profit to survive, flourish and expand, for without financial well-being neither its readers nor its shareholders can be served. But the function of the *Mirror* as a newspaper, and its service to its public, were now thrust low on the list of priorities.

Rothermere surveyed the battlefield, awaiting the first opportunity to pounce. It came with the death of Sir Edward Hulton.

The objective, which was gained in a remarkably short period, was simply to organise a series of financial swoops which would revolutionise Press control and achieve the maximum concentration of newspaper ownership ever seen in the world. His initial move became known when the Daily Mail Trust invited subscriptions for no less than £8,000,000, then swallowed the London and Manchester properties of Hulton's in one mighty gulp.

Such was public confidence in the Press as a field of investment that £40,000,000 was offered in a few hours, nearly one pound per head of the country's population.

Was the deal as prudent as it was courageous? One outcome is certain: the integrity of the Press as an institution was degraded to the stature of an auditor's nightmare. What a jumble of political opinion and social outlook there was in that group. Many were in front-line rivalry for the public's custom: The *Mirror* and the *Daily Sketch:* The *Pictorial* and the *Sunday Herald, Sunday Chronicle, Empire News,* and *Weekly Dispatch:* The *Daily Mail* and, in the north, the *Daily Dispatch.* The tangle did not end there. For a 49 per cent interest was also held in the Beaverbrook properties, though Beaverbrook himself retained personal control.

There now entered into the scene two men from South Wales – the Berry Brothers, the present Lord Camrose and Lord Kemsley, who were founding their own newspaper empire and were seeking expansion in Manchester. Three Richmonds in the field?

The ink on the Rothermere-Hulton deal was scarcely dry when the Berry brothers bought from the Daily Mail Trust all the Manchester properties except the *Daily Sketch* and the *Sunday Herald,* whose chief printing offices were in London. In 1924 these two journals became the subject of another flotation, involving more debentures, more guarantees by the *Mirror.* Then, within a few years the *Sketch* and *Herald* joined the rest of the Hulton properties already within the Berry camp.

There was activity, too, with the structure of the *Mirror* company. It increased its capital to £2,200,000 and capitalised £350,000 of undivided profits, distributing as a free bonus one new share for every two held. This bonus was repeated a few months later.

Rothermere now felt that his stature as financier and his sovereignty as Press proprietor were secure, unchallengeable. But in 1928 came fresh excitement with a bold but ill-conceived plan which punctured his prestige. It was born of vanity. A casual remark goaded him into making his classic blunder.

Rothermere was visiting America with his retinue, pondering new fields to conquer, seeking fresh outlets for the exercise of his financial prowess. And when he reached New York an acquaintance said to him: 'They tell me that the Berry brothers are now the biggest newspaper owners in Britain'.

This was too much for the imperious Rothermere. Incensed at the insult, he curtailed his journey and returned to London, brooding over his future plans, debating where next he would strike.

He looked around the provinces and examined its existing newspapers. They seemed to him to be unenterprising, Victorian, isolated economic units suffering from a lack of connection with a central organisation. Why not initiate a new chain? What the provinces needed was a pack of modern newspapers filled with London features, London talent, London skill. All these vital ingredients, together with a news service of *Daily Mail* standard, would be centrally supplied on a network of Creed machines and private phone links; local flavour, in each newspaper, would be superimposed by its editor and staff on the spot of publication.

Rothermere formed Northcliffe Newspapers Ltd, a £3,000,000 company, and announced that 'to the development of this great new enterprise all the ability and resources of the *Mail* and *Mirror* will be directed'. His own financial skill, and the enchantment of his dead brother's name, inspired the public to rush in with £25,000,000, and within fifteen minutes the lists were closed.

It was at this stage that some members, not all, of the *Mirror* board experienced their first misgivings. The Berrys had steadfastly entrenched themselves in the provinces: so had two other, smaller groups. Why did Rothermere so bluntly declare open warfare? Why did he raise the money so publicly and reveal his hand to his adversaries? Here, surely, was a case for individual sporadic purchase, for the nurturing of local confidence rather than the imposition of metropolitan dictatorship.

The scramble began, the maddest and saddest episode in newspaper history.

LORD ROTHERMERE

'In finance a titan to reckon with and fear. In other spheres his tuch was
less certain. Rothermere alone was not enough.'

Rothermere had prodigious resources behind him, but in some towns the Berrys succeeded in outbidding the new company for plant and publications already in existence. At the height of the contest

ROTHERMERE controlled fourteen daily and Sunday papers, with an interest in three others;

THE BERRYS controlled twenty-five dailies and Sundays.

Rothermere's boast that London could conquer the provinces, crush local financial interests and patriotism, and garner a harvest into the bargain was an hallucination. The Berrys from South Wales had a surer feeling for the provincial spirit.

The costly battle of the giants ended in the journalistic partition of Britain; an armistice, with casualties left maimed or unemployed all over the field. The curtain came down on Rothermere's bid for greater wealth and influence with the voluntary liquidation of Northcliffe Newspapers Ltd and the absorption of many of its properties by Associated Newspapers.

In 1929 John Cowley, *Mirror* chairman, told the shareholders at the annual meeting that the company's investments, which included even mining ventures in Newfoundland, were worth £8,000,000 apart from goodwill, plant and buildings.

Lord Rothermere's activities had not been confined to the purchase and sale of newspapers. There were ventures overseas in another industry, and the *Mirror* company as always had been used as his financial armoury.

In the early twenties he had built up wide interests in pulp and paper, and the *Mirror* and *Pictorial* were already big shareholders in British newsprint concerns and in the Anglo-Newfoundland Development Company. He now wanted to set up a mill in Quebec, buy timber limits, and make and sell newsprint to the rapidly expanding publishers in the US.

The Anglo-Canadian Pulp and Paper Mills Ltd was registered in 1925, and Rothermere became its first president. Again the two picture papers were involved, subscribing most of the preference shares, representing the major part of £1,640,000, and also guaranteeing £3,000,000 debentures.

The high promise of prosperity dissolved in the slump of 1929. Demand diminished and the newsprint debts of US publishers including William Randolph Hearst were frozen for years.

So that Anglo-Canadian could survive the depression there was a readjustment of capital in 1933, again guaranteed by *Mirror-Pictorial*. In 1940, the year of Rothermere's death, a major financial operation entailed sacrifices for the original shareholders, and Anglo-Canadian became a financial problem which the *Mirror* inherited from the Rothermere empire.

Fortunately conditions in the industry changed. The company became a vigorous concern under the direction of the Canadian Elliott M Little, operating on a financial reconstruction by two *Mirror* directors, Cecil H King and Arthur S Fuller, who surveyed the problems on the spot in Quebec in 1939.

Such were the fabulous deals of Harold Harmsworth, first Lord Rothermere.

In finance he remained a titan to reckon with and fear until his death. In other spheres his touch was less certain. For misjudgment marred his activities, and occasionally he scaled the peak of folly.

6
ROTHERMERE – JOURNALIST

Statistics yield no clue to a man's true personality: least of all to a financier's.

The Rothermere of the Stock Exchange was forever the buoyant optimist, juggling with millions of the public's money as well as with his own expanding fortune. Yet philosophically, and therefore editorially, he was besieged by gloom.

A wet blanket descended upon the *Mirror* from under which it was unable to crawl until Rothermere's financial dictatorship and editorial direction loosened.

In human and social affairs his perspicacity deserted him; ruthlessness alone was not enough. Politically he backed the wrong horses with a consistency which would have reduced a less affluent punter to penury.

The public trusted his financial judgment, snapped up his shares and were grateful for his dividends: unlike his brother, he did not know much else about them, did not understand their fears and aspirations, could not feel their pulse or sense their heart beat.

Such imperception and lofty isolation are not the hallmark of effective journalism.

As his editor of the *Mirror,* Rothermere inherited Alexander Kenealy, who had joined Hamilton Fyfe in 1904 and succeeded him as editorial chief.

Here was that very rare bird, the Inspired Editor, and his leadership more than any other man's built up the paper to the handsome sale which Rothermere acquired in 1914 – the world's largest circulation of those times.

Kenealy was the son of a Queen's Counsel and was christened in the Temple Church. But it was during his newspaper training in America that he absorbed the technique of sparkle, brevity and initiative that was to make his paper the most popular to come off the presses of Fleet Street.

He was a powerful man, and in his time a bar-room gladiator of note. Once, when he and Don McCarthy, an American cartoonist, had a dispute in Perry's, a bar parlour in the building of the *New York World,* the fracas cost Kenealy five hundred dollars including McCarthy's hospital expenses and the bills for broken glassware and furniture.

By the time he reached London he was less combative. When Fyfe threatened 'to knock his head off' in a verbal tussle over the handling of a story, Kenealy backed away, the colour draining from his ruddy cheeks. 'I would not have said it,' Fyfe recalled, 'if I had known the reason for his alarm – he was nervous of physical violence on account, I believe, of a weak heart. Nothing of the kind ever happened again. We got along very well.'

Kenealy had pride in his profession: serious news he treated seriously, light news lightly. But always he aimed to make the reader sit up.

Rothermere, unfortunately, was not to have the benefit of his experience for long, for in June 1915 Alexander Kenealy died and a memorial number with eight pages of text and photographs honoured *'The Man Who Made The Mirror'.* The front page showed Kenealy, short, tubby, with round and genial face, as his staff knew him best – at work at his desk in the office.

Ed Flynn, an American friend of Kenealy, followed him as editor for the greater part of the war.

The dynamic coverage of every battle-front by pictures and news assured success, and the paper ticked over with no apparent change of course.

In 1917, it is true, Rothermere emerged as the apostle of air power which to his credit he remained until his death in 1940. He was Air Minister for the last year of the war and became president of a public body known as the Air Council. When the Americans entered the war the *Mirror* commented:

> America cannot improve our men but she can enliven the whole conception of the task they have to perform. The air might well be a sphere of mobility to counteract the dreaded trench warfare of winter. Let us build and build until our command of the air be final. The air holds the secret, it may be, of final victory for us.

It was in the years which followed the first world war that the new chief proprietor's editorial influence became depressingly plain in a dozen dubious directions. The *Mirror* at that time appealed principally to women. Alas, the unhappy sex was inveigled into enduring a diet of politics and financial comment, a page a day of the latter, which would have halted a student of affairs in his tracks. From Rothermere, not once or twice but interminably, came the dominant ingredient of the paper – the ponderous political article. A surfeit of starch; little, if any, protein.

Ed Flynn was followed as editor in 1920 by Alexander Campbell, a Yorkshireman.

Campbell was harassed on the one hand by the pernicious system of buying readers with free insurance, free gifts, free competitions; on the other, he was beset by the political cupidities and time-consuming confabs of his millionaire master. Few in Fleet Street could have coveted the chair Campbell continued to occupy until just after the curtain fell on the Rothermere reign in 1931.

News was subordinated to political dogma: a galling, melancholy task.

The *Mirror* was committed to a protracted campaign for national economy, conceived and delivered with the same unctuousness and lack of verve as characterise a Sunday evening sermon on the virtues of thrift.

One word reiterated *ad nauseam* epitomised the crusade: SQUANDERMANIA. The Government could not expend a nickel without a rap over the knuckles from the sombre brother who had balanced Northcliffe's ledgers. Battleships? Outdated. The Singapore naval base? A white elephant. Labour Exchanges were 'pensioners' clubs'. Even air power, his cherished cause, must endure close scrutiny.

The Anti-Waste League was formed (president, Lord Rothermere) with some successes at the polls when he sponsored his own parliamentary candidates. The public were pestered to buy 'Solvency or Downfall', a reproduction of his exhortations. A South African Bantu, seeing an advertisement for the book in the *Overseas Mirror,* promptly sent off his money expecting to receive in return a salacious novel. It was clear from his letter that he was more interested in the chapters on downfall than on solvency. Owing, however, to the scarcity of dirty-minded Bantus, the book was a conspicuous flop.

Like another Press baron – the Messiah from New Brunswick, Canada – he ransacked the Old Testament for the language in which the prophets couched their forebodings. HAS THE DAY OF RECKONING COME? and THE SEVEN LEAN YEARS were the titles of his manifestoes.

The day of reckoning had not come for Harold Harmsworth – nor had the seven lean years. But the sincerity with which he conducted in private life his own campaign against squandermania disconcerted his associates.

He gave thousands to hospitals and universities. Yet in his personal sphere he practised frugality, moving from his hotel suite into a modest flat. His co-directors were entertained to austerity meals. Water was served instead of wine, and the host would discourse upon the coming bankruptcy of Britain.

Did he recall with chagrin in that period of parsimony the money he had lavished some years before upon Horatio Bottomley? When that plausible scoundrel was being paid hundreds of pounds an article to write for Rothermere's newspapers, the two gentlemen met while dining separately at the Carlton. Rothermere called across, 'I have long been wishing to meet my chief contributor.' To which Bottomley replied, 'On the contrary, I have long been wishing to meet *my* chief contributor.'

But japes about money were no longer acceptable.

One night, when he spotted Alexander Campbell in a seat at the Russian Ballet, he summoned him over and devoted the interval to reminding his editor of the country's impending collapse.

There were those who thought Rothermere's depression might have sprung from personal sorrow, for he had lost two of his sons in the war.

It was the province of foreign affairs that he earmarked for his most spectacular misjudgments.

His brother, Lord Northcliffe, had hated the Germans pathologically; indeed, this hatred and fear was one of the manifestations of the mental condition which developed in his later years. The Napoleonic blusterings and the satanic suspicions recorded in the last volume of *The History of The Times* have led to the misconception that the Northcliffe of the war and post-war years was the real man; his mind had in fact been unhinged for a considerable period, for he was suffering from the final stages of general paralysis of the insane. The brain which had created the *Mail* and the *Mirror* had corroded years before: the restless energy and truculence remained.

Henry Wickham Steed entered Northcliffe's suite on the fifth floor of the Plaza-Athenee in Paris on the evening of Sunday, June 11 1922.

He found him in bed, scantily dressed, obviously excited. For a moment, when the lights were turned up, his left eye showed a diagonal squint. His lower lip bore a dark scar as if he had been burned. Seizing Steed's hand he said how keenly he had felt the separation from him, and rehearsed in a gabbling voice the circumstances of his poisoning by the Germans, and the attempted assassination by his Secretary at Boulogne. [*The History of The Times* Fourth Volume.]

During Steed's absence from the apartment the founder of the *Mirror* had perceived the shadow of his dressing-gown hanging on the door and mistaken it for an intruder. Steed returned to find Northcliffe waving a

Colt pistol with seven chambers loaded at the shadow with his right hand and clutching a book of piety with his left.

When Northcliffe imagined in the 1920s that the Germans were pursuing him, he was demented. When Rothermere in the 1930s was pursuing the Germans he was at the height of his mental powers.

The rise of Benito Mussolini and Adolf Hitler made thoughtful people apprehensive. True, Lord Rothermere pressed for stronger British air power, but he did not share in the general anxiety. He saw Mussolini, in Pitt's phrase, as 'A Man of Destiny who had saved Italy by his exertions and Europe by his example'. He explained the first Nazi successes as the rebirth of Germany as a nation, the triumph of younger men in revolt against post-war depression and the old-world politicians. He sent G Ward Price as his emissary to hob-nob at the courts of the dictators and to explain, or explain away, their policies in his newspapers; even the activities of Oswald Mosley's British Union of Fascists were eulogised in the Rothermere Press.

Earlier, and more sensibly, Lord Rothermere had advocated the review of the Treaty of Trianon, a campaign which ended in the Hungarians offering the newspaper proprietor the crown of Hungary.

The monarchist party had been divided and the Hungarian people, then considered to be strongly monarchist by instinct, were without an acceptable claimant. Writing of 'Myself and the King question', Rothermere said: 'I have never discovered how or when the proposal that this high honour should be offered to myself first took shape. It seems to have occurred independently to a number of minds in the autumn of 1927, shortly after the appearance of my first articles on the subject of treaty revision. Though neither I nor my son knew it, the movement was spreading fast when he paid his visit to Hungary in the late spring of 1928 ... I was assured that, in the prevailing enthusiastic mood of the Hungarian people, a plebiscite in my favour would be practically unanimous.'

Rothermere declined, telling the Hungarians that although he believed a monarchy would have a steadying effect he could only recommend them to choose a ruler of their own race. After a round-robin from twenty highly-placed Army officers, a delegation came to London to persuade him to change his mind, but Rothermere was adamant.

The man who would not be king accepted many gifts which were 'pathetic evidence of the place which I had attained unsought in the imagination of the mass of the people'.

Among them, from Budapest Chamber of Commerce, was a magnificent writing table decorated with the coats-of-arms of the fifty-eight provinces and towns of Hungary. With a flag and a sabre which had once belonged to Hungarian national heroes he treasured this 'as evidence of the affection which my sympathy for Hungary's afflictions had aroused among her people.'

In home politics Rothermere's vagaries also confused his readers. David Lloyd George and Stanley Baldwin were both in turn to enjoy his flattery, but there was criticism of a vehement nature in store in later years for the Liberal and personal derision for the Tory. The Welshman was cynically amused, the Worcestershire squire aggrieved and wrathful.

A deviation from the *Mirror's* pre-war policy took place early in the years of peace.

Hamilton Fyfe had pledged the paper's general support to the Labour Party when it was formed as a separate Parliamentary force in 1903. When John Burns joined the Cabinet in the Liberal Government, Fyfe welcomed

> a Minister who wears a blue serge suit. The silly tradition which associates political ability with a frock coat and top hat is staggering under the blow.

Socialism, wrote Fyfe, was 'the creed of the future'. He campaigned for school meals for children. But humanitarianism to Northcliffe was squandermania to Rothermere. Bowler hats and blue serge suits were out; top hats and frock coats were in again.

Rothermere's policy, formerly Liberal, became fervidly anti-Socialist. All factions except one were given a Special *Mirror* Number in 1922: there was no issue for Ramsay MacDonald.

Even his patronage of the Tories was fickle, propelled by personal feuds with its leaders. None could wonder why the *Morning Post* called Rothermere 'the political Wibbly-Wob' when the *Mirror* and his other journals began their campaign against Baldwin which reached its crescendo in the thirties.

In the election of 1924, when the country threw Baldwin's protectionist policy overboard, and MacDonald, backed by Liberal votes, became the first Labour Premier, the *Mirror* told the Liberals they had committed suicide. Its advice that the older parties should combine against Socialism had been rejected.

Within a year Baldwin was back in power with a majority of 200 in the famous Zinoviev Letter election, and it was Rothermere's *Daily Mail* which had published the document. Fake – or genuine? Nobody knows to this day.

In Baldwin's 'Safety First' election of 1929 the *Mirror* again advocated a Liberal-Conservative line-up to keep the Socialists out, and when Labour won, though still lacking an overall majority, Rothermere turned to the Empire for consolation and linked with Lord Beaverbrook to form the United Empire Party.

Warnings of 'Solvency or Downfall' were now not so vociferous; fear of 'The Day of Reckoning' had eased; the spectre of 'The Seven Lean Years' had not been laid, but its eerie tappings were now not so audible. The United Empire Party held aloft a banner emblazoned with the one word PROSPERITY.

It is true that 'rigid economy' was included in the Party's programme to gratify Rothermere, and 'aid for the farmers' to appease Beaverbrook, but there was no explanation to the enthusiasts who rallied to the *Mirror's* recruiting office as to how both objects could be simultaneously achieved.

Two of the other precepts upon which the 'Wicked Uncles of Fleet Street' had agreed during their truce make curious reading to-day:

NO MORE SURRENDERS IN INDIA

NO DIPLOMATIC RELATIONS WITH RUSSIA

For one of the reasons why Lord Beaverbrook urged the public to vote for Winston Churchill in the post-war elections was that the Tory leader could speak to Stalin as man to man.

The United Empire Party was without concealment an organised onslaught upon the orthodox Conservative leaders. Why were there one-million-and-a-half unemployed in Britain? Why no protective duties on foreign goods? Why no sane system of Empire preferences? Why no tariff wall around the Empire?

When Rothermere 'on behalf of the readers of the *Mirror*' pledged himself to provide the organisation, candidates and money to fight fifty constituencies for the United Empire Party, Baldwin was visibly and vocally rattled.

He said Rothermere would be the first man off to France if revolution broke out in Britain. Rothermere replied in the same words, naming Aix-les-Bains as Baldwin's place of refuge; that was the Tory Leader's holiday retreat.

How childish it all seems now. And was then. But there was evidence to justify Baldwin's bitterness.

Rothermere, in an article, had written:

> Mr Baldwin is one of the greatest Prime Ministers who ever held office.

And then, four years later –

> Mr Baldwin is a completely incompetent person who got into
> high office by an accident of post-war politics.

Rothermere had demanded to be told in advance the names of the next Tory Cabinet – 'a preposterous and insolent demand', said Baldwin: it was a parallel attempt to dictate Cabinet appointments that had inflamed the wartime clash between Northcliffe and Lloyd George.

So the Press charade went on. *La Ronde,* with the *Mirror* playing a major role. Influential Tories pressed Baldwin to absorb some of the United Empire Party's proposals but Baldwin demurred. The pace hastened and the 'Wicked Uncles' themselves became confused. Lord Beaverbrook announced that he and Lord Rothermere had parted company, since they no longer saw eye to eye on all issues; Rothermere still advocated that Beaverbrook should be the next Tory Prime Minister.

There followed the unedifying farce of the by-election at St George's constituency in Westminster, with the slogan GANDHI IS WATCHING ST GEORGE'S.

Mirror readers, concerned with their own family affairs and unaware of the cause of the pother, learned at their breakfast table that

> this fanatic leader of a fanatic Indian horde knows that St George's is a
> test of the opinion of the people of Britain on the vital problem of
> whether India is to be surrendered or governed. Put Fetter in and you put
> Gandhi out!

For Baldwin the St George's fiasco was the breaking point. He told a public meeting that the papers conducted by Lords Rothermere and Beaverbrook were not newspapers in the ordinary acceptance of the term; they were engines of propaganda for die changing policies, desires and personal likes and dislikes of two men.

What they aim at,' said Baldwin, 'is power, and power without responsibility, the prerogative of the harlot through the ages.'

So far as the *Daily Mirror* at that time was concerned, the charge was justified.

7

YOU CAN'T SHOOT THE PROPRIETOR

The *Mirror* placed on record its mission to present all that was 'best and brightest', adding, with an unctuousness from which the industry rarely escapes, 'this does not mean a sort of journalistic ragtime or taking life in a clownish fashion'.

The melancholy campaign on Squandermania ensured that there would be no ragtime: that pledge was honoured to excess. Conversely, the undertaking that life 'would not be taken in a clownish fashion' was broken by political buffoonery.

Was the *Mirror* 'best and brightest?'

When peace revived competition and larger papers returned, there was a struggle, which ended in failure, to hold the million circulation. True the 1920s were a time of big news. But big news is a commodity Fleet Street has to share.

There was a creditable display of initiative in the gathering of news and particularly of pictures. The paper was proud of an interview with Queen Marie of Rumania, and Horace Grant succeeded in gate-crashing the Crown Prince of Germany, 'Little Willie', in his hide-out on the island of Wieringen.

Under Alexander Campbell's influence, the *Mirror* retained its social conscience. It exposed commercial rackets, avaricious house agents, promoters of snowball schemes who promised the gullible the chance of winning £150 for the investment of one shilling. There was a campaign for safety on the roads, police methods of obtaining evidence were criticised, and a demand was published for a restriction of the powers of the coroner's court. There was hand-to-hand fighting with the BMA journal over the right and duty of doctors to disseminate medical knowledge in the popular Press, and of solid practical value was the paper's work in raising vast sums for hospitals, a cause in which Rothermere and Campbell were interested.

Nor was the lighter side of life neglected.

A familiar friend reappeared – the beauty contest, this time a quest for the 'most beautiful woman war worker'. Highly-paid personalities were engaged to write for the feature pages, among them Ella Wheeler Wilcox. Miss Wilcox celebrated President Wilson's visit to Britain with a plea for British-American friendship entitled *Deep Unto Deep was Calling:*

> And one voice now and for ever
> Will speak from sea to sea
> Wherever the British Banner
> And the Starry Flag float free!

She was well rewarded for this tenth-rate ditty.

Humanity? That essential ingredient also was not overlooked in the hurly-burly of high and low politics, for there came into the news a terrier by the name of Bobs.

Bobs belonged to a thirteen-year-old girl in Fulham. He had bitten a policeman and had been condemned to death. A life for a bite? This the *Mirror* would not allow to happen. A picture of the whelp appeared on the front page with a placard round his neck bearing the words NOT GUILTY; he was described as 'the children's friend and the policemen's enemy', and twenty-two thousand people who agreed with this charitable view signed a petition.

Bobs was saved.

Unfortunately, orthodox enterprise and good printing do not alone make a newspaper a power in the land. The uncertain touch of clumsy proprietorship may be survived, but only if the journal is in step with the times, or more shrewdly a step ahead.

The *Mirror* of the 1920s and early 1930s was out of step; that is why, after it had failed to expand to any appreciable or permanent degree, it sank into a decline which nothing short of tempestuous change could check and reverse.

News photographs, on which the paper had built its world record sale, were robbed of their magic by the moving, and shortly the talking, picture of the cinema.

The *Mirror* was at variance with social trends. In a decade of brashness it offered gentility and sighed with nostalgia for the pre-war proprieties. The suffragette movement had succeeded and a new relationship was evolving between the sexes, but when young women were granted the vote at twenty-one instead of thirty it was in spite of Lord Rothermere and his picture paper. The change was derided as 'Flapper Folly', and the nation was pompously warned that the extended franchise would place men in a minority.

The 1920s were the age of political reform, for general education had encouraged an awareness of injustice and inequality. Labour twice took office, but the response of the journal which in the early days of Hamilton Fyfe had welcomed the formation of the Party was a protracted campaign of deep-dyed reaction.

This was the Century of the Common Man. Yet at the very time when the articulate masses were struggling to raise their standard of living and status in society, the *Mirror* directed its appeal to the dwindling middle class. Not only to the middle class, but to the middle-aged. All this, when youth was challenging tradition and rejecting the laws and modes of its elders with a boldness never before witnessed.

Failure was the forfeit which time exacted for these misjudgments, a failure which was deserved.

Folly was not confined to the offices of the *Mirror*. For the 1920s were the years when Fleet Street went mad on a grandiose scale.

A new concept was introduced into the newspaper industry, and it ran something like this: *To hell with editorial enterprise – give 'em a grand piano instead.*

The 1947-49 Press Commission condemned free gift schemes, and to-day to their credit the principal newspapers have an agreement not to revive them. Alexander Campbell, looking back upon this period of inanity, makes this tolerant comment: 'I have heard it said that *those* were the days. To remember or forget? If those *were* the days, there was something to remember – and quite a lot better forgotten.'

Fleet Street still bows its head when it recalls those years when the pursuit and presentation of news and views became a secondary activity. At the outset the *Mirror* held aloof from the scrimmage and sneered at its rivals 'resorting to all manner of desperate devices' to increase circulation: the *Mirror* indulged in the same desperate devices when it was drawn into the vortex in 1928.

Free insurance was the theme of the first act, and households were buying three or four copies of one newspaper or another so that each member of the family might be covered. The *Mirror*, not to be outmanoeuvred, offered a £25,000 free insurance policy against a fatal accident to man and wife provided either was a registered reader; before the Hitler war put a stop to the idiocy the paper paid out well over a quarter of a million pounds.

To the newsagent this quest for swollen circulations was a nightmare. Each paper employed battalions of doorstep canvassers whose duty it was to badger housewives into changing from the *Daily X* to the *Daily Y*, signing fresh forms and switching orders at the local shop from morning to morning. Newspapers which were the first to condemn intrusion by Press reporters into private grief were not slow to boast publicly of the booty they paid out after a rail crash.

The rivalry was not confined to free insurance, though the *Mirror* spent less on gift schemes than the others. Some papers offered free sets of works by popular novelists, and then came labour-saving gadgets and the forecasting of football results.

The *Mirror*, in association with the *Pictorial* and the *Sunday Dispatch*, two rival newspapers linked by the Rothermere interest, offered £20,000 for a correct forecast. Tom Hartley, of Blackburn, won the prize outright with twenty-four matches correct out of twenty-four. Tell that to your modern Pools fanatic.

When the courts ruled that newspaper football competitions were illegal, Fleet Street rejoiced, then embarked upon a fresh example of lunacy. The *Mirror* offered £7,500 for a forecast of the Derby's first five, but the courts again intervened.

The competition mania seemed endless and the *Mirror* once exulted in the distribution of £27,000 in one week in cash prizes, employing scores of people to check the entries. What are The Seven Best Qualities of Woman? Readers seeking a £500 award decided that 'love of home and children' heads the list, and that woman's 'most forgivable faults' are

Teasing,
Love of dress, and
Love of pleasure.

Then came puzzles, and the reign of 'The Guineas Man'. A representative of the paper went on tour handing guineas to train passengers he saw reading or holding that day's issue.

One final nonsense should be recorded and preserved as a monument to the days of thirty-two page issues. The 'Thirty two Live Pages', a well-drilled company of youths, toured the country in motor coaches 'to proclaim the triumph of the mammoth 32-page paper'. In blue uniforms piped with yellow and adorned with brass buttons, they numbered off at drill by hollering a feature of the journal – 'news', 'pictures', 'cartoons', 'leader', and so on. The drummer ended with the cry *'Daily Mirror, one penny'*. Then the thirty-two little chaps scattered over the town, each with a numbered disc on his cap.

One vanished, and by tracking down the remaining thirty-one and collecting their signatures a reader could name the missing page and win a ten-guinea prize.

But the *Mirror,* as a newspaper, did not contain thirty-two live pages.

8
THE BART REVOLUTION

At five a.m. in 1948 four men sat strapped in their seats around a table in the forward starboard cabin of a Sunderland flying boat gathering speed across the waters of Poole Harbour.

When the plane gained altitude and safety belts could be loosened, Harry Guy Bartholomew, chairman of the *Mirror* and *Pictorial* from 1944 to 1951, was closing his eyes. We were travelling twelve thousand miles to Australia to negotiate the purchase of a group of newspapers.

This was the first and last time I ever saw Bartholomew in repose. The volcano was dormant: Vesuvius was silhouetted against the Neapolitan moonlight with scarcely a wisp of smoke curling up to the sky. As he dozed off in his seat, a smile crossed his pink cheeks and his white hair fell over his forehead. Here was a deceptive study in innocence, for at sixty-four the volatile Press boss looked like a coddled, contented prize-winning baby, or an eminent divine.

Here was the man of whom, when he abruptly retired at the end of 1951, the *New Statesman* was to write:

> In some ways Bartholomew was like Northcliffe, a rough erratic genius fashioned out of an extraordinary mixture of shrewdness and naivety, toughness and sentimentality. He fought his way up from the very bottom of Fleet Street and in so doing carried the *Daily Mirror* with him to its present status as the most popular daily newspaper in the world... a working journalist, the first Englishman who really understood pictures and strips and realised that no-one reads more than a few hundred words on any subject.

Next to me was an Aussie returning to Sydney after nine months on an engineering mission to Metro-Vickers. He asked: 'Who is your friend?'

'Bart', typically, had imposed a rule of secrecy to apply throughout the journey. No surnames, no mention of newspapers, preferably no dialogue at all.

I replied: 'He is a well-known English bishop.'

'Well,' said the Aussie, 'he is certainly a fine old gentleman, a very fine old gentleman indeed.'

An early morning thirst is familiar to those who fly about their business at dawn, and I remembered that the sleeping bishop had placed a bottle at his feet in case of medicinal need. As I groped under the table for the prize, Bartholomew opened one eye and snapped: 'Take your thieving hands from that bottle of ------- Scotch!'

Throughout the eras of Northcliffe and Rothermere, Harry Guy Bartholomew played a prominent part in the story of the *Mirror*. He had never been in command, though his eventual ascendancy was inevitable.

Zest, originality and audacity were unrationed in this singular character, and he had few outside interests to divert his talents during the years of fretful waiting. The successes and the scope he enjoyed early in life were not enough, for Bart was restless. When he achieved ultimate power in 1944 his colleagues were to pay for the frustrations he endured in earlier years at the hands of uninspired men who were jealous of their own seniority. Bartholomew spat the bit from his mouth and snapped the guiding rein; he galloped on at a furious pace, outdistancing all around him, clearing all fences, trampling down all opposition, contemptuous of caution, heedless of danger, foaming and neighing, sparing neither himself nor others.

And in his headlong, headstrong rush, he raised the paper to the greatest daily sale the world has ever seen. Northcliffe was the first genius whose name appeared in this narrative, for he created the *Mail* and the *Mirror*. Bartholomew is the second; he re-created the *Mirror*.

I have met men who feared him, many who respected him, none who loved him, but only one who said he hated him.

Bart joined the paper in January 1904 (circulation 25,000) on the eve of its conversion into a picture paper. His name appears in the first Wages Book: 'H G Bartholomew, 30s.'

He came from the engraving department of Northcliffe's *Illustrated Mail*, and Hannen Swaffer, speaking of Bart's years as his assistant art editor, has praised his technical skill: 'If the staff had gone home, Bart would develop a negative, make a print and then make a block, which he handed to me finished.'

It was necessary once to transport an elephant from the Continent, and no one was surprised when young Guy Bartholomew volunteered for the job.

HARRY GUY BARTHOLOMEW

'Brilliant, truculent, mercurial. His normal means of communication with his staff was the hand-grenade; if urgent, the thunderbolt; if it was necessary to denote displeasure as well as urgency, an atom bomb would do. He decided to divide and rule.'

He also specialised in schemes to bedevil the opposition, particularly if the opposition newspaper was in the same financial group.

During Swaffer's regime as art editor Northcliffe issued the galling order that the *Mirror* should hand some of its best pictures to the *Mail*. Here was a direct challenge to Bartholomew's ingenuity; here was the situation in which he developed, perhaps over-developed, the sense of showmanship which was never to desert him.

To retain a scoop for his paper, circumvent Northcliffe's instruction, and deceive the *Daily Mail,* the assistant art editor smashed a photographic plate across his hand, deliberately cutting his fingers. On another occasion he plastered his face with greasepaint and stumbled from the art room green and ill; when the *Mail* messenger arrived for the pictures it was discovered that Bartholomew had taken them to hospital in his pocket.

In 1913, at the age of twenty-eight, he became a director, Appointed by Northcliffe at one of the two *Mirror* meetings over which he presided. The Legend began to form and grow. Bernard Grant described Bart's zeal in a race to London with the first pictures of a royal visit to Paris in 1914, recording how the driver of the French train 'seemed to forget all else but the rustling of banknotes in the hands of our art director as he urged him to break the record for the run to Calais'. Grant described, too, the trials of blockmaking during a stormy Channel crossing:

'There was Bart, unable to keep his feet, on his knees doing something with a heavy frame – a man forever gingering up the speed of things.'

The Rothermere regime cast a blight on the paper's contents in the twenties, but in the photographic field the enterprise which had brought fame continued. Bartholomew built up a service of pictures by telephone, telegraph and radio, and recruited a team of fliers to rush pictures from news-spots in Europe and Africa. The faces of Alan Cobham, Captain W L Hope, a King's Cup winner, and Captain Birkett were familiar in the office art room. The paper usually led in the air race to bring pictures to London: it also led in the evolution of the system which made the air race obsolete.

In the history of radio transmission of pictures Harry Guy Bartholomew holds a notable place, for he and an assistant named Macfarlane produced the Bartlane process, basing their developments on the early experiments of a German professor. Bart would arrive at the office long before the day staff and devote the early hours to adjusting his transmitters and plotting electric circuits.

In 1923 he succeeded in cabling across the Atlantic pictures of the Shamrock's race for the America's Cup. 'Cable a portrait of Sir Thomas

Lipton, and you won't be able to tell it from a portrait of the Dalai Lama,' gibed the critics. The challenge was accepted, and the Lipton features were plainly recognisable.

The *Mirror* and the New York *Daily News* installed the new apparatus and used it to flash pictures of big fights and other international events across the ocean.

George Greenwell, one of Fleet Street's most experienced cameramen, describes Bart's activities in this period: 'There was not a younger man in the office physically or mentally. He was on duty day and night if a big story was coming in, always ready to choose the negatives, usually half-fixed, and to spur on the edition. A sure sign of a job well done was a friendly dig in the ribs for the photographer, with the comment 'Good stuff!' But there could be a hell of a dressing down, too, if there had been a slip-up. It was his personal interest, his fiery enthusiasm, that got the best out of us. He knew what he wanted and how to brief men to get it.'

He was immersed in the technical problems of telephoto transmission and the coupling up of portable transmitters with the telephone system. Yet, as an artist and cartoonist himself, he always found time to improve the paper's attractiveness.

In the early thirties he revolutionised the presentation of pictures, rejecting the traditional rectangular shapes and heightening the appeal of dramatic 'shots' by bold cutting. He evolved a series of pictures, announced as 'a study by Lensman', which portrayed the rich beauty of the British countryside and the Holy Land.

The early thirties brought an expansion in Bartholomew's activities, a step nearer the position that was to make him the centre of national controversies.

John Cowley was still chairman, and was to hold on grimly until his death at the age of seventy-four in 1944. His sphere was the commercial and mechanical side of production, and he had a shrewd insight into the financial strengths and weaknesses of most of the newspapers in Fleet Street. Editorially, his contribution to the paper's eventual success was painfully undistinguished; indeed, he viewed the Bartholomew Tabloid Revolution with hostility, or at the best uneasiness. He became concerned at the eyebrow-raising strictures of his personal friends.

By the end of 1934, three years after Rothermere had sold his shares in the newspaper, editorial direction was in the hands of Bartholomew. Bart at fifty-one was not a well-read man, and he had never attempted to write for the Press himself. His approach to the problem was not scientific: he relied on his instinct and his instinct rarely failed him. The picture paper had lost its novelty. Public interest waned and by 1934 diminishing circulations were causing dismay in both the *Mirror* and the *Daily Sketch* offices. With a sale of below 800,000, gradually sinking towards 700,000, the *Mirror* was in peril of extinction; the danger point had been reached in newspaper economics and a new policy was imperative.

Leigh Brownlee, who had turned from school-teaching to journalism, had succeeded Alexander Campbell as editor in 1931 and occupied the chair for three years. He had played cricket for Oxford and Gloucestershire, and it was natural that he should elevate sport to a prominence unequalled up to that time in the *Mirror*. But cricket exclusives were not enough.

Bart found himself in command of a newspaper which had sunk into a coma. For years it had fed its readers upon a diet of 'big names'; day after dreary day statesmen and churchmen, novelists and dramatists contributed their views on the past, present and future of mankind. Lord Birkenhead, Sir Oliver Lodge, J B Priestley, Osbert Sitwell, John Galsworthy, Julian Huxley, Lovat Fraser, Philip Guedella, Ian Hay, John Buchan, Andre Maurois – a homily from one or other of them would arrive at the breakfast table with enervating regularity. There were humorous prose and stories in rhyme. And there was endless advice on how the readers should invest their money; a single issue occasionally carried up to three pages of company prospectuses.

The *Mirror* printed news and views that all the other papers printed; it had no identity, no personality of its own, no *raison d'etre*.

It directed its appeal to the declining but still well-to-do middle class. It was the paper for the folk who annually holidayed for a month or so in Scotland or the South of France, enjoyed the long weekend, had tea at the tennis club and motored in the country. And it was upon this newspaper, with these pressing problems, that practical, resourceful, energetic, theatrical Harry Guy Bartholomew was turned loose.

For thirty years he had helped to organise some of the paper's finest pictorial triumphs: now, though still occasionally subdued by the baleful glances of an ageing chairman, he could begin to put into operation his own ideas in every department.

The professional impertinence which transformed a newspaper demise into a newspaper resurrection began to gather momentum.

In November, 1934 Bart launched his experiments with heavy black type, the trade mark that was totally to distinguish the *Mirror* from its straight-laced competitors until the post-war years when nearly every other popular newspaper purloined in full or in part the typographical technique they had affected to despise.

The appearance and style, the social and political outlook of the paper, were transformed by easy stages; two more years passed before it was possible or prudent to complete the revolution which made Fleet Street rub its eyes, the public dip into their pockets, the prelates protest, and rival journals squirm.

By 1936 little remained of the former pale production except the title, and the *Mirror* was soon to taste to the dregs the unpopularity of success. Bart was still pioneering. He did not yet have the men he needed. He was the director in charge of the contents of the paper, but he still had chairman John Cowley above him and a board to whom he was responsible for the conduct of the paper.

The exciting story of how he changed the *Mirror* will be told in the remainder of this book. The curious story of how the *Mirror* changed him will be told in the next chapter.

9
BARTHOLOMEW THE BOSS

The coming of power affects men in devious ways: it leaves no man unchanged.

A common manifestation is megalomania, which in its milder form may go no further than an admiration of one's own talents, a contempt for the inadequacies of one's lieutenants, accompanied by outbursts of unreasoning intolerance. To lesser characters the coming of power brings mental anxiety, physical exhaustion, and a general shortening of their span on earth. Some develop qualities hitherto dormant or untested; others, who from the passenger seat urged vigorous action, become paralysed by the weight of final responsibility and are numbed into cautious inactivity.

Few men prepare themselves either spiritually or philosophically for their ultimate task. And Harry Guy Bartholomew was not among the few.

'Shall I control events from on high, or drown myself in detail? Concentrate on the spheres where results have proved me pre-eminent, or dominate the whole operation? Lead, or drive? Encourage the intelligent critical co-operation of a team of individualists, or demand the dubious allegiance of a group of drilled sycophants?'

Bart' was not given to soliloquy.

He chose to walk alone, instinctively.

To divide and rule.

He succeeded John Cowley in the chairmanship in 1944, and became at sixty-one the *enfant terrible* not only of the two newspapers of which he was now in command but of the newspaper industry in Britain and in certain foreign lands as well.

To any course of action suggested to him he would say; 'No. Do it this way.' A hint that X would be the right person to accomplish Y would yield the immediate order that Z should do the job. He would telephone his principal executives when they were absent from the building; favourite times were 8.55am. and 1.45pm. When he knew they were at their desks he would ignore them, or be 'out' himself.

His normal means of communication with his staff was the hand-grenade; if urgent, the thunderbolt; if it was necessary to denote displeasure as well as urgency, an atom bomb would do. Everybody who mattered in the office, except the recipient, knew just when the explosion was about to occur; everybody, except the victim, was told: *'He won't like that!'*

'Bartholomew,' said a Labour Cabinet Minister, 'is the most cantankerous ------ I have ever met.'

Cantankerous, wilful, cunning. If that was all there was to The Bart Legend the result would have been disastrous, but the outcome of most of the operations of this thickset, sawn-off-shotgun of a man was resounding success. The paper which had only 25,000 readers when he joined it in 1904 was selling 4,350,000, the highest daily circulation in the world, when he retired in 1951.

It has often been said that Bartholomew is a reticent publicity hater, but that is not the case. He created around himself the atmosphere of oriental mystery, and nothing delighted him more than to know that Fleet Street had been stunned by his latest action and was wondering what on earth the 'Old Man' would do next. In his previous incarnations he was the fly in the ointment and the thorn in the side.

Public functions he abhorred; not, again, because of innate modesty but because he suffered from a social inferiority complex; he did not make speeches because he could not make speeches; he avoided intimate contact with his equals in other industries because he did not know what to say to them. His powers lay in other directions.

Journalistically, like the other few giants of the industry, he had his blind spots. The part which sport plays in the life of the British nation was a factor he could not or would not understand, and as a result the *Mirror* in his time was encumbered by some of Fleet Street's worst sports pages in its struggle to pass the *Daily Express,* which had Fleet Street's best. Only in recent years has this blemish been rectified: with sport from the start the triumph would have come sooner.

Curiously, in supreme power, the industry's finest picture expert turned against pictures. The decline of 1934 established that pictures could no longer remain the paper's dominant attraction, but Bartholomew's latter-day lack of interest in his photographers and active animosity to the picture agencies did not hasten the paper's development.

There was, too, the inexplicable reduction and destruction of the library of four million pictures and Press cuttings. A new machine for photographing newspapers and recording their contents on a strip of film had captivated Bart's imagination. The result was that a reporter or sub-editor anxious to check his memory over an item in a previous issue was obliged to peer for twenty minutes into a projector built on the principle of the 'What the Butler Saw' machines on seaside piers. Bart considered that his adoption of this damned silly device was a revolutionary step forward in newspaper production: I thought, and said, that it was the most calculated example of unthinking vandalism since Goering's stooges set fire to the Reichstag. No one could persuade him the system was dangerous nonsense: few dared to try.

His colleagues, too, found it difficult to play their own instruments in a one-man band. Unlike Beaverbrook, he did not dedicate the twilight of his career to the discovery and elevation of the younger men who would one day, inevitably, succeed him. He too often befriended the mediocre. He was heavily engaged in recapturing the lost years of his youth when utter power was withheld from his grasp. There could be no sitting back for Harry Guy Bartholomew in his sixties: he was on the bridge, in the engine room, and forever on the look-out up in the crow's-nest. He was the incandescent flame: his executives were moths who flew at a respectful distance, singed their wings, or burned to death according to the talents, cowardice, or courage with which nature had endowed them.

Yet, in a career of mammoth achievement, Bartholomew's foibles were as few as they were obvious. He was ruthless and capricious, but he was never slow to display his rugged charm and generosity to those who were temporarily in favour.

Bart saved the *Mirror*, and there are other spheres in which his influence as chairman was decisive.

War conditions, and then later the economic restrictions of the post-war years, reduced British newspapers to pygmy proportions. Bart searched for, and found, new outlets for his energy and for the company's great assets.

For nearly three years during the war he produced with Basil Nicholson and five others a secret newspaper, *Good Morning*, for submarine crews. In addition to its own material the paper reproduced the most popular strip-cartoons. With the grateful connivance of their lordships at the Admiralty sealed bundles of *Good Morning* were delivered at operational bases at home and abroad to be opened daily by the coxswain as the morning watch ended and passed around to each mess. Papers were numbered but not dated. By these ingenious means, however long the cruise might last, the submarine men were kept in touch with affairs at home and, depth-charges or no depth-charges, did not miss their daily dose of Jane.

The rule that the coxswain should distribute only one issue a day as the submarine's journey progressed is on record as having been broken only once:

One submarine, hit by a depth-charge, sank to the sea bed. The engines were out. A tense quiet settled on men about to die.

Then the coxswain came round with a large parcel. He peeled off the copies tomorrow – and tomorrow – the tomorrows they did not hope to see. It was a jest and a gesture. Every man knew the truth.

Then the engines throbbed. The engineers had won. When the short cheer ended, an embarrassed coxswain had to explain that they had had their *Good Mornings* for the rest of the trip.

First Lord A V Alexander described the submarine paper as 'one of the happiest inspirations in journalistic enterprise.' In Dunoon *Good Morning* started a 'Good Evening' Club for submariners off duty.

After the war came the astounding success of *Reveille*. Is there anything to equal it, for rapid success, in the history of the newspaper industry?

Reveille was an obscure weekly journal before it was purchased by the *Mirror*, selling under 100,000 copies to the more uninspired, grousing type of serviceman: it was the barrack-room lawyer's Bible. No new newspaper could be launched in those days, for such enterprise in post-war Britain was against the law. It was permissible, however, to purchase and develop existing productions provided their titles were unchanged.

Bart jumped in, bought *Reveille*, evolved his plans, and put the experienced Roy Suffern in charge of expansion. In spite of its abominable name, which its readers pronounce in a variety of ways, the paper leapt to a sale of over 3,000,000 by the year Bartholomew retired.

As chairman, Bart also played the pioneering role in widening the company's interests overseas to Australia and West Africa.

Throughout all these major operations he retained to the end the atmosphere of mystery, breakneck speed, and nosetapping keep-your-mouth-shut secrecy which he had cherished since the early days when as art director he stampeded the French engine driver into setting up a new record for the Paris-Calais run.

Fleet Street lives by publishing stories about other people, and journalists occupy their leisure hours by telling stories about each other. What are the stories they tell about the ebullient Bartholomew?

They remember the night during the Abdication Crisis when he came to the office at midnight wearing an Anthony Eden hat and a lounge suit pulled on over his pyjamas.

They talk about the notorious poster in the early war years. People were scared about the new German spherical magnetic mines. When the first two were washed up on an English beach Bart seized upon a bright idea of Ted Castle's, had them photographed side by side and enlarged to the size of a placard. Next morning they appeared outside the newsagents' shops in main streets and sedate suburbs with the truculent colloquial rejoinder:

AND THE SAME TO YOU!

Old ladies in Bournemouth, Malvern and Bath may have missed the point.

They exchange reminiscences about the night he fired so-and-so, the trap he laid for A, how surprised he thought B would be when C got his job; how he was filled with remorse after some outrageously eccentric behaviour, and then half-an-hour later laughed it off over a drink with a future victim.

Above all, they talk about that passion for secrecy.

When John Walters met him aboard an incoming liner at New York, Bart whispered: 'I am Colonel Bartholomew on the passenger list. I have nothing to do with the *Mirror.*'

He insisted on Walters taking him to the improvised Press Room where a horde of American reporters were interviewing distinguished passengers; he enjoyed, with puckish satisfaction, his escape from the barrage of questions which would have embarrassed him.

Asked if he would like to 'see the sights' of the skyscraper city, he said: 'No, Walters. I haven't the time. Besides, these places don't interest me.' What did he think of San Francisco? 'Scarcely noticed it.' At a New York cocktail party he spent as much time talking to the switchboard operator and young reporters of his own New York bureau as he did to Henry Luce and Randolph Hearst Jr.

When a war correspondent returned from the front and stayed at the Savoy Hotel in London, Bart was angry in the belief that the man was 'giving himself airs'; he ordered him to cease war-corresponding and become a sub-editor.

Northcliffe traversed the world in a chariot filled with his cleverest editors, writers, and financial executives. Beaverbrook's country house at Cherkley and London apartment at Arlington House are the rendezvous for social wits, politicians and the favoured leaders of his newspapers. Bartholomew was different; his confidants and social companions for many years were Bill Jennings, the company secretary, and Fred Onslow, on the managerial side.

At weekends he drove his Rolls Royce at seventy-to-eighty miles an hour to his boat on the Norfolk Broads. There he would potter around with lathes and spanners and drills, mingling in a pair of old grey flannel bags with the local boatmen, talking about the *Mirror's* annual outboard race.

One daily relaxation was pursued with regularity and enthusiasm. At five-thirty in the afternoon he would straighten his tie, adjust his black Homburg hat and stroll down Fetter Lane with Jennings or Onslow to Fleet Street's wine bar, El Vino. There, standing with his back to the door, he was a familiar though not a popular figure. To the man who had decided to walk alone the attention of other journalists and even of his colleagues, if uninvited, was not welcome.

Friends? 'A newspaperman can't afford them,' he would say, and his unhappy underlings were forever aware that to be seen with a knot of rival journalists was, in the Old Man's eyes, an unforgivable crime.

Enemies? He could not care less.

Nothing, nobody, could intimidate him, and no journalist who worked for Bartholomew could say that he was ever requested to suppress or embellish his attitude to a public personality because that man was a friend or enemy of the boss.

To Northcliffe, says Tom Clarke, newsgetting was a battle in which all was fair in love and war. News to Northcliffe was a commodity no true journalist could possibly think of ignoring, whatever its source and however it was come by. If it fulfilled the one and only condition, truth, the journalist's duty was to publish it whatever the pleasure, pain, satisfaction or annoyance it might induce.

Bartholomew held similar views. A man of few words, he expressed the creed succinctly:

'Publish and be damned'.

This was the only occasion on which he quoted the Duke of Wellington. Or any other duke.

10

SHOCKING 'EM AND SOCKING 'EM

The ageing readers of the Gossip Column had been accustomed for years to a diet of refined, soporific chit-chat on social and booksy affairs.

Was Dame So-and-so, the actress, more effective in this comedy or that tragedy? What a coincidence that Brigadier Purpleface's book on his experiences on the North-west Frontier should be published on the same day as General Godamnit's demise in Cheltenham. Was it generally known that George V was an enthusiastic philatelist? Sure it was. The column had told the readers half-a-dozen times before. Who was the tiniest debutante, the best-dressed member of parliament, the tallest cabinet minister, the most handsome bishop?

One Monday morning in 1935 the readers were informed, just as they had been in 1934, 1933, 1932 and 1931, that the swans on the lower reaches of the Thames were mating. Three weeks later they picked up their *Mirror* to learn that Queen Ena of Spain had shocked the guests at a dinner at the Savoy by using a toothpick after the succulent savoury and before the dreary orations; furthermore, that an actress had found it absolute hell to dance at the Dorchester Charity Ball because of her screaming corns. Her husband, a famous actor, threatened to horsewhip the columnist.

From Bath and Bournemouth came letters of protest; from Newcastle guffaws of delight.

First eye-opener was the transformation of the news pages. Sledge-hammer headlines appeared on the front-page in black type one inch deep, a signal that all could see of the excitements to come. Human interest was at a premium, and that meant sex and crime. The retired colonels, dowagers, professional gentlemen and schoolmistresses who still constituted the bulk of the paper's old faithfuls were astonished to learn on picking up their *Daily Sedative* that MOTHER SLAYS BABE IN WOOD TO MAKE WAY FOR LOVER. The headline occasionally occupied twice as much space as the story itself, and there was no mistaking the strident appeal of the stories:

MARRIAGE AT 9 SHOCKS U.S. WOMEN

UMBRELLA IN COFFIN MEMENTO OF ROMANCE

GIRL FINDS MOTHER AFTER 20 YEARS IN STREET VIGIL

In Geraldine House, where the *Mirror* was produced, nobody cared what the rivals published; we were living dangerously. A different type of newspaper was being evolved, and the mounting circulation established beyond all question that the public adored it.

The editorials were vociferous on the need for rearmament, and when Hitler or Mussolini startled Europe with a threat or act of violence the news was given front-page prominence; as a general rule, however, day-to-day developments in international affairs received scant attention. Britain's new popular paper cast its net nearer home, and cast it deep.

Gay smile-raising items were sure of a place, but it was the unorthodox approach to serious social issues that stimulated the talk and the criticism. The news editor's daily duties list took a new appearance. Instead of the expected '10.30, interview Lord Helpus re reported sale of half Devon estate', the reporter would find:

JONES: Evils of the slum.

SMITH: Organised vice exposure.

THOMPSON: Cruelty to children. NSPCC campaign.

The exposures were effective enough, but there was a regrettable sequel to a case in which a man was fined £25 for forcing his five-year-old son to hold live coals. When the *Mirror* published a photograph of the child's injured hands two thousand angry citizens besieged the father's house all night, flourishing copies of the paper and crying 'Lynch him'. Police had to be called out to protect the man and control the mob, for the picture, published as a deterrent to others, unfortunately also acted as an incitement to citizens to try to take the law into their own hands. The paper's own attitude to lynching had been made abundantly clear by the front page publication of a photograph from America; it was a revolting study of mass lunacy, but its appearance indicated that the *Mirror* intended to expose unpleasant truths as well as to report titivating niceties. The sale rose the day that picture was published and has risen ever since. Convention was thrown out of the window.

Broadcasting - Page 24

Daily Mirror

THE DAILY PICTURE ● NEWSPAPER WITH THE LARGEST NET SALE

DRESS-SUIT ORDER FOR NEW POLICE —PAGE 2

No. 9,365 Registered at the G.P.O. as a Newspaper. WEDNESDAY, NOVEMBER 29, 1933 One Penny

TRIAL BY FURY—U.S. LYNCH LAW

Frenzied Mob Storm Another Gaol

SOLDIERS' BOMBS DEFIED

Lynch law is spreading in the United States. Here are two contrasting pictures:—

IN MARYLAND
Something like civil war broke out yesterday when a mob attacked the State Armoury in an attempt to release four lynchers arrested by order of the Governor.

IN CALIFORNIA
The Governor publicly pardoned people involved in the storming of a prison and lynching two kidnappers, which was "a fine lesson to others."

The situation in Maryland grew so serious that the State Militia had to be mobilised. They hurled tear gas bombs at the mob, which replied with bricks. Shots followed, but it is not known whether they were fired by the crowd or the troops.

Martial law has been proclaimed.

SECRET SEARCH

Police Guarded by Troops Armed with Machine Guns

BALTIMORE, Tuesday.

A fierce clash between an infuriated mob and soldiers at Salisbury (Maryland) in which tear gas bombs and bricks were hurled and shots fired, came as a climax to the arrest of four lynchers by order of Governor Ritchie.

The men are alleged to have killed a negro who had attacked an aged white woman.

When the State Attorney refused to arrest the men a secret house-to-house search was ordered by Governor Ritchie.

Police, under the protection of troops armed with machine-guns, tear gas bombs and riot guns, hauled the wanted men from their beds last night. They were taken to the State armoury at Salisbury.

Yelling Crowd

The report of their arrest spread like wildfire, and crowds of townspeople soon gathered around the armoury.

Antagonism against the Governor's action flared up, and later a yelling crowd surged against the building.

The State Militia was called out, and a pitched battle took place.

Troops hurled tear-gas bombs into the advancing mob, but still they came on and drove the soldiers into the armoury.

A general fire alarm was sounded, and brought a fire brigade full speed to the assistance of the troops.

CAR OVERTURNED

A fusillade of bricks was launched against the armoury and shots followed.

The firemen appeared to be sympathetic towards the crowd, because they poured water into the tear gas apparently in an effort to deaden the effect of the fumes.

After the riot had died down the troops departed in motor-cars, apparently heading towards Baltimore. It is not known if the arrested men were with them.

The crowd did not molest the troops, but they seized and overturned a motor-car which was said to belong to the State Attorney.

The negro, for whose lynching the men were arrested, was done to death by a mob at Princess Anne.

Defying a barrage of tear gas bombs and the truncheons of twenty police, more than a thousand people burst into the county gaol and carried off the negro.

The victim was stripped and dragged through the town by a rope round his neck and hanged to a tree next to a Judge's house. Later the body was cut down and burned in the public square.—Reuter.

According to Exchange, the Maryland authorities have proclaimed martial law.

Telegraphing and telephoning were banned during the arrests.

SHOTGUN GUARD

Four Gangsters Cleared of Kidnapping Charge

A jury at St. Paul, Minnesota, yesterday acquitted four gangsters, led by Roger Touhy, who were accused of kidnapping Mr. William Hamm, junr., a young and wealthy brewer, states Reuter.

The gang were also indicted by the grand jury in Chicago for the alleged kidnapping last July of Jacob Factor, the financier accused of share-pushing frauds.

Crowds jammed the corridors of the courthouse to learn the verdict. Guards around the court were reinforced and sheriffs stood on each stairway with shotguns ready.

Factor Case

After their acquittal the four men were served with "fugitive warrants" accusing them of participation in the kidnapping of Jacob Factor.

They will be taken to Chicago for trial in the Factor case, regardless of their acquittal yesterday.

Mr. William Hamm, junr., was kidnapped in June, but was released a few days later after a ransom had been paid. It was stated at the time that this ransom was much less than the £20,000 originally demanded.

Leaders of the mob battering in the doors of the county gaol at San Jose, California, prior to the lynching of Thurmond and Holmes, two alleged kidnappers.

Governor Ritchie, of Maryland, who has had four lynchers arrested.

Governor Rolph publicly pardoned people involved in the San Jose lynching.

The sentence of lynch law carried out at San Jose. Thousands of onlookers cheered the spectacle. (Pictures by radio.)

A NEGRO IS LYNCHED

'A revolting study of mass lunacy, but its appearance indicated that the *Mirror* intended to expose unpleasant truths as well as to report titivating niceties…'

73

The rank and file in the Services found a new, intrepid champion. The case was put for serving men who received no marriage allowance until they were twenty-five; 'if I were I selling matches I could give my wife more money,' wrote one sailor. When another had his pay docked for sending a letter to the paper without first submitting it to naval censorship, the *Mirror* gave publicity to his punishment. There was no support for barrack-room lawyers and messdeck moaners, but the battle conducted in pre-war years against the smothering of legitimate grievances by military red-tape explains much of the paper's war-time and post-war acceptability to the Forces.

Another quality now began to emerge; courage was accompanied by candour. Frequently, with an urchin grin which even the staid at times found appealing, the *Mirror* put its fingers to its nose at tradition and protocol.

In 1938 the Birthday Honours List was announced with this comment:

> The Honours are out, a dull catalogue of names. True, they are worthy names, but many of the people who nave put all they know into bettering this great country of ours Are not there. They are shunned ... but, if you are still interested, turn to the details on Page twenty-five. Frankly, we ourselves are bored.

Causes similar to those of the new *Mirror* had been espoused by other journals, and similar views expressed; what was refreshing about this new technique was its youthful vigour. Many newspapers, including those who took excessive pride in their respectability, had given, and were still giving, prominence to the sexual misdemeanours of the populace; but none so audaciously.

The methods which Harry Guy Bartholomew originated himself, and in other cases approved with relish, were shocking in the true sense of the word. There was no concealment of the facts. Nothing was said by innuendo. The pompous platitude was discarded. Politicians who had made mistakes were no longer advised to consider transferring to another Ministry where their undoubted talents might better be employed on the nation's behalf; they were denounced as blunderers, fools, or damned fools.

The British public loved it, though the effect on the Old School in all spheres of life was alarming. They felt that a crowd of hooligans had desecrated St Paul's, raided the pavilion at Lords, ploughed up the Oval, broken the windows at White's, stolen the mace in the House of Commons and staged variety at Sadler's Wells.

CECIL THOMAS

And so they had.

Bartholomew was getting around him a band of young journalists who had to be wide awake and on their toes.

Oddly enough, at their head was Cecil Thomas; cherubic, courteous and unobtrusive, he was the last man a Hollywood producer would cast in the role of the ruthless tabloid editor. He was a journalist of wide experience; he simply did not look the part. Roy Lewis, who once endeavoured to unravel the mystery of the paper's success for the review *Persuasion,* wrote that in Rothermere's days Thomas, then night editor, returned malodorous copy to its nasty-minded author holding it twixt finger and thumb, but that 'after 1935 a comparable reaction by editor Thomas ensured it a banner headline.'

Few of the *Mirror's* detractors in those early uninhibited days of the Tabloid Revolution were aware that the editor of the newspaper was the son of a Cambridgeshire rector. Inside Geraldine House the relationship between the explosive Bartholomew and the tranquil Cecil Thomas, who was editor for fourteen years, was understood by all. Bart was the architect, Thomas was in charge of the builders – or, in the view of some, was the superintendent in charge of the madmen.

He was good-natured and needed to be, for one of Bartholomew's favourite pranks involved a plank of wood. In the presence of a member of the staff, or of a petrified visitor, Bart would creep up behind the editor and crash the plank on his head. The weapon was eight feet long and a foot wide, and those beholding the homicidal attack for the first time would nearly faint. The plank, in fact, was made of balsa wood and weighed less than if it had been made of cardboard. Although it was quite light I always suspected that it hurt the editor more than he admitted: he regarded the caper as part of the duties of being Cecil Thomas.

One day, when walking down Fetter Lane towards Fleet Street with Cassandra, I saw Bartholomew and Thomas a few yards in front.

'There,' I said to Cassandra, 'go Don Quixote and Sancho Panza.'

'Who,' asked Cassandra, 'is the donkey?'

The donkey worked hard during the hectic days of the late thirties. He had several brains and many legs.

Many of the journalists who worked in the news room subsequently filled the top jobs on Fleet Street papers. Among them were Edward Pickering, managing editor of the *Daily Express;* Stuart Campbell, managing editor of *The People;* Ted Castle, who became editor of *Picture*

Post; Bill Farrar, night editor of the *Daily Herald:* Roland Thornton, who was editor of the *Daily Graphic;* E M Dougall, for years night editor of the *Daily Mail.*

But the man who primarily shaped the new-style news pages was Roy Thistle Suffern, now a director of the *Sunday Pictorial* and editor of *Reveille.*

Suffern is a short-tempered, energetic Ulsterman with a nasal accent and a staccato method of issuing orders, two characteristics which do not instantly commend him to subordinates. From the Manchester office of the *Express,* where he had been news editor, he brought to the *Mirror* as night editor a soundness of judgment and a shrewdness in assessment between pathos and bathos which were essential at that time. There could be no high-falutin' formula in the handling of human news. This crazy, hell-raising journal called for bold decisions, and Roy Suffern was the man who made those decisions at night.

The whole appearance of the *Mirror* changed. The picture-paper tradition of photographs on the centre pages was blown sky-high and sensational news took their place. Forty-page issues were frequent.

Suffern, directing night operations, became feared for the sharp note of urgency in his voice. But he could give the soft answer, too.

Len Jackson recalls a night when the edition was six minutes late, a serious matter. The make-up sub-editor was sent for and Suffern demanded shortly: 'What held you?'

Now it happened that the make-up sub was not inarticulate. Boiling with rage, for he had been sweating to get the paper away to time against pestilential odds, he proceeded to tell the night editor what had 'held him' in no uncertain manner – so forcibly and at such length that the staff in the news room downed their pencils and cocked their ears to hear the fun.

Suffern listened without a word, stood up, put his hand on the shoulder of the embittered sub-editor, and said, smiling:

'You're right, old boy. We're a set of illegitimates!'

11
JANE GIVES ALL!

When the government threatened the *Mirror* with suspension in 1942, Prime Minister Churchill could not have realised just what he was doing. Jane was the heroine of the British Army and the Yankees. A GI drafted from Calcutta to China went pell-mell to the SEAC Forces' newspaper for a private preview of the remainder of the Jane sequence before he would fight for Uncle Sam; she was in *Stars and Stripes,* and another American Services' newspaper analysed her effect on military morale.

Captain Reilly-ffoul, with his alliterative invective, explosive language and roving eye, was Tommy Handley's favourite cartoon character. The fruity captain, created by Bernard Graddon, was also painted on many an RAF fuselage and flew on bombing raids as air crew mascot.

Popeye, the sailor whom spinach made mighty, was indispensable to the Navy, and messages reached him from battleships on active service. Churchill himself, in need of a daily smile in Downing Street, turned to Jack Greenall's Useless Eustace.

Marlborough won battles without the aid of strip cartoons, but in the twentieth century they were 'secret weapons' not to be lightly cast aside by his descendant!

Strip cartoons are a sphere of popular journalism in which pioneered. Other newspapers were *(a)* hasty in deriding the development, *(b)* apprehensive of their rival's success, (c) flagrant in apeing the new technique.

The story which ends with Jane, Garth, Belinda Blue Eyes, Buck Ryan, Beelezebub Jones and Jimpy begins in 1904 – second year of the paper's existence – when W K Haselden, a tall, elegant insurance clerk called on the editor with a portfolio of specimen drawings.

Haselden's work became renowned. His method was to illustrate the topic of the day with a series of four or five sketches. How did woman emerge from servitude to equality? His panels showed four men exacting obedience from their wives. The caveman intimidating the cowering woman with death by stone axe; the Elizabethan frightening her with a whip; the Victorian forewarning her that his displeasure would be incurred; the Edwardian diffidently mouthing the admonition 'Obey, or ...,' with the militant woman, eyes flashing, quelling him with a defiant '– OR WHAT?'

Haselden, now in retirement on the Suffolk coast, was on the paper for nearly forty years.

The German Emperor and his son became his victims as Big and Little Willie, and British Tommies threw *Mirrors* into the German trenches to exacerbate the humourless enemy. Sometimes the Germans retaliated with grenades, but occasionally laughter was heard. Those cartoons were 'damnably effective', the Crown Prince admitted in 1918 to a *Mirror* photographer who was the first man to interview him.

With his English characters Burlington Bertie, the 'knut with a k', Miss Joy Flapperton, the sweet young thing, and Colonel Dugout, the departmental bureaucrat, Haselden showed the way for future cartoonists.

The first authentic strip, of the type which to-day has millions of followers, appeared in 1923 – Mutt and Jeff, by the American artist Bud Fisher. New York newspapers had long been producing comic sections, but to Britain the technique was an innovation. New characters, English as well as American, emerged all over the paper, and the public contracted that pleasant disease of stripitis of which it will never now be cured. Dud, Jay, Tich, The Jinks Family, The Pater and The Newlyweds were the forerunners of the *Mirror*'s own creation, Pip, Squeak and Wilfred.

Pip the Dog and Squeak the Penguin made their debut on May 12 1919, christened after their creator's war-time batman, a gentleman known as 'Pip-Squeak'. Wilfred the Rabbit joined them a little later, and with this trio Bertram J Lamb, who recorded their adventures as Uncle Dick, and his illustrator Austin B Payne achieved a phenomenal success.

It became apparent that strips did not enchant the children alone; the *Mirror,* indeed, owes much of its popularity to appreciating this truth years before other British newspapers, who to this day are stumbling far behind in the marathon. Letters applauding the antics of Pip, Squeak and Wilfred came from bishops, politicians, industrialists and authors, and on one birthday anniversary of the pets Viscount Ullswater, former Speaker of the House of Commons, sent a greeting in rhyme.

Bertram Lamb, a genial soul who dwelt in the clouds, died in Switzerland in 1938 after a long illness, but Austin Payne continued to draw the animals for the Children's *Mirror* on Saturdays and the strip has now been revived in daily form by Hugh McLelland.

Many men are puzzled by the fact that dress bills are not lessened by the brevity of material used by the modiste. Is it because the modern girl buys six frocks to every one bought by her grandmother?

W K HASELDEN: 'A tall, elegant insurance clerk called on the editor with a portfolio of speciment drawings. His work became renowned. He showed the way to future cartoonists.'

How curiously slow the rest of Fleet Street was to follow, for there could be no doubt at all about the triumph of 'P, S and W' among all ages and standards of intellect. Uncle Dick obviously could not shake hands with all his family, so he compromised. He asked the boys and girls to take hold of Mum's hand or Dad's hand, or even Baby's hand, and to say: 'How do you do; how *do* you do, how DO you do?' 'Good,' wrote Uncle Dick, 'now we know one another.' Even in the tiny makeshift *Mirror* produced in the General Strike it was considered prudent to find space for a message to the children: 'Wilfred says goo-goo to his little friends'.

Only when the pets appeared in public before seaside crowds of 20,000 did the spirit of amity break down. Pip was hauled before the magistrates at Clacton for performing on the beach unmuzzled, and Uncle Dick was fined fifty shillings. The penguin bit a mayor on the nose and once spent two hours frisking about in the sea. Worse still, he bit the hand of his guardian, Bert Canty, who yelled out a curse that delighted the wide-eyed kids and perturbed their mothers.

'How sweet they are,' said the Queen when she saw the pets at a garden party. Sir William Orpen painted them, without fee. They were honoured in pantomime, ballet and film, and raised thousands of pounds for charity through the Wilfredian League of Gugnuncs [WLOG for short]. Meetings began with the Gugnuncs' Own Chortle, which as a former Gugnunc I well remember:

> Gug, gug! Nunc, mine!
> To friends of all degree.
> Give gugly hugs to nuncly gugs
> Of the WLOG.

Bartholomew had studied the success of Pip, Squeak and Wilfred. Was it possible to create strips with the same mass-appeal for young adults?

Norman Pett arrived with the answer in December, 1932. Nobody realised when Jane first appeared under the title Jane's Journal, or the Diary of a Bright Young Thing, that she would become the pin-up of the British and American Services in the second world war.

Round-up, the US paper in the Far East, described Jane as 'a highly patriotic comely British lass whose one affliction at odds with her otherwise sterling character (if affliction it be) is that she has just one hell of a job keeping her clothes on.' The Yanks, admitting that tweeds were seldom allowed to gum up the plot, waited a while to catch Jane *au naturel.* It happened, and *Round-up* under the headline JANE GIVES ALL commented: 'Well, sirs, you can go home now. Right smack out of the

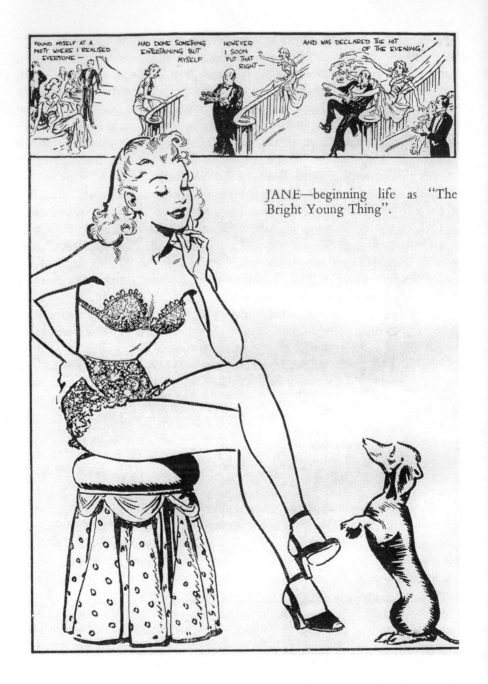

'Jane peeled a week ago. The British 36 th Division immediately gained
six miles…'

blue and with no one even threatening her, Jane peeled a week ago. The British 36th Division immediately gained six miles and the British attacked in the Arakan. Maybe we Americans ought to have Jane, too.'

The first episode in 1932 showed Jane in pyjamas, not yet in cami-knickers, reading a telegram: 'Expect Count Fritz Von Pumpernickel over from Germany. Can't speak a word of English. You will love him.'

Occasionally Jane shed a dress or a skirt in moments of crisis or adventure, but she did not reveal all until the Nazi menace was close upon us. Her new artist, Mike Hubbard, has given her a youthful, less brassy, expression which her long-standing record of immodesty scarcely justifies.

When Bartholomew became director-in-charge-of-editorial in 1934, and chairman ten years later, it was clear that the strip-cartoon activities would develop.

His interest was stimulated afresh by the arrival at Geraldine House of Basil D Nicholson, who had studied the latest American methods, and came with tales of the proven pull of story-cartoons in British advertising.

Over the years new characters appeared, and the *Mirror* was so impressed by their immense reader-interest that by 1936 a forty-page issue contained a page-and-a-half of cartoons and strips. They were given more space than serious news, and the readers still asked for encores.

Is there any need to search in this day and age for the secret of the lure of strips? The *Express,* the *Mail,* the *Herald* have all discovered it at last. In their 1949 survey of the Press, Mass Observation made this comment: 'Much of the popularity of the *Mirror* strips may be due to their blending of reality and fantasy in such a way that people are easily stimulated into identifying themselves with the strip characters'.

Mass Observation, an independent research organisation, quoted a 'Man, 35, artisan class' whom they had interviewed; he 'wanted a body like Garth's'.

Psychologists talk of 'reader-identification'. Why be lonely when you can begin your morning as the desirable Jane with her posse of admirers and a carefree attitude to handsome fiancé Georgie? Why should key-tapping at an office desk or standing at a factory lathe be humdrum when you can take time off every day to hunt for clues and track down desperate crooks with Buck Ryan? Why be plagued by frustrated maternal instincts when Belinda Blue Eyes is there on page so-and-so to be mothered every morning? Domestic problems? So has Ruggles. And why be worried that you're short and skinny, brother? Throw out your chest, ripple those muscles, adjust your Time Helmet and fly to future centuries to be fawned upon by passionate Karen and faithful, yielding .Dawn.

'Reader-identification' or escape, the demand for strip cartoons in this nerve-wracking, highly-competitive, war-torn world is proved by their success. There is no harm in a flutter with the Flutters, and there is a great deal of good for a bride-to-be in a lesson from Patsy, the cookery student created by Bill Herbert and Ambrose Heath with Jack Dunkley as artist. Intellectuals condemn strips in public, but most of the critics follow them keenly in private.

Strips are now big business in Britain. Talent is scarce and cartoonists are highly paid, but the enthusiasm of Bartholomew placed his newspaper far ahead of competitors by building its own team of artists.

Hugh McLelland, creator of Jimpy, was the first head of the department, succeeded in turn by Philip Zec and Julian Phipps. Strips are planned months in advance so that there is no clash of interests; they are rarely the work of a single artist, for the high production rate of a cartoon a day calls for specialists working together on ideas, continuity, script and drawings.

A distinctive reputation has been established by Buck Ryan's Jack Monk, who takes great pains to get his background detail correct. Aeroplane instruments, surgical apparatus, and so on, are not sketched in from imagination. Monk cross-examines the real-life equivalents of his characters to ensure that the language and mannerisms of his policemen, criminals, professors and professionals of all degrees are authentic; he has become a master of dialect and an authority on cockney rhyming slang. The customers insist upon precision.

Should strip-cartoon characters step into real life and rub shoulders with living people? Is the fantasy destroyed, or does reality strengthen the appeal? Stephen Dowling conducted this experiment with his Ruggles family. They took a trip to Margate, and the portraits of Mrs Pearson and her family whom they met aboard the steamer appeared in the cartoon. The morning greeting 'I saw you in the *Mirror* to-day, Mr Smith' was heard in hundreds of English streets. When the Ruggles Family showed how self-help groups built their own houses, an organisation of two hundred people was formed to emulate the achievement in Newcastle upon Tyne.

Public taste is forever changing, and the secret of the *Mirror* in cartoons as well as in other editorial activities is that it marches 'Forward with the People'. No newspaper can succeed without men in charge who *instinctively* know what is right, who can assess the temper of public opinion without moving from their desks. Fleet Street calls it FLAIR. But Basil Nicholson taught the *Mirror* never to depend on one man's hunches on strip cartoons; as public taste transforms itself before, during and after wars, its new desires are studied and fulfilled.

Investigations are occasionally conducted by outside agencies or advertising concerns; frequently by the newspaper itself.

In January, 1947, when strips were occupying 12 per cent of the paper's total space, a survey by the London Press Exchange disclosed the cartoon tastes of women readers:

80 per cent looked at Jane,

73 .. .. Belinda,
70 .. .. Ruggles,
69 .. .. Garth,
63 .. .. Buck Ryan,
61 .. .. Jimpy.

Five years later the *Mirror* itself probed the varying appeals of the regular cartoons to men and women:

	Women	*Men*
Jane	82 per cent	71 per cent
Belinda	79	54
Buck Ryan	66	73
Patsy	56	17
Jimpy	22	35
Just Jake	19	42

Women readers, it seems, are not outraged by Jane's occasional immodesty.

The paper's own investigations, the results of which have not hitherto been made public, clearly show the trend of popular approval and explain to those who were perplexed the hotly-debated demise of Just Jake and Jimpy.

Here are some of the results of tests conducted in 1937, 1939, 1946, 1949 and 1952 with sample batches of readers:

JANE

She has always headed the list of the most popular strips with 86 per cent readership in 1937, 85 in 1939, 90 in 1946 – she reached her peak of popularity at the close of the war – 79 in 1949, and 77 in 1952.

GARTH

Admiration for the superman has steadily increased from 72 per cent in 1946 to 73 in 1949 and 75 in 1952.

PIP, SQUEAK AND WILFRED

GARTH

BELINDA

RUGGLES

THE FLUTTERS

BUCK RYAN

CHARACTERS FROM THE STRIPS
'Strips are now big business'

BUCK RYAN

The gentleman sleuth has lost a few Dr Watsons over the past six years, but is still accompanied on his adventures by nearly three-quarters of the readers.

Buck rated 54 per cent in 1937, rose rapidly to 78 in 1946, but fell to 69 in 1952.

BELINDA BLUE EYES

81 per cent followed her triumphs over misfortune in the sentimental years which preceded the war; she stood at 77 per cent in 1946, 58 in 1949, rising to 66 in 1952.

THE FLUTTERS

Up from 50 per cent in 1949 to 55 in 1952.

RUGGLES

In 1937, when Mr Ruggles and his wife were implicated in domestic problems of the type that concern millions of their readers, they were the intimate friends of 74 per cent, expanding to 76 in 1946. Did his followers enjoy as much Ruggles' fact-finding missions and his encounters with real-life personalities? The answer perhaps is in the figures: Ruggles fans diminished to 51 per cent in 1949 with a small rise to 55 in 1952.

JUST JAKE

Declined from 48 per cent in 1939 to 31 in 1952.

JIMPY

This ingenious strip was the favourite of the intellectuals, but their fancy, alas, was not reflected by the public at large. Jimpy rated 33 per cent in 1946 climbed to 36 in 1949, and fell ignominiously to 29 per cent in 1952. That was the year Jimpy died.

There are other procedures employed by the cartoon staff to keep abreast of public opinion, and there is no newspaper in Britain which could conscientiously claim to come anywhere near their skill and insight in this field.

Will the day come when, in a newspaper strike, the Lord Mayor of London will read out the strips over the BBC so that the followers will not be deprived of their daily thrill, throb and sob? It happened in New York last year with Mayor Impellitteri: it could happen here.

The only tragedy is that the strip technique has been degraded to flood the country with foreign, cheap, appallingly drawn, vulgarly worded, multi-coloured weekly comics crammed with sadism and sub-normal sex. Their heroes are thugs, molls and monkey-men; their plots are liberally sprinkled with coshings, blackmail, cowardice and corruption. And British parents allow their children to swallow them as their regular – and sometimes sole – literary diet.

12
AIN'T LOVE GLAND?

Are popular newspaper staffs motivated by the sentiment expressed in Ivor Novello's Coronation Song, 'We're One Big Family'? Such thoughts should be dismissed at the outset of this chapter.

No successful newspaper has been generated by 'the team spirit'. Northcliffe knew it. Beaverbrook knows it. So did the staff at the *Mirror* during the Bartholomew Revolution. The world's largest circulation, and the second, third, and even the nineteenth, are strictly the product of internecine warfare, departmental unarmed combat – or, to be polite in front of the customers, a headlong clash of ideals, techniques and ambitions.

One school of thought at Geraldine House was founded by the unruly, introspective, wildly imaginative and self-destructive Basil D Nicholson. Nobody liked him except his disciples, and it is doubtful whether Nicholson liked himself.

He arrived in 1935 knowing little about newspapers, but this was no major defect since an entirely new sort of newspaper was about to be conceived and delivered. So little did he know about newspapers that he phoned the respected Wallace D Roome who happened to have been a director since 1904, appointed by Northcliffe, and demanded if there was the slightest possibility of having a goddam desk and a red telephone, thus swelling his cohort of enemies by one that day.

His relationship with Bartholomew, who did not have a great deal of time for intellectual types, rested upon similarly uneasy grounds.

Nicholson had often been puzzled by a whining noise that came from the process department above our room. It would rise to a screech, then droop to a plaintive, 'cello-like hum-m-m-m. When Bartholomew wandered in one day Nicholson put the question bluntly to him:

'Bart, who in the name of hell do you think is making that excruciating din?'

The Old Man was annoyed, but admitted eventually that the noise was coming 'from an invention of mine'. Secrecy, of course, must be preserved.

'What is the invention for?' asked Nicholson.

'I cannot tell you that.'

'Well – what sort of thing is it for?'

Bartholomew, angry at this impertinent, unceasing cross-examination, blurted out that his invention 'could do anything'. Nicholson screwed up his face in wonderment and then asked: 'Can it, for instance, make love to a guinea-pig?'

One of his better-known eccentricities as the newly-appointed features editor of the *Mirror* was to advertise in the *Telegraph* for 'bright assistant features editor with ideas, able to take charge'. I was at that time working on the *Sunday Chronicle* at the minimum union wage, applied for the job, was interviewed by Nicholson, pointed out the unconventional wording of his advertisement, was informed by Nicholson that he 'didn't expect to last long there himself the way things were going', and was hired.

'Can you start to-day?' he asked. 'Otherwise I might be fired before you get here.'

I observed his green tweed suit, his octagonal spectacles, and the immense cigar that obliterated half his face. I heard his gritty humour and maniacal, derisive laugh as he unfolded a grandiose plan by which, together, we would change the direction of the human race. 'Yes,' I said; 'I could start very soon.' It was apparent that no time should be lost.

Six months later Nicholson beckoned me to go with him to 'the roof'. The wind was at gale force, it was raining, and it was impossible to light the giant Corona he had thrust in my mouth. 'Bartholomew has fired me,' he shouted. 'He wants to see you now.'

The months in the madhouse together had been enjoyable and I was sad that the collaboration seemed about to end. What I did not know on the rooftop was that Nicholson had been peremptorily ordered time and time again to tone down our handiwork but had ignored the instructions on the grounds that the directors who issued them did not know what they were talking about.

For some reason, now hard to discern, I was under the impression that the brand of headlining in which I was at that time specialising –

JOHN COWLEY (Chairman 1919-1944)

MATCH-MAKING MAMMIES
SHOO SPINSTER LOVELIES TO GIBRALTAR
TO GRAB A JACK TAR HUBBY

REVELLER VANISHES FOR DAYS –
COMES BACK AS POP-EYED DRAGON
SHOUTING 'WHOOPEE! WHAT A NIGHT!'
BOSSY WIFE GETS HUSBAND'S GOAT –
HE WANTS A VAMP AT 40!

was the subject of universal applause in the boardroom; in fact, and understandably, they were giving chairman John Cowley heart failure. His friends had come to the considered conclusion that *he* had gone mad.

'I think they want to give you my job,' shouted Nicholson. 'Take it, or everything we've done will be wasted. All the other people here are fools.' Internecine warfare is internecine warfare.

Nicholson, who had wandered into advertising after mooching around Oxford, had written a book called *Business is Business,* full of wit, confusion and downright brilliant nonsense. A curious cuss by any standards; a fish out of water who was suddenly thrown into the whirlpool of the changing *Mirror* simply because he wondered why newspapers did not publish more strip-cartoons and told as much to Cecil H King, then the young advertising director. King was impressed, and still places the outrageous Nicholson high on the list of the cleverest men he has met.

Newspapers, said Nicholson to me at 2am in such conference rooms as the Gargoyle Club, did not know their business. What was the use of worrying readers about obscure revolutions in Bolivia if they could not sleep at night through indigestion? Was a pregnant woman, whose husband could not possibly afford her fourth child, interested in a Parliamentary debate on foreign affairs which would obviously result in nothing at all? What was the point of publishing pompous articles by avaricious big-wigs when figures proved that nobody would read them? Did newspapers really care what their customers read, or didn't they know how to find out? Why had the profession of journalism attracted such little talent and originality? Had it ever occurred to Fleet Street that people didn't want to read anything at all? Or was I the sort of bloody fool who believed that the newspapers knew what they were doing?

Basil Nicholson crossed swords with so many people simultaneously at Geraldine House that he was obliged to fold up his tent and move on, though he did return to the old camping ground for spells on future occasions. Much of the gospel, or heresy, he preached contributed to the success of the newspaper he understood but which did not understand him. And he did not move on until he had founded a sect which in the years to follow displayed many faults, to be sure, but also some virtues.

Alas, he died this year in Dublin at the age of forty-five, and William Connor, who wrote the only obituary that appeared in print, thus summed him up: 'Intelligent and daft. Sardonic and silly. Clinical, cruel – and downright soppy. Brilliant and bemused. He has gone, but for those who appreciate mental explosions the dust will not settle for many years.'

The features staff of the Bartholomew Revolution was in later years to be spread far and wide. Some were fired during temperamental clashes; some inter-married.

Tony Clarkson became editor of *John Bull*. Mackenzie Porter went to Canada. Cyril James went to a literary agency. Bill Herbert is now in the New York bureau. Eileen Ascroft joined the *Evening Standard*. Brian Murtough was transferred to the *Sunday Pictorial*. As for the circus of writing priests, psychologists, gourmets, soothsayers, politicians, doctors and dog experts gathered around them, they were dispersed to the winds and others more or less sagacious took their place. Cassandra alone of that feature staff stood his ground: nothing less important than the British Government could move him on.

The pages were stimulating and aggressive, as crammed with excitement and surprises as a Bertram Mills Christmas Show or a Blackpool pleasure garden.

Articles became brief and punchy. Gossip, barbed and bright, offered such titbits as the story of the millionaire who gave his dance partner a double-decked bus because he liked her tango. And the headlines! For a public nurtured on shock-free newspapers the effect was startling.

Behind the barking and the tinsel, however, was a closely reasoned scheme. The plan which these young men evolved was simply this – to get under the readers' skin and to stay there. They were all, in their way, lay psychologists. Most of them had come from working-class or middle-class families in the provinces; they really knew and had personally experienced the aspirations and setbacks, the joys and the heartaches of the millions of ordinary people whom they set out to entertain and instruct. The down-to-earth feature pages became more and more like a letter home to the family, and that was their secret.

Readers accustomed to ploughing through the mild views of established authors were now expected to think and write for themselves.

Are you glad you married, or sorry? What was the most embarrassing moment of your life? Is your family crazy, too? Tell us about the worst nightmare you ever experienced. Tell us about the skeleton in your cupboard, the misdeed you are ashamed of. Tell us about your Greatest Adventure. What are your Eight Sane Rules for Happy Marriage?

The paper was homely, too: it wanted to hear readers' stories of their children's pranks on holiday. Small prizes were offered as inducements for letters and it was soon apparent that readers considered that confession was good for the soul and were anxious to read the confessions of others.

An intriguing type of headline never before seen in Britain's morning newspapers began to emerge:

BETWEEN MIDNIGHT AND DAWN
I MET A MURDERER

POISON-PEN FIEND'S
ASTONISHING CONFESSION:
I SMASHED A GOOD WOMAN'S LIFE

HE DROVE HER FROM HOME
THEN SHE NEEDED HELP. NOW HE ASKS
– 'WHERE IS MY DAUGHTER?'

I AM THE WOMAN YOU PITY

One series was called 'Truth'. Prizes were offered for letters which husbands, wives and others got off their chests the things they would like to say about their nearest and dearest:

'If only I could tell.'
These words are often on the lips of every husband and wife.
'If only I could tell him about that irritating habit of his that drives me mad!' 'If only I could tell him that he is killing my love by being so secretive!' 'If only I could tell her that I don't really love her!' 'If only I could tell her that she is the most wonderful wife in the world!' 'If only I could tell him of my past. It is haunting me!'
Well, here's the chance to open your heart and tell the truth. Don't boyyle iy up any more. Tell the *Mirror*. Address immediately to 'Secrets', *Daily Mirror*. Names and addresses will not be published.

There arrived this heart-rending contribution from 'Worried':

My wife sometimes complains that I leave unfinished some splendidly cooked meals. It would no doubt surprise her to know that she is the cause by continually smacking her lips while masticating food. It nearly drives me to distraction.

'Dismayed' had a real grievance:

> While courting I was very dissatisfied with the shape of my nose. I drew out my savings for a 25-guinea facial operation. Not a word of this did I breathe to my lover. To my horror he did not notice the difference!

The relationship between reader and newspaper became more intimate, and tantalising problems of the heart were much in favour.

'Dick's gone, and it's my own sister who has taken him away from me,' a young lady from Paignton complained. She found the sister's diary in which the missing husband was listed among many more boy-friends. Was it fair to show the diary to Dick? Readers, instead of being told to mind their own darn business, were asked: What would YOU do?

A shrewd old lady now came on the stage named Dorothy Dix. She was, in fact, an American, but she dealt with universal human problems in an adult and racy manner which no other writer has ever excelled. Is petting advisable at sweet seventeen? How far should a fiancé be allowed to go? How do you differentiate between a snake-in-the-grass and a young gentleman of honourable intentions? Should married couples have separate holidays? How can I make my husband look forward to the arrival of baby with the same emotional thrill that I experience myself? How can I induce my wealthy father to treat my impecunious admirer with one iota of respect? Is a young lady in peril of being adjudged a tippler if she enjoys more than two cocktails? Is cooking really as important as Mother says?

Dorothy Dix positively stood for law and order. Excessive petters should be slapped; Good-time Charlies are those who skedaddle as soon as a girl says 'No'; wealthy fathers never approve of their daughters' down-at-heel lovers; and yes, cooking is just as important as Mother says. But Dorothy always contrived to give her advice in an amusing, worldly, acceptable way. One felt she had been petted herself, had known the odd Lothario, and maybe enjoyed a tipple or two.

There was no mealy-mouthed hypocrisy in her advice; it came straight-from-the-heart, particularly to the over-competent Mother whose children were brought up on text-books:

> It may make you feel good and competent to treat your baby like a machine and spend all your time working out his diet, but you are laying up trouble for yourself if you don't mix a little perfectly good and practical love into the day's routine, said Miss Dix. Why are modern

children often hard-boiled and priggish? Because they have never had any affection in the cradle. They don't know how to love or be loved.

Eileen Ascroft was sent away with a typewriter to the French Riviera for three weeks with orders to return with a complete course of twenty-four lessons on how to be beautiful, charming and popular or, failing that, how to make the best of what God Gave You. This series, presented as *The Charm School,* caused much excitement among the ladies and inspired sixty thousand letters from readers in six weeks.

The *Mirror* announced an anthropological investigation of its own: 'We are going to get to the bottom of this love business.' It put a questionnaire to its women readers asking them how old they were when they first went out with a boy, when they were first kissed, and so on. No fewer than 50,432 filled in the forms, and when their answers were analysed it was possible to release to the waiting world the information that the first kiss, on average, came five months after the first 'hello' and was received at the age of fifteen-and-a-quarter, usually between 6pm and midnight.

Lonely wives complained to the *Mirror* about their husband's jobs; loneliness, indeed, was a subject which brought in pathetic letters whenever it was mentioned, and in many cases it was possible to give advice that really helped these neglected unfortunates.

Young men and women were invited to send in the story of their First Love. Said the paper:

> People used to sneer at calflove. Parents laughed at its tenderness and infinite sincerity.
> 'You must be in love' they would say to their 15-year-old son. And they would grin to see him blush so heatedly and rush so furtively from the house.
> Yet each one of us treasures the memory of the first love that meant so much to us and only seemed to make the others laugh. Write to 'Calf Love', Daily Mirror. A half guinea will be paid for every story chosen.

The series soon rocketed to a start with a reader's story headed: 'She Was Sweet Seventeen: I Loved Her Then and − I Love Her Still!' Next day's story began: 'He died at 16 − And I Shall Never Love Another'.

The customers in those days had a fair piece of homework on their hands if they obeyed the call to write to the editor, the feature editor or the editress whenever those executives needed outside advice. Yet tens of thousands of people were eager to assist. We were setting out to prove that the experiences of ordinary men and women could make exciting reading, and it was not the meagre prize of ten-and-sixpence which attracted them; here at last was a national newspaper dealing sensibly, sympathetically and understandingly with their own problems and which published their own views.

There is nothing so good for a newspaper as getting itself talked about. And people were beginning to talk about the demure picture paper that was now so pert and frank. Rival journals observed its progress with some concern: to denounce it was tempting but unhelpful, to emulate it might be unwise.

The young were talking about it, and every newspaper from *The Times* to the *Daily Worker* cherishes its younger readers for the simple reason that older folk already have one foot in the grave: the dead don't pay newsagents' bills.

The accent was on youth, and invitations such as this appeared with frequency:

> Knock! Knock!
> Who's there?
> It is the younger generation.
> What is your ambition?
> Youth is painfully fighting for an outlet which will offer escape from obscurity into the public eye. The *Mirror* is offering that outlet.
> If you are under twenty-five and have something to tell the world about yourself and what you want, send in your entry, now. Write 100 words on 'What I am', 100 words on 'What I can Do' and not more than 200 words on 'What I Want'. Address your entry to 'Ambition'.

Among those who talked were a section of citizens much I neglected by newspapers of the time. Girls – working girls; hundreds of thousands of them, toiling over typewriters and ledgers and reading in many cases nothing more enlightening than *Peg's Paper*. How were they persuaded to become readers of a live daily newspaper?

One step which made the grade with these future wives, mothers and family subscribers was a provocative attack on their working conditions. It angered more girls than it pleased, but it set them arguing.

They do the work – why don't they get the pay?' asked the *Mirror*. Girls of decent education could be hired for office work for 25s. a week, said the story. 'Big business walks in silk stockings, but they are threadbare and have holes in the feet.' Then came some home-truths:

> You do most things in an office rather less efficiently than men.

Deny it if you will but it is true. Take a simple thing like filing and indexing. You would not think that men could do this job better than you? Well, they can. Quite a lot better. Their minds are more orderly. They move more quickly. Ask the people who install and instruct on the use of these filing systems. They plump for men every time. Then even a thing like being a telephonist. Men again. In newspaper offices, where time is short, there are men on the switchboards. They are quicker — more effective. But — and here is the whole point — *YOU COST LESS*. You do things a shade worse, but you do them for a whole lot less.

No newspaper had addressed itself to large sections of the community in quite this manner before.

There was an article later on Pin Money Girls. 'She steals your job... or tries to! And she wants to know 'Why Not?' She needn't work, but she does. Girls tell her she is the cause of the low wages paid to women workers. Men tell her she holds the jobs they should hold. But she said: 'Who would benefit if I stayed at home?' Is she right?'

The *Mirror* was now pushing its nose into every conceivable controversy.

Death on the roads was frightening parents, for the toll was rising and there was no end to the slaughter of children. The sharp-eyed feature staff observed that, nevertheless, Mr Leslie Hore-Belisha, then Minister of Transport, always appeared to be smiling in his pictures. He is, it is fair to say, a genial character by nature, but his jovial face was published prominently under the headline: WHAT HAS HE GOT TO LAUGH ABOUT?

Cassandra dealt with the medical profession. 'Of course I'm biased,' he wrote. 'I'm agin doctors. I don't like 'em. For one thing their mumbo-jumbo, their smooth, lying inefficiency, and their blunt assumption that the disease-laden clients have the mentality of sick cattle. They are traders in the most valuable commodity we have — life itself. And they give poor value for money.'

Cassandra opined that the General Medical Council was 'unparalleled in bigotry and autocracy' and described the ordinary doctor as a man with 'neither the wit nor the means to break into the big money'.

'Dog-fights' were staged on human issues of the day: Should Breach of Promise be Scrapped? Is the Marriage Bond Cruel? Can Marriage be Happy Without Children? Both sides of the question were presented, and readers then stated their views. Landladies, for a change, were given the chance to say what they thought of their boarders, and an inmate of a workhouse contributed a piece of his mind under this challenging headline: YOU CAN KEEP YOUR CHRISTMAS PUDDING.

There was no hesitation, none at all, in upsetting accepted middle-class ideas. No subject was taboo, even funerals. When Cyril James, one of the paper's provocative writers, contributed a piece entitled 'And When I Die', the illustration showed a tombstone with the inscription:

> HERE LIES CYRIL JAMES – HE NEVER
> KNOWINGLY HARMED ANOTHER, BUT
> DIED IN THE FIRM BELIEF THAT HE HAD
> NOT MATTERED

The introduction to the article asked:

> What sort of a funeral will you want?
> Flowers?
> A long service?
> Tears and black clothes?
> Cyril James wants no one to mourn his passing. 'I want nobody to grumble because he had to wear stuffy, depressing clothes on my account', he says. 'When I die I want people to be honest with me.'

Books of the month, one thriller and one romance, were recommended with the advice 'There is no need to waste time on a boring book if you follow our selections.' There were questionnaires to test intelligence and courage.

Dorothea Brande required ten-minutes-a-day of every reader's time to impart the Secret of Her Formula for Success.

The *Mirror* psychologist explained how to ask the boss for a rise. Noel Jaquin decided whether readers were in the right job by analysing their hand-prints. T Georgius, with a sample of handwriting, was able to assess whether a lady would make a Good Mother. Father Owen Dudley warned 'these foolish girls'. Mark Benney, author of a best-selling book called *Low Company,* instructed readers on How to Burgle a House: the intention of course was to warn the public against the average burglar's method, but Scotland Yard were worried and called to remonstrate.

For those unconcerned about such mundane matters as success, money, work, motherhood, and burglary, Shaw Desmond announced that he had lived before and invited letters from readers who were convinced they had previous incarnations.

There was sentiment, too.

Patience Strong wrote a daily poem about the simple problems of life, and her obvious sincerity brought her an immense circle of friends. George

Lansbury wrote about his mother; from her, he said, he had learned that love is the greatest thing.

Love? A different sort of love was the theme of the most favoured series which appeared in those days of the Tabloid Revolution. Its title was 'Ain't Love Gland?', and its writer was a witty, well-informed lady named Katherine Townsend. 'Here is a series everyone will talk about,' said the *Mirror* confidently. 'It is the gayest ever. Glands, says Miss Townsend, rule our lives – and our loves. To-day's types are the streamlined girl, dominated by her thyroid, and the square head with very active adrenal. On Monday the pre-pituitary male will be dissected for your instruction.'

And the next day:

'Do you look like this – wide-eyed, petite, with well-turned ankles, a small face broad yet oval, a high-pitched voice and small plump hands? Then you are probably POST-PITUITARY!' The text outlined the characteristics of the post-pituitary girl and what she might expect from life. For the male reader there followed a few paragraphs of advice on How to Date this Girl.

Advising on partners for an evening out, Miss Townsend wrote: 'There are no complications with the excess adrenal. She will enjoy a lecture or a debate. A political meeting is right up her alley. The thyroid is a different proposition. She likes big parties and places with lots of people. She has a zest for almost anything. She can drink plenty – with a preference for cocktails or whisky.'

Fleet Street was puzzled. Was nothing sacred between the *Mirror* and its readers?

13

THE ABDICATION: SHOULD A NEWSPAPER TELL?

I quote from *A King's Story, the Memoirs of the Duke of Windsor:*

> Publicity was part of my heritage, and I was never so naive as to suppose that my romance was a tender shoot to be protected from the prying curiosity of the Press. But what stared at me from the newspapers that were brought to my room on Thursday morning really shocked me. Could this be the King, or was I some common felon? The Press creates: the Press destroys.
>
> The bitter unanimity with which the so-called 'quality' newspapers lashed out left little doubt that they reflected the Government's attitude toward me. By that action the Monarchy was brought violently into politics...
>
> It was all extremely unpleasant, to say the least. And to the degree that the daily Press reflected British opinion, the Prime Minister had certainly won the opening engagement, as Max Beaverbrook had prophesied he would...

> ...while I was absorbed in writing, Wallis entered the drawing room. In her hand she had a London picture newspaper.
>
> 'Have you seen this?' she asked.
>
> 'Yes', I answered. 'It's too bad.'
>
> The world can hold few worse shocks for a sensitive woman than to come without warning upon her own grossly magnified countenance upon the front page of a sensational newspaper.
>
> 'I had no idea that it would be anything like this,' she said. Nor had I. And, trying to reassure her, I expressed the hope, but without conviction, that the sensationalism would soon spend itself.
>
> 'You do not seem to understand,' she said in a troubled voice. 'It is not only that they are attacking you personally, or me. They are attacking the King.'

> To me Wallis has always been a blithe spirit – gay, quick, unconquerable. She has an article of faith that enables her to face the future with untroubled heart – 'Don't worry. It never happens'. But that morning her face was tragic.

The newspaper to which the Duke refers in his Memoirs is the *Daily Mirror*. His erroneous account can only be attributed to the naivety he denies in his first sentence, to a defective memory, or to a curious sense of ingratitude to the few British newspapers which did demand a fair hearing for a King in torment.

The 'grossly magnified countenance' was in fact a delightful portrait posed by the lady herself and taken by a photographer of her own choosing. The *Mirror* did not attack the King or his future Duchess: on the contrary it battled for his cause – a campaign in which it had few allies and which it honourably lost.

Here, at all events, is the inside story of The 1936 Abdication Crisis, Fleet Street, and the *Mirror*.

Edward first met Wallis Warfield Simpson after his return from South America in 1931. She and her husband were fellow guests at a country house, and the dialogue between the lady and her future spouse was as banal as is customary on such occasions. The romance that was to pin back the ears of the world and send a British monarch packing from his throne and his palace was born in a chat about plumbing.

Did Mrs Simpson miss American central heating? No, she didn't. In fact she liked our cold houses. Then, with the archness of which her sex alone is capable, came the remark that made it apparent that here was a woman who was different.

'I am sorry, Sir,' she said, 'but you have disappointed me. Every American woman who comes to your country is always asked the same question. I had hoped for something more original from the Prince of Wales.'

The Duke himself has recorded how occasional meetings took place among mutual friends at dinner parties and at the Simpsons' flat in Bryanston Court during the next few years. He was 'struck by the grace of her carriage and the natural dignity of her movements' when she was presented to his parents at Court at Buckingham Palace. She had 'exquisite taste'. Her food was 'unrivalled in London'. She had 'a magnetic attraction for gay, lively and informed company'. And the talk at Bryanston Court was 'witty and crackling with the new ideas that were bubbling up furiously in the world of Hitler, Mussolini, Stalin, the New Deal, and Chiang Kai-shek'.

The friendship could not interminably escape official attention, and before his death in 1936 King George V found cause to discuss his successor's infatuation with the Archbishop of Canterbury. The talks were described by Dr Lang as distressing; in his view the life of George V was shortened by this anxiety.

To the public, one year later, the news of Edward VIII's intentions came as a shock for which they had been unprepared.

There had been few outward signs, and their significance had not been appreciated. At Ipswich Assizes on October 27 1936 Mrs Simpson was granted a decree nisi on the grounds of her husband's adultery, but the case was obscurely reported in deference to the King's wishes. On December 1, the Bishop of Bradford made a public reference to the King's behaviour in an address to his Diocesan Conference and the *Yorkshire Post* simultaneously published a leading article on the character of the monarch. On December 2 *The Times* obliquely referred to 'a marriage incompatible with the Throne'. Then came the bombshell and the nation for the first time heard that the King wished to marry Mrs Simpson.

In Fleet Street alone the full force of the gathering crisis had been known and understood.

Behind the scenes there had been much activity since early October. Powerful men had formed themselves into opposing groups and for one reason or another were conspiring to influence historic events.

Much would have been learned by an eavesdropper on the telephone lines between Buckingham Palace and Stornoway. There lived Lord Beaverbrook. Activated by two motives – his deep-seated contempt for Stanley Baldwin, then leading the forces of conventional respectability, and secondly by a genuine desire to succour the King who had called him to his side – the wily Press proprietor strode into the drama with ill-concealed relish. He counselled silence until the time might come when the case could be presented to the people in the manner most favourable to Edward VIII. The King valued his advice, so much so that when Beaverbrook was travelling across the Atlantic in November he besought him by cable and telephone to return. The Press lord is periodically troubled with chronic asthma and he had planned a rest in the desert of Arizona; he came back in the same ship on November 26 and drove immediately to Fort Belvedere.

The lines were also busy between Stornoway House and Warwick House, St James's. There lives Esmond Harmsworth, the present Lord Rothermere, an intimate friend whose aid the monarch also sought; the *Daily Mail* became an ally. Talks of a different nature were taking place between 10 Downing Street and the offices of *The Times,* for Stanley Baldwin and the editor, cronies and fellow clubmen, were in frequent consultation.

The existence of the Royal romance had long been known to the *Mirror* in detail. I was at that time presiding over the features department, and John Walters, head of the New York bureau, was daily despatching cuttings from the New York Press; there was no secrecy in Wallis Simpson's native country, and the interest of the American newspapers had been stimulated by several inescapable clues.

During the period of six months mourning for King George V, Mrs Simpson occasionally joined the new King's friends at Fort Belvedere. Further she attended two official dinner parties at York House at which the guests were Mr and Mrs Baldwin and the Churchills; her presence was recorded in the Court Circular, for 'secrecy and concealment', writes the Duke of Windsor, 'were not of my nature'. In the summer of 1936, when the period of mourning was over, Edward VIII set off on a Mediterranean cruise in the *Nahlin* yacht with his assistant private secretary, an equerry, the Minister for War, Mr Duff Cooper and Lady Diana Duff Cooper. 'Wallis was also a member of the party, although she and I were both by then well aware that my interest in her had attracted attention and speculation.'

That the King had fallen in love with Mrs Simpson was beyond reasonable doubt, but the items in the American Press which I was daily receiving were ripe with rumour, conjecture, innuendo, lies and double doses of disrespect.

New York's *Sunday News* referred to 'suppressed rage in the Royal household'.

Another American newspaper published this titbit: 'Declaring that it was Crown property, policemen shooed loiterers away from Cumberland terrace, site of the new home of Mrs Wallis Simpson. A sergeant and two constables patrolled the district. Every time anyone dallied outside Mrs Simpson's home they were told 'ordinary garden people don't live here, y'know. This is Crown property.' Someone asked what would happen to people who insisted on standing in Cumberland terrace. 'They'll likely get in serious trouble,' rejoined a constable.'

A popular theme was the purchase of extravagant gifts. 'King Edward has given Mrs Simpson a 125,000 dollar emerald necklace, it was learned to-day. There have been other gifts but it is understood they have not nearly reached the rumoured total of one million dollars. One gift is believed to have been a big black sedan. The King ordered two, and only one was delivered to him.'

Another newspaper said: 'Edward, the day before his departure from Vienna, walked by himself from the Bristol Hotel where he was stopping to a shop on the Kaerntnerstrasse. He bought huge quantities of silk stockings, underwear and dresses. All Austria knew about it by grapevine.'

Long before the people of Britain were at all aware of the romance, the Americans were informed by their newspapers that the King and his lady had parted. Said the New York *Daily News:*

> King Edward VIII will marry a hand-picked Princess and not Mrs Wallis Simpson, after all. The King and Commoner interlude has ended, and London believes that Edward was breaking the news tonight to his American sweetheart at a rustic rendezvous far from Buckingham Palace. Any one of six princesses whom he might have married, but ignored, will be chosen as the next Queen of England. It will be a marriage of convenience, a concession to the Victorian temper of modern England. The King has told his Court advisors to name the girl.

One paper announced: 'Mrs Simpson all set to tour her empire'.

The same cuttings were reaching Mr Baldwin and were causing him much concern.

Should a newspaper tell? How much should a newspaper tell? When should a newspaper tell?

In Britain there was no desire on anyone's part to intrude prematurely into the King's private affairs, nor indeed to allude to them at all until they made their impact on the welfare of the nation. But that state was reached when Mrs Simpson's divorce became imminent in October.

The King was determined, if he possibly could, to control the attitude of the British Press, and the first step he took was to consult Lord Beaverbrook. The result was a secret and hurried conference at which Beaverbrook and Harmsworth achieved what the King himself described as 'the miracle I desired – a gentleman's agreement' among editors to report the case without sensation'. It was agreed in principle at that stage that the King's friendship was of a private nature and was therefore no concern of his subjects.

Within four days a different view was taken by Prime Minister Baldwin. He saw the King, mentioned the stories which were appearing in America, and expressed the view that the monarchy was in danger. The divorce petition, he said, should be cancelled. It was not cancelled, and the reports which appeared on October 27, circumspect as they were, sharpened the conflict between the opposing forces.

The King's men were powerful, for Beaverbrook and Harmsworth were soon to be joined by Churchill. But the rival group was no less illustrious.

On November 11 Geoffrey Dawson, editor of *The Times* and the diligent courier of those who were horrified at the trend of events, discussed the situation with the Archbishop of Canterbury. Dr Lang was deliberately standing aside from the controversy, but volunteered the information on George V's 'distressing talks with him about Edward's infatuation': from this conversation sprang the phrase which appeared in *The Times* editorial of December 8 – '*King Edward's father, whose closing days were clouded with anxiety for the future*'.

On the same day Dawson was consulted by the Prime Minister on the problem of publicity, for Baldwin was as stupid on newspaper matters as he was ignorant of foreign affairs. How should the news be announced, and when?

Thus Dawson moved behind the scenes building up the case against the King. He desperately desired that his newspaper should deliver the first public admonition. On the rise of the Nazi menace *The Thunderer* was silent: could it remain silent on the approaching constitutional crisis without forfeiting forever its claim to guide opinion?

Too timorous to act in defiance of Baldwin's plea for postponement, *The Times* bided its time. There was a complicating factor, for the King was about to visit a distressed area the Government had neglected. Could he be criticised just before, or just after, an important public appearance?

It was on this side issue, curiously enough, that the preliminary Press skirmish was centred, but only the initiated were aware the opposing factions were showing their hand. On November 23 the *Daily Mail,* under the headline 'A Contrast', acclaimed the King's humanitarian concern for the workless and implied that the Cabinet was indifferent to their plight. The following day *The Times* denounced this attitude as improper and mischievous; the King's constitutional position, said that newspaper, was above and apart from party politics.

At the request of the King the Cabinet met on November 27 to consider the possibility of a morganatic marriage and the Dominions were consulted. Then, on December 1, some months before the Coronation was to take place, the silence was broken by the Bishop of Bradford, who spoke of the King in a manner to which the people had not been accustomed in their lifetime.

'I ask you to commend him to God's grace, which he will so abundantly need if he is to do his duty faithfully. We hope that he is aware of his need,' said Dr Blunt. 'Some of us wish that he gave more positive signs of his awareness.'

Had the Church chosen the moment and the man to cast the first stone? No. Bishop Blunt acted alone and without consultation; he afterwards claimed that he was referring merely to the King's apparent indifference to religion. His words were interpreted by Fleet Street as an official rebuke by the Church of England and a warning that the friendship with Mrs Simpson must cease if a crisis was to be averted.

Perhaps the newspapers should have told the public long before, and there can be no doubt that had Bartholomew at that time been in supreme command of the *Daily Mirror* the news would have been published in terms that all would have understood. He now resolved to act – alone – after chairman John Cowley had left the office for the night.

Fleet Street embarked upon its most exhausting and exciting week for a generation. There were hours of hesitation and anxiety, but on December 3 the nation was to know the secret of the tremendous struggle between the King, the Church and the Cabinet.

The *Mirror's* first two editions contained no news of the crisis. The third spoke of Baldwin's 'audience of the King on urgent and political matters not connected with foreign affairs'. Next there were hints of 'grave issues'. Not until the edition that came off the presses at 3.53am. were the facts revealed with a portrait of Mrs Simpson. It was the only crisis ever known to bring Bart into the office in his pyjamas.

What attitude did the *Mirror* take? The leader writers in most newspapers weaved tortuous sentences to cloak their temerity and indecision, but Geraldine House had a new tradition to live up to. No evasions. No innuendos. Boldly and brashly the *Mirror* plumped for the King in the biggest, blackest type in store.

It had good reasons to suspect that the politicians in Westminster were not being entirely frank with the King, the people, or the Dominions, and the autobiographies which have since been written about the ten days of the Abdication Crisis have justified those suspicions.

'Until this week the *Daily Mirror* rigidly refrained from commenting on or publishing news of this situation. We have been in full possession of the facts,' the readers were informed, 'but we resolved to withhold them until it was clear that the problem could not be solved by diplomatic methods. This course we took with the welfare of the nation and Empire at heart. Such is the position now that the nation, too, must be placed in possession of the facts.'

God Save the King appeared as a front-page banner-line, Mr Baldwin was harried to take the people into his confidence, and two pages were devoted to the stories I had collected from the American Press. 'These were the lies,' the headline proclaimed, 'which poisoned world opinion.'

The *Mirror* demanded of the Prime Minister: 'THE NATION INSISTS ON KNOWING THE KING'S FULL DEMANDS AND CONDITIONS. THE COUNTRY WILL GIVE YOU THE VERDICT.' Two days later there followed: '45,000,000 DEMAND TO KNOW the answers to five questions AND THEN THEY WILL JUDGE'.

Cassandra was also heavily engaged in this rearguard action for the King who gave up his throne for love. His article was titled 'I Accuse!'; it began with these words:

> I am writing about what I regard as the biggest put-up job of all time. I accuse leaders of the Church of England of putting our King in a position from which it was almost impossible to retreat. I accuse the Prime Minister and his Government of manoeuvring, with smooth and matchless guile, to a desperate situation where humiliation is the only answer.

There was no doubt about whose side the paper was on. With sincerity, and in company with the *Daily Express* and the *Daily Mail*, it had backed the wrong horse. Baldwin won, the King abdicated, and the public accepted the course of events with equanimity. A curious factor is that though the *Mirror* had miscalculated public opinion, its circulation increased more than that of any other newspaper during the crisis and it maintained more of its increased sale than any other newspaper when the crisis subsided.

It shed inevitably the last of its older conservative readers. Cheltenham, Bath and Bournemouth had watched the changes in their favourite sedate paper with curiosity, dismay, horror and apoplexy in successive stages; the handling of the Abdication was not the last straw, it was the one after.

Should a newspaper tell?

The *Mirror's* decision to end the secrecy and publish the facts was recalled some years later when the *World's Press News,* a trade periodical of the industry, invited the views of editors on the practice of interviewing bereaved relatives. editor Cecil Thomas replied:

What is a newspaper? Does it or does it not exist to provide news for its readers? Well, then... are news editors to be asked to say that this or that is not 'nice' news? Are they to be constantly acting as nursery censors? A news editor with that type of mind would be like a general with a conscientious objection to killing.

The truth is that the London Press is already too niminy-piminy, too nice altogether, too refined, too ready to leave out, too reluctant to print without fear or favour.

Just recall, they said nothing at all about Mrs Simpson until December 3 when the *Daily Mirror* gave her name and picture. Then all, with terrific unanimity, came out next day with pages about her.

Remember Bishop Blunt? When he began the abdication row by publicly criticising the King – a thing, it is true, which has not been done for a hundred years – two evening newspapers (overflowing with the inscrutable wisdom of sub-editors) deleted the paragraph which was the only news in the story.

A newspaper that wishes to retain the confidence of its readers should be ruthless and remorseless in revealing all the news it can get.

Editor Thomas's epistle had nothing, completely nothing, to do with the problem of Press intrusion into private grief. The revelation of the King's romance with Mrs Simpson was an intrusion into private joy. But Fleet Street raised its eyebrows at his frankness. More people bought the *Mirror*, and who except Fleet Street could be surprised?

When George VI was crowned six months after the departure of Edward VIII the paper produced a forty-page Coronation Number. A full review was given of the crowd arrangements, even to a list of public conveniences along the processional route. The list was appropriately headlined:

ALL THE NEWS YOU WANT
TO KNOW AND WHICH NOBODY ELSE
WILL TELL YOU

The darned paper was irresistible.

THE ABDICATION

At last, the news broke…

14
THE NEW CRUSADERS

When chain cafes proposed to increase the cost of a cup of tea from 2d to 2½d most papers recorded the event in a few obscure lines. To the *Mirror* and its readers this was big news indeed; the cafes were named with page one prominence and an immense hullabaloo was generated.

It was a cheeky pup of a newspaper. In addition to wagging its tail, sitting up and begging, and running and fetching, it developed the disconcerting habits of barking and biting, and many a time sank its teeth into the seat of the pants of an official bungler.

As well as a sense of humour and humanity, the *Mirror* had a conscience, and it conducted its crusades with a sincerity and a brand of courage which commanded wide attention and aroused the wrath of its victims.

Politicians with something new to say, like Cripps, could always find an outlet for their views in the *Mirror,* and thinking men behind the scenes – men of the calibre of Lord Vansittart – observed with interest the trend of its policy on major affairs.

On the most cogent issue of those times, war or peace, the paper bears minute scrutiny. It emerges with a record which makes the pro-appeasement of *The Times* look cowardly and reduces to asininity the *Daily Express* promise that 'There will be no war'.

From 1932, when Churchill warned Britain of the dangers of a rearmed Europe, the *Mirror* consistently urged that appeasement would lead to disaster and that aggressors could be checked only by realism and preparedness. 'The policy of talking, trusting, yielding, explaining,' said an editorial, 'will go on failing. We want peace. But we see that others do not want it.'

Front pages were used as early as in 1936 for advocating the appointment of Churchill as Defence Minister. Prime Minister (Honest Stanley) Baldwin was roundly attacked for his squalid 'sealed lips' confession that he had ignored the need to rearm so that he would not lose an election; he was bluntly accused of false pretences. The paper complained loudly, too, when Lord Caldecote, then Sir Thomas Inskip, was appointed custodian of Britain's military security – 'there has been no stranger appointment since Caligula made his horse a consul,' said Churchill.

David Walker toured Europe to warn the British of the repressions to which the people of Germany, Austria and Czechoslovakia were being subjected; Cassandra visited the Spain in which Franco had triumphed.

Somewhat sourly, in the final volume of its History, *The Times* recalls its suppression of the portion of a letter signed by nine prominent Liberals led by Lady Violet Bonham Carter in which they advocated that if Chamberlain wanted to show that national unity existed, he should include Churchill and Anthony Eden in his Cabinet, for they had consistently advocated the policy Chamberlain was at last taking up.

This was an act of overt partiality by the editor, Geoffrey Dawson, and his action is defended in the History merely by the paltry assertion that he 'was clearly right not to provoke attacks on a public man of the greatest potential value'. It is interesting that no attempt is made to justify a reader's letter, which Dawson published on August 12 1939 and which contained these remarkable words: 'The deep and widespread admiration of the English for the German people, and indeed, for Herr Hitler, is, it seems, being destroyed of malice *prepense* by the German propagandists themselves.'

Says the History: 'The *Daily Mirror,* which had long been amusing Printing House Square with its references to *'The Times* Fifth Column', excelled itself.' It then quotes the *Mirror* condemnation: *'The Times* has pursued a policy that has put heart into every reader who has the Fascist and the antidemocratic cause at heart. The latest incident (banning the Liberal letter) is well in the Himmler tradition. *The Times* is still regarded abroad as the foremost journal of considered British opinion. But it cannot be long before it is universally known that the *Daily Telegraph* [which published the Liberal letter in full] has taken up the reins discarded by Dawson in his death-throes of journalistic suicide.'

The *Mirror* was also in the front-line of national controversy in more domestic matters. Just as its gaiety attracted the light-hearted, so its outspokenness and new political integrity increased its importance as a newspaper.

Wrote Cassandra of the Coronation celebrations for King George VI:

> The latest insult to the unemployed has been announced by the Minister of Labour, Mr Ernest Brown.

He proposes that the Unemployment Assistance Board should make special Coronation payments of 2s. 6d. to all persons who Were unemployed during the week ending May 8 next. Haifa crown! What a contemptible gesture! They will fill their Stomachs all right. They will have a good time on thirty pence. The whole nation will be united at this gladsome time and not a word of complaint will come from the great army of workless . gratefully clutching their half crowns. Oh nuts!

When unemployment figures fell below two million the paper focused attention on the problem by publishing a bitter protest against 'the smug satisfaction all round, except among the derelicts left behind, jobless, hopeless.'

Under the headline 'I AM THE TWO-MILLIONTH MAN' the writer complained that while thousands were underfed the House of Commons 'drivelled' for seventy-five minutes over little Maud Mason, a Manchester schoolgirl whose essay praising Britain as the best country in the world brought a rap on the knuckles for her teacher from a stupid school-inspector for imparting 'old-fashioned imperialism'.

The paper tested the theory of Professor L Sargent Florence, expounded to the British Association, that it was possible for a man and wife with three children to live on 34s.10d. a week. After her first day's shopping the guinea-pig housewife said: 'I don't mind telling you I am mighty thankful I have got £2 a week in the ordinary way instead of 34s.10d. I can see that already.'

A cause which particularly attracted the new crusaders of Geraldine House was the protection of children from cruel parents: then, as now, the paper was vigilant in exposing the evil-doers and in demanding punishments which would act as a potent deterrent to others.

Said one writer, initiating a campaign under the headline 'THE CRY OF A CHILD':

> I have just read a sentence that should make every father and mother in Britain physically sick. Twenty-three formal words, but a sentence which tells a tale of horror much more nauseating than all the harrowing chapters written about the atrocities of the Great War. A tale of the Slaughter of the Innocents. This is the sentence. I want you to read it over and over again: *'During the past twelve months the number of cases of violence to children reached the highest figure in the history of the NSPCC.'* The number is 4,814. Nearly 100 children, that means, suffer at the hands of adults every week. One hundred children enduring a living death.

The article closed with an appeal for public help:

> There is spreading among us to-day a spirit of raging resentment against cruelty to infants. This spirit must spread more and more! Do not be content to say: 'That child is living a life of hell'. Bring those parents to justice. Tell the police! Tell the NSPCC! Tell Britain!

Occasionally the paper's methods of campaigning incurred the distaste of its more squeamish readers. There were protests when a photograph was published of a greyhound which had been allowed to starve to death, but the *Mirror* returned to the battle next day:

WE DO *NOT* APOLOGISE

> Our picture of the starved and dying greyhound shocked you. Maybe it made some of you sick. If it did we are glad. It was good for you. We intended to shock you, and we shall shock you again and again if by doing so we can help to stamp out the wanton cruelty—so often born of thoughtlessness—that lives in Britain to-day. ...
>
> Forty-six people wrote to complain about it. But only 4,800 letters of praise were received. It is pitiful to think that only 4,800 people were roused sufficiently out of their apathy to write to support us. We want you to join us in a great crusade to end cruelty.

When the complaints continued to arrive Cassandra took the matter up in his column.

'I wish to protest about the disgusting picture you published' wrote one reader. 'This is cheap sensation at its worst. My two children who saw the picture were quite upset by its horror and ugliness. As I cannot allow gruesome illustrations like this to be left lying about the house I have asked my newsagent to stop sending the *Daily Mirror.*'

Commented Cassandra: 'Well, we have lost a reader. But we can take it, and we are not very downhearted by losing the attention of a mind so monumental in its stupidity and bigotry. We are going to publish more of these pictures, and if we lose another handful of readers, well, that will be just too bad.'

Millions of new readers were drawn to the paper over the years by its vivacity and youthful attitude to life, but there were hundreds of thousands who found its expanding sense of reality unpalatable. They wanted life to be one unending strip-cartoon.

Why, they asked, do you persistently mention unemployment and slums? Why must you stick your nose into politics and depressing social problems? Why not write about the parents who are kind to their children instead of about the monsters who are cruel? Why not tell us about happy marriages and leave divorces and broken homes alone? It is almost impossible, they complained, to pick up the *Mirror* without finding yet another warning to the nation to be prepared for war.

As the day of reckoning approached on September 3 1939, the *Mirror* sensed that there was in many people a deep-rooted desire to turn their backs upon it all and escape to a life of unreality and pleasure. The paper's reply to these escapists was to stage a fascinating social experiment – 'Seven Souls in Search of Sanctuary', an idea much copied since by journals at home and abroad.

Seven men and women were selected from different walks of life – a young bachelor, an unemployed man, a ledger clerk, a glamour girl from the West End stage, a young married woman, a spinster and a married man of forty.

Together they lived for a week in Flower Cottage, a Tudor retreat on Effingham Common in Surrey, cut off from life. So that the facilities could be rapidly acquired the mother of a member of the features department was removed from this abode and parked in an hotel.

The telephone was disconnected, no radio or newspapers were allowed, and in the paper the following week the Seven Souls wrote exactly what they thought of one another and their reactions to their experiences as fugitives from life.

The bachelor deserted before the time was up. His verdict was: 'You can't escape from reality'.

The *Mirror* agreed with the bachelor.

15
THE FABULOUS
GODFREY WINN

Godfrey Winn, novelist and erstwhile actor, arrived at the *Daily Mirror* in the autumn of 1936 to start work on a daily page.

The title was 'Personality Parade', and the equipment the young man brought to the task was unique in this or any other country, in this or any other age.

There were his mother and his powdered-white Sealyham terrier, Mr Sponge; he wrote about them with regularity and public devotion. There was his garden at Esher, which he constantly described in his page. Next, his unbounded energy and self-confidence, plus a determination to absorb himself in the lives of his readers even if he became a wealthy young man in the process. Plus a hide as thick as a rhinoceros, for he was impervious to criticism. Plus a floating birthday, for nobody other than himself and presumably his mother knew then or knows now how old he was or young he is.

As success came his way, his stock-in-trade was expanded by the acquisition of a secretary, also mentioned in 'The Page', a dozen silk shirts embroidered 'G.W.' in blue silk thread, and a pale blue coupe known to the machine-men of Fleet Street as 'Winn's Blue Boudoir'.

He had come to preach the gospel of This Happy Life, and the only problem which troubled his soul was a certain sensitivity about his thinning hair. This, however, he concealed in his many photographs by the device of looking at his readers straight between the eyes.

There was something else in the equipment which he called (with sincerity) 'my sincerity'. Winn knew he was sincere and his readers knew he was sincere: what the sophisticates and the cynics thought did not matter to him. So far as he was concerned the writers who lampooned him were 'madly jealous', and the fact is that Winn out-smarted and out-distanced most of the people who wrote him down as a pampered gilded lily. If proof were needed of his resilience the war provided it, for he voluntarily flew on bombing raids, sailed the Arctic seas, and then joined the Navy on the lower deck.

Within a year the *Mirror* was telling its readers that 'Winn, at twenty-eight, has become the most famous newspaper writer in the land. We wanted a man who could tell the truth in a world in need of a new message. Winn, who has written a quarter of a million words in the past year, was the idealist we needed.'

He was also the idealist other newspapers needed, for as soon as he left the *Mirror* in February 1938 he was signed up by the hard-headed John Gordon of the *Sunday Express* and in postwar years by the circulation-hungry Charles Eade of the *Sunday Dispatch*. Winn gave them value for their money; his claim that he 'works like a black' is justified.

He does not write or type his epistles. He walks them, or trots them, or canters them, or gallops them. He circles round the room shouting to his secretary at the top of his voice, wringing his hands in dismay when the word he needs escapes him, waving them petulantly in the air when an interrupter enters the door. A passer-by peering through the window would assume that General Winn is dictating his final terms to the beleaguered garrison. In fact, the words are honeyed; Godfrey is talking about gardens and friendship.

Winn knew famous people like Louis Mountbatten, Somerset Maugham, Noel Coward and Ivor Novello, and he wrote about them. But that was not at all the principal idea behind his page. Not many of the readers were famous, though they all had a mother, many had a dog, some had a garden, and few would turn their noses up at a new blue coupe. This page was something different; Winn wrote about himself and about his fans.

He is happy now to recall his hectic days on the *Mirror*. He talks at machine-gun tempo without punctuation or reserve, interlacing his philosophy with harsh financial details. Like this:

'At the start I was getting £20 a week. Then it was raised to £30 a week and expenses, and at the end I think I was getting about £40. To begin with I was on a month's trial. Then, at a ten-minute lunch in Fleet Street – just a scrappy half-crown do – I was asked: "Will you stay another three months?"... I said I was going to Italy for the winter, and was doing a new book. I still didn't see myself in newspapers, but I said Yes... I still thought it was going to end. But then came Jarrow. Jarrow, and the march of the unemployed, made me realise that I wanted to do some good. I shall never forget going there to write my page. To one of my informants I made a stupid remark about the emptiness of the shops. I noticed there was nothing in the windows, and asked why. Then the truth occurred to me. It was useless putting anything in those shop windows. The people had no money with which to buy... We did a lot of good. There was a stamp fund which raised hundreds of pounds for deserving causes. Christmas turkeys – dolls – the page became a terrific power... None of the tricks of the trade was known to me. I was getting 600 to 1,000 letters a week. The work was a tremendous emotional strain... My page was successful because it was the first time the reader had been brought on to the page. I used to make it a rule to go to tea with one of my readers every week, arranging for a photographer to be there as well... When I opened my garden for charity – it wasn't a big place, just a nice garden – 1,400 people came to meet me and my mother and to shake our hands. It pleased me when people said: 'You look just like I imagined you would be from your writings'... The whole thing is to write about what everyone else possesses... When I write a page I always think of an invalid in a darkened room, and how you have to bring the world into that room.... The letters were wonderful. I signed on for another year, which took me to February 1938. Then the *Express* offered me £5,000 a year to write once a week for five years. I felt absolutely whacked by the work I had been doing every day and accepted... The *Mirror* offered me £80 a week and expenses to carry on. But I couldn't do it. I had been writing my page six days a week, then five days... There haven't been many successful new columns since those days – in fact I can't think of any. The reason, I think, is that London journalists are obsessed with the West End, which is absurd... I now make £15,000 a year – never less – and my contracts for the next three years are certainly up to that. That is the position sixteen years after I started on the *Mirror*... You have to remember that the people who pay your salary are the ordinary people. That you cannot deceive them. And you have got to believe in yourself as a writer... When I had 200 messages of congratulation for my last birthday one brought me a pair of socks from a lady in Scotland who first wrote to me when I was writing Personality Parade.'

What did Godfrey Winn write about, day after day for twenty-four months?

He first intrigued women readers with an article called: 'In 1936 I Hope to Meet my Wife'. It is now 1953 and Mrs Godfrey Winn has still to be launched on society. His first Personality Parade began with this burst of enthusiasm: 'I am sitting at a desk in a newspaper office for the first time in my life. I thought I was going to have a holiday this August. But a new job is worth all the holiday in the world – and I feel fine!'

Blatantly he asked for women's support and got it. 'I like working with women,' he wrote one day. 'It is only men, jealous of feminine success, who assert that women are lazy, indiscreet, unimaginative in their work. That myth must die.'

Occasionally there appeared such unexpected stories as this: 'Yesterday a pair of pink silk knickers were found dangling from the Squadron flagstaff at Cowes. Instead of pulling that 'flag' down they ought to keep it flying from every flagstaff in the place. Such a gesture to gaiety would make Cowes less like a cemetery during racing week.'

Winn believed that his most private thoughts were the ones he should share. 'Thank God there is Sunday – one day at least when we can all be ourselves.' Early in 1936 he asked God to teach him not to be a snob about anything in the coming year.

When, after six months work he took a holiday in South America, he described his feelings to the faithful flock with detail and intimacy. 'The old jersey that I wear when I am working will stay on its peg in the corner as a hostage against my return from South America.'

Talented Pamela Frankau took over while he was away, matily introducing herself with the wisecrack: 'If you want to do me a favour ring up Gilbert, my father, and ask him if he is any relation to Pamela.' Such brittle humour was short-lived, for the maestro one month later to the day had a welcome home from Mr Sponge.

'Mr Sponge was waiting at the corner of the lane that leads to my cottage. How had he guessed? There is no need to ask or answer that question if you have kept a dog yourself. It was just the same as if I had never been away. And then my mother said: 'Tell me all about your trip.' And I started to tell her as to-morrow and to-morrow I shall tell you... I am fighting fit and at your service.'

Whatever Godfrey told his mother, he was pretty frank with his readers about the night life he had seen in Rio. He wrote of the conditions in the brothel area, where all the houses had names like *Dolly* and *Conchita* painted on them. 'I suppose there were close on a thousand women boxed up in that square, peering out at the passers-by, screaming their wares, for which, our guide told us, the highest charge was the equivalent of a shilling.' A blush must have come to the cheeks of the more sedate of his admirers that morning, for he added this further saucy note: 'Some of them were already practically undressed in their efforts to entice within strangers outside their gates.'

Sometimes he sounded the note of acerbity.

Agitating against a revival of cockfighting, he wrote: 'I *hope with all my heart that before this week is over the aeroplanes of the RSPCA will bring off a victory of which Christ would have approved.*' The country gentlemen who indulged in the sport were upbraided as 'swine'.

The Duke of Windsor's detractors provoked him to another outburst. 'It is a cruel fallacy to imagine that you can better prove your loyalty to our present King by being disloyal to the name of his predecessor. In any case throwing mud at someone who is not in a position to answer back is the behaviour of a coward who will find that most of the mud has stuck to his fingers.'

The page contained some good descriptive writing. But it was at its best, and he was at his happiest, in the cosy atmosphere in which he and his fans exchanged their innermost thoughts, doubts and aspirations. To spinsters and unfruitful matrons he was an attentive son; to neglected mothers he was the boy who regularly wrote home (every day, no less); to humble folk who found life uncomforting he brought the salve of gushing friendship.

Only occasionally was indignation about the cockfights of Yorkshire or the brothels of Rio permitted to intrude upon the blissful atmosphere.

Winn liked writing about his mother and Mr Sponge, his garden, his secretary and his sincerity.

The only problem, really,
    was Godfrey's
    thinning
    hair.

16
CLEAN AND CLEVER

The new sensational paper did not enjoy universal approbation: its competitors, in particular, were discouraging.

The *Daily Express* watched with some anxiety the rapid growth of the tabloid and began to be concerned about its own claim to being 'the world's greatest newspaper'. Was the claim based upon its world's record sale, still secure in pre-war days? Or upon its intellectual appeal? Or upon what? Arthur Christiansen, the splendid editor of the *Express,* observed the *Mirror's* antics with curiosity, and his newspaper began to publish unctuous boasts about its own freedom from 'salacity'.

The *Daily Sketch* swooned. Its proprietors kept a Black Book of its lusty rival's misdeeds and launched a campaign which proved to be the most side-splitting boomerang the newspaper business had ever known.

The idea of the campaign was simplicity itself. Instead of attributing the failure of the *Sketch* to proprietorial inelasticity, the blame was placed upon the *Mirror*. It was successful because of the methods it employed. Its news and features were frank enough – but look at its pictures!

Glamorous young ladies smiled out of the picture pages, and there were examples even of beauty unadorned. When two African girls brazenly bathed in a stream on page eighteen and were followed later on by 'The Glory that is Perfect Womanhood', a fine study of a sports girl from the London Salon of Photography, the *Sketch* had the vapours, and resolved that the time had come to sound an alarm.

Thus was launched the 'Clean and Clever' campaign. The *Sketch* announced to the public that 'All the News and Pictures Fit to Print' were to be found in its chaste pages; unprecedented and unparalleled, here was an example of a delicious incongruity – militant virginity.

And it was taken frightfully seriously by the *Sketch* itself. In addition to publishing only the News and Pictures Fit to Print, whatever that may mean, it filled its space with letters from prelates extolling its virtues. The Bishop of London was all for their efforts to produce a daily paper free from vulgarity, suggestiveness or sensationalism; he was apparently unperturbed by the prospect of a newspaper free from interest and free from reality. The Bishop Suffragan of Whitby assumed, quite wrongly, that 'the *Daily Sketch* must have a big circulation and therefore can be a real weapon for good'. The Rev J A Porter, of Cathedral Clergy House, undertook to recommend the paper to those under his charge – a Christian gesture which, judging by the future circulation of the *Sketch,* was of small avail. The Very Rev Mgr John M T Barton DD welcomed a reaction against the tendency to bring out 'all that is most beastly in men', a remark which must have been read with some surprise by the *Mirror*'s poetess, Miss Patience Strong. The Bishop of Manchester hoped that the *Sketch* would increase its circulation: so, forlornly, did Lord Kemsley. The Rev Bernard Grimley DD declared that the British public 'would rally round a paper with decent standards', then added with caution – 'if it keeps up to date'.

One of the solicited testimonials went so far as to hint darkly at the *sins* of 'a certain other paper'. The *Sketch* had, of course, written to these distinguished but in some cases not fully informed gentlemen advertising its own righteousness and guaranteeing not to use 'sensational, ribald and pornographic pictures'. Meanwhile, an entirely different drove of divines were happily and effectively writing for the *Mirror* and reaching far greater congregations than they could ever reach from their pulpits.

The 'Clean and Clever' campaign, in which the two Sunday picture papers were also involved, was brimful with humour.

Pictures were taken one Saturday of Barbara Ann Scott, the comely Canadian world champion. Miss Scott was leaping elegantly in the air displaying the briefs which seem to be inseparable from the art of ice-skating. When the *Sunday Pictorial* published the picture a letter arrived from a reader drawing the editor's attention to a discrepancy between that version and the one which appeared the same day in Lord Kemsley's weekend essay in gloom, the *Sunday Graphic.* The *Pictorial* was accused, 'in the pursuit of salacity', of interfering with Barbara Ann's clothing by slicing a few inches from the legs of her panties: 'I am in the newspaper industry myself', said the reader sagely, 'and I know how these things can be done.' I had the joy of revealing to the mistrustful reader that his lordship's wowsers had in fact (and to Miss Scott's surprise) painted a few inches *on.*

Society ladies preening themselves in the height of fashion with décolleté necklines turned to the *Sketch* the following morning fearful lest their dresses were no longer designed by Norman Hartnell but by some zealous blue-stocking who worked for the art editor. Would the *Sketch* have risked a charge of lèse-majesté had Princess Margaret been twenty-one in 1938 and worn the styles she favoured in 1953?

I even heard tell, after the war, that the *Sketch* got into trouble with a farmer for printing a picture of his proud prize-winning bull with the most important part callously obliterated by a few deft touches from an artist's paintbrush. Who on earth, the farmer wanted to know, would bring his cow to that dejected freak? I cannot vouch for this story because I do not know the bull.

In addition to a smug full-page advertisement in the *Telegraph,* the *Sketch* used the fronts of London buses as a battle-ground for their purity campaign. The *Sketch* bus would announce –

ALL THE NEWS AND PICTURES
FIT TO PRINT
or
CLEAN AND CLEVER

Following closely behind, the *Mirror* bus would announce more palatable and intriguing fare:

THE CHARM SCHOOL BEGINS
THIS WEEK
or
READ GODFREY WINN EVERY DAY
or
FRANK! LIVELY! DIFFERENT!

Lord Kemsley discovered to his chagrin that he had wasted his money on running a first-class publicity campaign for the rival newspaper. The *Mirror* did not publicly reply to these expensive tut-tuts; but it was grateful, privately, for Lord Kemsley's largesse.

Did the 'Clean and Clever' nonsense spring from obvious unadulterated envy of a competitor's triumph? There have been critics who were guided by loftier motives.

When the paper achieved the world record daily sale of more than four millions in post-war years *The Economist* commented: 'The success of the *Mirror* is a sore reflection upon a democracy, sometimes called educated, that prefers its information potted, pictorial and spiced with sex and sensation'. Yet in 1945 this same excellent journal, *The Economist,* expressed the opinion that the *Mirror* was one of the decisive influences in the General Election, since it preached to many of the unconverted.

Can a newspaper be 'potted, pictorial and spiced' and 'a decisive influence' at one and the same time? The answer is Yes: the *Mirror* reflects life *as it is,* but it has always shown an awareness of the world *as it might be.*

The Royal Commission on the Press displayed a shrewder, broader-minded insight into the secrets of popular newspapers. Though critical of other aspects, the Commission described the mass circulation journals as remarkable value for money.

'Readers,' it said, 'find a brightly coloured kaleidoscopic picture of the world day by day. They find exciting incidents at home and abroad; they find pathos and tragedy mixed with sentiment and comedy; they find personal gossip about the great or notorious and about people in the news who are neither great nor notorious but have caught the popular imagination for the moment; they find well produced photographs of people and places. Great affairs of national or international importance may not always get the space or the dispassionate treatment that is their due, but they are not neglected, nor are serious features lacking, even if the lighter predominate.'

The *Mirror* was curiously frank about itself in the years of the Tabloid Revolution and frequently printed vigorous attacks on its own technique.

Brian Murtough toured the provinces asking the public: What Do You Think of Us? From Stella Walter, a young shop assistant in Carlisle, came the forthright answer:

> You are corrupting the provincial view of life. Your *Pledge of Secrecy* stories are presented with a crude over-emphasis. They just don't click with me or my friends – they don't ring true. Glamorous lovelies? You can have too much of a good thing. After all, girls are quite a common occurrence, aren't they? You cram an artificial view of life down the throats of people in the country, and so do other London papers.

Readers joined in the affray, some praising, others damning the paper as 'a sickening rag'.

'You write too much about society nobodies,' said one. 'You also write too much about ordinary nobodies. You flash people up in enormous type just because they are young and in love or old and out of love, because they live extravagantly or die horribly. What will you do when something important happens? Burst?'

Unperturbed by criticism from rivals or readers was Harry Guy Bartholomew.

When at an annual general meeting of the company a shareholder expressed his gratitude for the 30 per cent dividend but his misgivings at the general tone of the paper, Bart likened its popularity to that of the well-known condiment, Colman's.

'Well, sir,' he replied, 'if you take the tin you must expect to take the mustard in it.'

17
BEHOLD – THE READER!

WAITRESS, 30, to Mass Observation investigator: 'I like any bloody paper that has the horse racing results in'.

Editors of rival popular newspapers would give the gold in their teeth to meet The Average *Mirror* Reader and His Wife, buy them a slap-up lunch in Claridge's, take them to see the finest show in town, lead them gently by the hand to their own offices and then keep them securely under lock and key. There they would be observed through a microscope, dissected by skilled and supple fingers, put together again and cross-examined for the remainder of their breathing years.

What worries the other papers principally is the age of this couple, for the *Mirror* has a greater proportion of readers under forty-five than any other national. Advertisers like this: competing newspapers do not, for a paper which has learned how to magnetise youth has grasped the holy grail of prosperity and power.

Northcliffe put the point succinctly when he glowered at the death notices in *The Times* and reminded its staff that every name in those long columns represented the loss of a subscriber. He would have no such qualms about the robustness to-day of the tabloid he founded in 1903; one in three of Britain's adult population is aged between 16 and 35, and 42 of every 100 *Mirror* purchasers are under 35.

This chapter collates what others have found out about these people, and discloses what the paper itself has discovered.

The Average *Mirror* Reader might be visualised as an under-35 artisan, a well-meaning chap, not always as handsome as the one who appears in the paper's trade advertisements; he has a wife who is conscious of her own appearance, and one or two children at the local council school. To know this couple intimately it is necessary to analyse their fads and fancies, their attitude to life in general and to their chosen daily paper in particular.

Behold now the *Mirror* Readers – a composite picture constructed from reports by Political and Economic Planning in 1935, P Kimble in 1943, the Hulton Readership Survey of 1948, and principally the large-scale survey by Mass Observation for the Advertising Service Guild in 1949:

THEIR SEX
In 1935, 70 in every 100 were women. In 1943 just under 49 in every 100 were women. Today readership is fairly evenly divided.

THEIR AGE
Predominantly under 45, with 42 out of every 100 under 35.

THEIR INCOME
Predominance among the lower income group.

THEIR POLITICAL VIEWS
Out of every 100 readers questioned in 1949, 58 supported Labour, 24 supported no party [were undecided], 15 were Conservative, 2 were Liberal, 1 other factions.

The *Mirror* reader, more than the reader of any other newspaper, is politically 'unattached to any party'.

THEIR ATTITUDE TO THE MIRROR
Out of every 100 readers,
   29 like the letters,
   27 the strips and cartoons,
   18 the pictures, and
   17 the news.
   16 are vague but generally approving.
   6 don't know what they like.
The remainder have miscellaneous views. The total exceeds 100 because some like more than one item.

More than half say they read the news, and two-thirds of their reading time is spent on news as distinct from features and sport.

Letters: Nearly one-third of all readers are 'fond of them'. For some, the letters are the chief reason for buying the paper.

Strips and cartoons: One reader in every four likes them. Very nearly half say they read them. Strips get as much attention as the second page feature or the page of home news.

The *Mirror* reader spends an average of six minutes on his paper in a train or bus and slightly under three-and-a-half minutes in a public library.

At home a great deal more time would be devoted, but no figures are available.

Politics: Nearly one-third, a higher proportion than for any other daily paper, do not know which political party the *Mirror* supports. 55 out of 100 say it is Labour. 5 say it is Conservative. Women readers particularly do not know the paper's political outlook.

There are lies, damned lies, and statistics; the object here is to present the reader as he is, not to explain why he is so, or to imply that he might be better or worse.

Let any newspaper which assumes a high intellectuality for its own readers over those of the tabloid beware. The indifference to politics, as an example, is general; Mass Observation concluded that 'although the majority of readers (of all papers) look at the political news, it is only to glance at it'.

One-third of all *Mirror* readers do not know which party their paper supports; one-fifth *of Mail* readers questioned, and nearly as many *Express,* are in the same boat. It is not only the *Mirror's* women readers who are particularly ignorant of their paper's political outlook; women readers of all papers are equally ignorant – or, a cynic might think, sensible.

Only five per cent of *Mirror* readers could recall what the paper's critic had said about the last film they saw: the total of all papers was merely seven per cent. On the other hand, how many film critics remember what another film critic said about a film?

Mass Observation were getting closer to the secret of the tabloid when they reported what men and women they interviewed had told them. The club porter (45) who liked the paper because it called a spade a spade. The unskilled working-class mother (30) who read the Live Letters while feeding the baby. The male cleaner (30) to whom the 'home truths' in the letters appealed. The man, artisan-class (35), whom we first met earlier in this book, who wanted to have a body like Garth's.

They are the folk who puzzle the papers which want a circulation like the *Mirror*'s.

Now we know them better we may continue the narrative of the strange escapades, the bold ideas, the crazy stunts and the courageous thinking that dragooned them together as the readers of one newspaper.

18
THE MAN HITLER CHANGED

It is now necessary to select a fine fretwork saw, stand on a chair, cut around the craniums of two men, lift up the lids and peer into their brains.

Richard Jennings as leader writer, and Cassandra as principal columnist, were cast to play dominant roles in the adventures which befell their newspaper during the Hitler war. We need to know something about these two gentlemen, or political saboteurs.

Both wore spectacles. Both were highly individualistic specimens. Both annoyed the British Government. There the similarities end, for they laboured on separate floors, never lunched together, seldom talked or exchanged ideas.

Jennings abhorred noise, particularly whistling boys, against whom he wrote many a fussy leader. William Neil Connor, who is Cassandra, played a harmonium in his office.

Tall, thin and testy, Jennings gave one the impression of a distinguished but sardonic schoolmaster, with neat drainpipe trousers and a deprecating sniff; young reporters and subeditors automatically took hands from pockets when passing the sage in the corridor. Connor, tough, rough, thickset, has the appearance of an insolent truant, with shapeless bags and a heavy scowl.

Jennings absorbed all that is good in English culture. Connor created his own culture; he was unable to fit into any other.

It is with the fascinating transformation of the leader writer that this chapter deals.

In carpet slippers, and with two books tucked under his arm, Jennings was once descending in short shuffling steps from his lone perch on the fourth floor to the editorial deck on the second floor when two racing hooligans disguised as messengers rushed past him on the stairs. They nearly collided with the dignified leader writer and then rushed upwards, the second throwing an apple-core at the first. Jennings stepped aside in disdain, muttering 'There goes the rising generation, the flaming, golden, lustrous, rising generation'.

He came from and lived in the world of books; indeed, he held a unique position as a collector of first editions. 'Good enough for Richard Jennings' was for many years the warm recommendation with which London's second-hand dealers cajoled a reluctant purchaser.

The harum-scarum of the tabloid revolution of 1935, '36, '37 swirled around Jennings but left him unaffected. He had been there working on the paper almost since its inception, and he had seen changes before. He had been writing the editorials in Northcliffe's and Rothermere's time, succeeding Hamilton Fyfe; he saw no reason why he should loop-the-loop because Harry Guy Bartholomew, assistant art editor when Jennings first arrived, was now the editorial director.

Nor did Jennings, or Bartholomew, know then that the coming war was to transform 'WM' into the best known, most quoted and hated leader-writer to emerge in the struggle.

Why 'WM'? No-one knows. But those were the initials he chose to write under and used for forty years. Perhaps he was paying respects to William Morris. Could be. For Jennings was a Socialist, influenced from his university days at Oxford by the writings of Shaw and the Fabians.

His father was a leader writer on *The Times,* and it was not surprising that Jennings' own style was mature and world-weary. Here is an example, his musings on money inspired by a gold-rush:

> How sweet is the idea of not slowly toiling and earning and putting by a little, but of adventuring and digging and picking up a lot. We are told of the ineffable sweetness of money earned by the sweat of the brow. But money earned (thinks the clerk now getting on fifty, with eight children to support) is mere payment for woes endured – the daily journey to the office, the boredom day in and day out. For that boredom you get something – the right to go on being bored. Such money is necessary stuff, like bread without much butter, necessary, dull. One must live, in spite of Voltaire, and one must work to live. Therefore the villa where the ageing clerk lives is only kept up in order that he may go on working to keep it up. So he goes on paying rates, rent and taxes. Money inherited is more amusing. It is, according to the extreme view, very immoral, like jam. But jam is nice and so is money inherited. It is a luxury, a setting free. And money found in Eldorado? That is the best of all...

What did it mean? Little enough to the unthinking moderns, but much to the reflective middle-aged. For more readers wrote to Jennings than to any other leader writer in Fleet Street. The initials at the end of his fragments and pleasantries attracted them, for editorials in other newspapers are delivered in Olympian anonymity as if they were the pronouncement of a committee, which they usually are.

When WM discoursed on roses his readers sent him bouquets of the choicest from their gardens. 'I followed this up with a leader on banknotes,' he said, 'but next day my postbag was empty.'

One incident of which Jennings was proud, and which will surprise the *Mirror* reader of to-day, is that it was due to him that two of the Sitwells had their poetry first published. Osbert Sitwell acknowledges the debt in his autobiography and tells how his sister Edith decided she must be free from parental 'bondage' if she was to realise her ambitions as a poet.

'Just as it may seem strange that a poet of my sister's order should arise out of the circumstances I have described, so it may be unexpected that a paper such as the *Daily Mirror* should be the first to publish her work. This was due to the perspicacity of the leader-writer and literary editor, Richard Jennings, the well-known bibliophile, and to him I also owe my own first appearance in print.'

Edith Sitwell's poem appeared over her name in the spring of 1913. Osbert's first published poem appeared in *The Times* in 1916 – also 'through the good agencies of our friend.'

Jennings, who came from a family of eight but remained a bachelor himself, was happiest in the company of books and authors. Yet he kept in touch with political reality, and there were portents in his earlier leaders of the Cato he was to become in Hitler's war.

When Churchill first warned Britain in 1932 of the danger of a rearmed Europe, WM's' editorial welcomed his survey. As the years went by he preached in his sixty-word leaderettes the vital message:

The dictators mean war.
Be strong.
Re-arm.
Seek allies.
Appeasement will not save us; it is
leading to disaster.

It is to WM that most of the credit must go for the *Mirror's* sane record in foreign affairs since the Nazi spectre first appeared, but it was not until 1938, when the Germans had invaded Austria, and the Czechoslovak crisis was upon us, that Jennings attained full stature as a nationally-acknowledged commentator on the grim and hurrying events that were to engulf the civilised world.

When Chamberlain, with a naiveté which in retrospect is as bewildering as when the words were first spoken, asked 'all concerned' to continue their efforts towards peace, Jennings wrote:

> Does this include Hitler or Goebbels or the pale spy Ribbentrop, so recently the darling of the treacherous upper-crust riff-raft in this country?
>
> Mr Chamberlain must be aware of the hardening of opinion here. Even the old lion Garvin is roused at last. The journal which slobbered over dear Von Ribbentrop, admired that inspiring leader Mussolini, and called Franco a gallant gentleman, has now given up its sickly diet of spaghetti and begun to eat roast beef again. Surely opinion is hardening!
>
> If it weakens among 'those concerned' in the Government we had better stop handing out gas masks and hand round swastikas instead – for use a few months hence.

The bibliophile who nurtured poets and loathed whistling boys now set aside the parable and the graceful allusion with which his writings had been sprinkled in the years of peace. For Jennings now the long, sharp-pointed lance.

Had the second world war not crashed about him, WM might well have reached his retirement still writing about Eldorado banknotes and Christmas trees made of aluminium. What happened to him had happened before to David Lloyd George. The man who cut LG's hair for several decades observed that when his customer moved to No 10 Downing Street not only did he change his attitude and his deportment, the actual size of his skull increased to such an extent that the overall area of hair-cutting was noticeably greater after greatness had been thrust upon him.

Civilisation was in peril, and men of culture like WM must rise in wrath to defend it.

Chamberlain brought back from Munich the Anglo-German agreement; 'peace with honour' had been reached between a German fox and an English rabbit, and the *Mirror* warned that the pact was a scrap of paper – 'and we know what the Nazi word is worth'. Churchill, anticipating a demand from Hitler for restraint on Press freedom, spoke prophetically but with unconscious humour of 'the next stage of our journey, with every organ of public expression doped or chloroformed'.

When Chamberlain set off for a talk with Mussolini a picture of an umbrella summed it all up with the laconic caption 'Gone to Rome', and WM offered the Premier another Shakespearian quotation for his next speech: 'I eat the air, promise-crammed'. When Czechoslovakia joined

Austria in enslavement, and the points of German bayonets turned towards Poland, Jennings urged immediate consultations with Russia, America and the Scandinavian countries. Two months before the devastating proclamation of the Nazi-Soviet pact he wrote of the 'anti-Bolshy bogy' and demanded of the 'ditherers'

> What will you say when you hear that Hitler himself has approached Stalin and made a friendly agreement with him? Won't that be rather awkward? Suppose the dear Fuhrer goes red? He turned the Japs into Allies. He won't strain at Reds after he has swallowed Yellows.

When war came the paper, with justice, proclaimed its leader writer as 'The Man Who Made All England Sit Up'. Jennings had arrived, 'the one voice in this country' said his newspaper 'that has unswervingly warned our people of what would happen next, who has revealed the ultimate aims of the dictators, who has hammered home the lesson that Britain must be strong'.

The one voice?

In its enthusiasm for WM the paper had forgotten Churchill's own contribution to realistic thinking. Just as Churchill, when his Cabinet threatened to suppress the *Mirror* in 1942, forgot what Jennings had written in earlier years, and how he had considered WM's' editorials the best in Fleet Street and had sent the leader-writer his congratulations.

At all events the erudite Richard Jennings, petulant, serious, sincere, was on his rostrum. Ready to urge and scourge, to cajole and lampoon, to exult and censure, until they threatened to set the law on him.

19

WHAT MAKES CASSANDRA CLANG

William Neil Connor, already famous as Cassandra when war began and soon, to his critics, to become infamous, is a stronger, headier brew than Richard Jennings. XXXX instead of Tio Pepe.

Psychiatrists might linger over the titbit that he was born a dissimilar twin, or make heavy weather with the plausible theory that a man so aggressive must be concealing a whopping inferiority complex, or cherish as a material clue his rejection by the Royal Navy on leaving school as 'not up to optical standard'.

His father was Irish and worked in the Admiralty; his mother is an Aberdonian. Connor, now in his early forties, is a married man with three children – the cause, no doubt, of the soupcon of sentimentality that occasionally peeps into his column. He lives in the last place where you would expect to find him, an old country rectory in Bucks.

Yet the biographical details shed little or no light. The measure of the matter is that Cassandra is a medical and mental problem: physically and spiritually he suffers from blood pressure.

For a few years, like many another thwarted individualist, he endured the sticking of stamps, minor clerical work and junior accountancy in various offices. Then he drifted into advertising, eventually writing copy for J Walter Thompson's. He learnt a lot in that spirited American-influenced concern, for they were the pioneers of consumer-research, high-pressure marketing, 'point of sale', and all the rest of the paraphernalia of convincing the public they cannot possibly do without something they have never previously heard of – or needed. Some of Connor's best stories concern this black art, for it was in advertising that he grasped the power and the value, though not the danger, of words.

I have never heard whether JWT's were sorry to see him go. The young man looked unhappy, and was. Now, as a newspaperman, he just looks unhappy.

He would have been content to run a lucrative bookmaker's agency, but the fact is – for good or ill – he drifted into journalism and swiftly progressed in the only profession where big-scale, incessant rudeness (skilfully written) is highly paid.

I give this plum to Cassandra's critics for what it is worth: the last advertising campaign upon which he was engaged was in the commercial interests of the producers of 'Harpic'. You may recall the horrified accusing eyes which 'would judge the hostess in the only room where she could not be present'. The immortal, purchase-compelling prose which appeared under the eyes, pointing out among other things that 'the old-fashioned brush-work is out-of-date', came from the pen of William Neil Connor.

We joined the paper the same day, August Bank Holiday, 1935. So did Peter Wilson, whom the *New York Journal* once described as 'the handsome gentleman with the rakish blonde moustache'. He is now the *Mirror*'s top sports writer, rejoicing in the title of The Man They Can't Gag. Another man they couldn't gag was Freddie B Wilson, his father, who did the same job years before him and who became notorious at Cambridge by winning the table tennis championship when playing sitting down and using a breadknife instead of a bat.

When I first met Connor I felt that I was involved in an extremely unpleasant motor crash; even the exchange of orthodox civilities, the casual 'Good Morning', was accompanied by the awful din of screeching mental brakes. It has never been a question of What Makes Connor Tick, but What Makes Connor Clang.

He is industrious, no doubt of that, and a well-informed sort of cove. For he has an appetite for newspapers, magazines and books; he 'does' *The Times* every day from the first Personal Ad to 'printed by' at the foot of the final page; studies the American political columnists, keeps an eye on *Pravda,* an ear to Iron Curtain radio, and masticates Hansard before meals in the evenings. He remembers every point of detail to the slightest disadvantage of the victim he picks up on the tip of his pen for public scrutiny in his column. When memory fails, and the enormity of a politician's early misdemeanour temporarily escapes him, Cassandra taps his head and says: 'My private librarians are looking it up'.

The value of the man is that he writes superbly, is a born journalist, means what he writes, and writes without fear.

According to subject and the state of his liver, he can make his column purr or bark, nuzzle or bite, canter or gallop, soothe or repel. And, a rare gift, his words appeal alike to men and women, young and old, intellectuals and ignoramuses, priests and atheists, judges and old lags, heterosexuals, homosexuals and hermaphrodites.

Cassandra became a Fleet Street success story, just like the ones he used to think up as an advertising copy-writer.

'Never trust an underdog,' he said to me when he had worked a few weeks on the *Mirror*.

A man had been sentenced to a stiff term of imprisonment for stealing milk in South Wales. Why had he stolen it? The thief told the magistrates his crime was inevitable, that his children were starving, and that whatever the consequences he had to take the risk for their sake.

'Prison,' said the Bench. And Connor fell for it hook, line and sinker. The things he called those brutal JPs. Had they ever heard a baby whimpering for milk? What would they do, subdue the mite into silence with a bludgeon? What Cassandra did not know was that the time-server had been caught for the umpteenth time. He had no children; he was a professional whipper-upper-of-other-people's-milk-bottles.

Since then Cassandra has rarely had the wool pulled over his eyes: not, at any rate, by an underdog. Nor, without investigation, does he believe all complaints against 'the authorities', for he has also learnt that the facts are rarely what they seem.

One man Connor simply could not help being rude to was Godfrey Winn. It was he who christened Winn's luxurious blue coupe the 'blue boudoir'. Winn, in return, upbraided Connor as a cynic.

The trouble between them broke when a reader of Cassandra sent in a clipping from a newspaper article as an example of over-emotionalised slush worthy of comment. He reproduced the paragraph and knocked out its wisdom teeth, not knowing or not admitting that he knew the cutting came from the page of the man who worked two doors away.

Winn was piqued, but later magnanimous. Connor was invited to a dinner – with me, as features editor and peacemaker. It was a slap-up, evening-dress affair at the Dorchester, with the 'blue boudoir' as transport. Winn could not have been more pleasant, patient or generous. But the first ugly rip in the fragile seams came with the second cocktail.

'Winn,' said Connor, 'how do you like being a performing clown in Cudlipp's Feature Circus?'

CASSANDRA (William Neil Connor)

The charm of the host withstood the remark; he smiled and ordered another cocktail.

The second and fatal rip came with the entree.

'Godfrey,' said Connor, warming to his task, 'you know I don't like your column. It's not my sort of stuff. Dogs and mothers – I don't write about them and I don't like reading about them...'

Winn's dismay was alleviated with the next sentence.

'...but I want to be fair and tell you this. A man I know, a friend of mine, thinks your page is magnificent. He swears by it, never misses it...'

Winn beamed and poured out the wine.

'He says it is the sincerest piece of writing in any newspaper He doesn't know how you can keep it up every day. And furthermore, he is always badgering me to arrange an introduction to you.'

Our host was delighted: 'Well – why not arrange it? I d love to meet him.'

'Difficult, Godfrey, just at the moment.

'Well – give me his address and I'll write to him. I always write to my fans.'

Connor spelled out the name with care. And then the address – a well-known lunatic asylum.

When-he arrived in Washington to interview Senator Joseph McCarthy; Connor opened the conversation by informing the American: 'I detest everything you stand for and will do my best to denounce all your horrible persecutions and the filthy nation-wide witch-hunt over which you preside.'

McCarthy's offer to autograph his latest book was rejected with the genial rejoinder – 'I have not the slightest desire to have either your signature or your book.'

Cassandra is the guest who is seldom asked twice.

WANTED!

FOR MURDER . . . FOR KIDNAPPING . . .
FOR THEFT AND FOR ARSON

Can he recognised full face by habitual scowl. Rarely smiles. Talks rapidly, and when angered screams like a child.

ADOLF HITLER
ALIAS
Adolf Schicklegruber, Adolf Hittler or Hidler

Last heard of in Berlin, September 3, 1939. Aged fifty, height 5ft. 8½in., dark hair, frequently brushes one lock over left forehead. Blue eyes. Sallow complexion, stout build, weighs about 11st. 3lb. Suffering from acute monomania, with periodic fits of melancholia. Frequently bursts into tears when crossed. Harsh, guttural voice, and has a habit of raising right hand to shoulder level. DANGEROUS!

Profile from a recent photograph. Black moustache. Jowl inclines to fatness. Wide nostrils. Deep set, menacing eyes.

FOR MURDER Wanted for the murder of over a thousand of his fellow countrymen on the night of the Blood Bath, June 30, 1934. Wanted for the murder of countless political opponents in concentration camps.

He is indicted for the murder of Jews, Germans, Austrians, Czechs, Spaniards and Poles. He is now urgently wanted for homicide against citizens of the British Empire.

Hitler is a gunman who shoots to kill. He acts first and talks afterwards.

No appeals to sentiment can move him. This gangster, surrounded by armed hoodlums, is a natural killer. The reward for his apprehension, dead or alive, is the peace of mankind.

FOR KIDNAPPING Wanted for the kidnapping of Dr. Kurt Schuschnigg, late Chancellor of Austria. Wanted for the kidnapping of Pastor Niemoller, a heroic martyr who was not afraid to put God before Hitler. Wanted for the attempted kidnapping of Dr. Benes, late President of Czechoslovakia. The kidnapping tendencies of this established criminal are marked and violent. The symptoms become an attempt are threats, blackmail and ultimatums. He offers his victims the alternatives of complete surrender or timeless incarceration in the horrors of concentration camps.

FOR THEFT Wanted for the larceny of eighty millions of Czech gold in March, 1939. Wanted for the armed robbery of material resources of the Czech State. Wanted for the stealing of Memelland. Wanted for robbing mankind of peace, of humanity, and for the attempted assault on civilisation itself. This dangerous lunatic masks his raids by spurious appeals to honour, to patriotism and to duty. At the moment when his protestations of peace and friendship are at their most vehement, he is most likely to commit his smash and grab.

His tactics are known and easily recognised. But Europe has already been wrecked and plundered by the depredations of this armed thug who smashes in without scruple.

FOR ARSON Wanted as the incendiary who started the Reichstag fire on the night of February 27, 1933. This crime was the key point, and the starting signal for a series of outrages and brutalities that are unsurpassed in the records of criminal degenerates. As a direct and immediate result of this calculated act of arson, an innocent dupe, Van der Lubbe, was murdered in cold blood. But as an indirect outcome of this carefully-planned offence, Europe itself is ablaze. The fires that this mad has kindled cannot be extinguished until he himself is apprehended—dead or alive!

THIS RECKLESS CRIMINAL IS WANTED—DEAD OR ALIVE!

All the above information has been obtained from official sources and has been collated by CASSANDRA

With this page, by Cassandra, the Mirror declared war on Nazi Germany. An order was issued by the German High Command that *Mirror* directors were to be immediately arrested when London was occupied.

20
ENTER SIR WINSTON

The *Mirror* needed no second thoughts in determining the path it should pursue in the Hitler war. Here above all was the newspaper of the masses, the Bible of the Services' rank and file, the factory worker and the housewife. No daily journal was in a better position to register the people's pulse-beat, reflect their aspirations and misgivings, and make articulate their elation or censure on the progress of the war. All the clues were in the *Mirror's* postbag from its readers. The paper's executives knew the way the wind was blowing long before Westminster or Whitehall; writers were free to record these zephyrs, gusts, gales, hurricanes and tornadoes and state their views without fear or favour on what should be done.

An early collision with the politicians was, perhaps, inevitable.

This Parliament, unrefreshed by direct contact with the critical electorate except in by-elections, had been formed four years before war was declared, and once war began no general election was possible until 1945. Small wonder, then, that the Chamberlain Cabinet of 1937-1940 and the Churchill Coalition of 1940-1945 so frequently misjudged the trend and temperature of public opinion on political events.

In the headlong clash between Parliament and Press which I am about to narrate, who was right – Churchill or the *Mirror'?* Whose ear was closer to the ground? Who more clearly sensed the people's dissatisfaction with the past, their deep-laid suspicion of the bunglers who were allowed to remain in office, their apprehension over the future?

The *Mirror* group recorded more swiftly and encouraged more surely than any other newspapers the surge of public opinion which demanded Churchill's entry into the War Cabinet and his subsequent Premiership in 1940. The man himself, after eleven years in the wilderness, was astonished at the spontaneous acclamation of confidence in his own personality; he failed to perceive that in turning to him the public were also expressing their desire to break with the Tory Party's past ineptitude and present timidity.

140

Six years later, when he was cast down from the pinnacle of power, he was again surprised and again misunderstood the motives. What he misread as public ingratitude to himself was in fact public mistrust of the pre-war failures, appeasers and Cabinet job-jockeys he had retained in his retinue.

On the day the Germans attacked Poland, September 1 1939, there appeared on the front page of the *Mirror* the head of a determined lion. The years between the wars had produced 80 new national symbols; a lion still expressed the British spirit.

Winston Spencer Churchill visited Neville Chamberlain in the afternoon at Downing Street and was invited to become a member of the War Cabinet. After midnight he wrote a confidential letter to the Premier expressing misgivings which the *Mirror* was frequently to express in the coming months: 'Aren't we a very old team?' asked Churchill. 'I make out that the six you mentioned to me yesterday aggregate 386 years or an average of over 64! Only one year short of the Old Age Pension! If, however, you added Sinclair (49) and Eden (42) the average comes down to fifty-seven and a half.'

At 11.15 on the morning of Sunday, September 3, Chamberlain went to the microphone to inform the world (and Churchill, to whom he had sent no further communication) that Britain was already at war, and the following day the *Mirror's* front-page lion was suitably snarling. Jennings wrote:

> For months, even years, past, we have tried to warn the public concerning the aims, the threats, the secret intentions of Adolf Hitler. We have been accused of provoking those warlike thoughts that we have endeavoured to defeat by urging that readiness which alone can save us now. But we now forget these dissensions... to-day and henceforward and until the end, *endure!*

Cassandra published a page proclaiming:

WANTED! FOR MURDER... FOR. KIDNAPPING...
FOR THEFT AND FOR ARSON...
ADOLF HITLER
ALIAS ADOLF SCHICKELGRUBER

The editorials up to the resignation of Chamberlain as Prime Minister followed a simple pattern. We were in the war. Let us fight it. No truck with the Nazis. Throw out the muddlers. Get on with the job. Jennings pressed for war to the end, with no 'sinister truce leaving Hitlerism better equipped to turn in all savagery upon France and Britain', and there was a prayer that among the leaders who conducted the war would be found a few active or attacking minds.

When Leslie Burgin, Supply Minister, appealed to the public for 24,000 oil lamps to illuminate Army huts, he was headlined as *The Foolish Burgin*, caught with his lamps untrimmed. Daily, under the single word MUDDLE, examples of red tape, managerial stupidity and trade union restrictionist practices were arraigned before the public; the more outrageous cases were labelled

JUST DAMNED SILLY.

An editorial on October 27 1939, gave a glimpse of the shape of things to come:

> Our recent criticism of the domestic blockade on the home front has brought us an unexpected response in reproach.
> This is that we ought not to indicate incompetence in high ,. posts or to denounce muddles because if we do that
> 1: The Nazis will be encouraged.
> 2: The public at home will be alarmed.
> We have to admit at once that we do not care a rap whether the Nazis... read that a democracy openly discusses its own muddles.
> As to the alarm of the public – we are amazed at the sweet ignorance of those who imagine that colossal and continuous muddles can be concealed from the man in the blacked-out street.

In the Spring, when Hitler invaded Norway and Denmark, the *Mirror* suffered from the national disease of over-optimism and suffered as severely as the rest of the patients. Cassandra had already written that the Nazis would find the Dutch no easy nut to crack. Now a cartoon appeared showing Hitler sitting on a branch labelled Scandinavia, sawing it through. And Jennings wrote:

> At the Maginot Line, the Allied Armies stand alert. If the Hun did not pass at Verdun and Ypres, how shall he pass now with the magnificent engine of France ready to strike, and the ever-growing armies of Britain building up their indomitable strength?

Over-optimism, at least, was not subversive. Indeed, one of the few realists of those times was General Ironside's schoolboy son who, after being conducted around the Maginot Line and asked what he thought of

France's renowned static defence, replied with youthful prescience that he was 'not deeply impressed'. In the awkward silence that followed someone asked the fifteen-year-old what he intended to do in the war, and he replied, briskly, 'Join the Navy'. He did.

The setback in Norway was the signal for the campaign against the vain, disastrous Neville Chamberlain to be conducted in earnest. He was daily scourged by the satire of Jennings. The Premier, said one editorial, was an expert at the art of explaining away failure – he had so much practice at it.

Would Hitler obligingly wait until our Government had thought out another eyewash explanation which would turn failure into success?

Another glimpse of the shape of things to come appeared in an editorial on May 7. Another example, too, of the irritating style in which Jennings revelled and by which men in high places were repelled:

> Today – let us press this point – the sole issue, the real issue, is not the failure in Norway, with its repercussions in Italy and in America and in the Balkans: in fact, all over the world.
>
> Let us, if you like, wipe out the Norwegian episode, which is not a side-show – though what it is we have not yet been told.
>
> The questions for MPs of any patriotism, the questions for Conservatives who have the strength of mind and character not to quail at the crack of the Margesson whip, are these –
>
> What of the next phase? What of the next possible failure? What excuses are ready for the next crash in the prolonged 'too late' campaign? Have we been warned? Have partial or local failures taught us their lessons? Or will the technique, the 'sickening technique', of muddle have to be exemplified again and again, till its disasters rouse even those poor mutts who moan that it is better to drift to defeat under the men who muddle than to call upon new men to pull the war machine together in good time...

Cassandra, also, was an enthusiastic sniper in the anti-Chamberlain campaign. When the Prime Minister left Downing Street for a weekend in the country, armed with fishing rods, Cassandra observed:

> If he does as well fishing as he has done in his manoeuvring with Hitler – then he will catch a packet.

There was a third contributor who should be mentioned. For on November 1 1939, Mr Herbert Morrison warned the public in one of his series of fortnightly *Mirror* articles that the war was not a joke.

The Chamberlain Government fell on May 10, 1940.

A few minutes before six in the evening Churchill stepped into a car outside the Admiralty and drove along the Mall to Buckingham Palace.

> I was taken immediately to the King [he records in his memoirs]. His Majesty received me most graciously and bade me sit down. He looked at me searchingly and quizzically for some moments, and then said: 'I suppose you don't know why I have sent for you?' Adopting his mood, I replied: 'Sir, I simply couldn't imagine why.' He laughed and said: 'I want to ask you to form a Government.' I said I would certainly do so.

The *Mirror* was now heavily committed in the political battle. But it continued to inform, intrigue, entertain and shock its readers in other directions. It condemned the Government for conducting business as usual; to some degree it conducted business as usual itself.

Defensibly, in various headlines, it recorded:

LOVE STILL GOES ON

GIRL IN SLACKS CANED

SHE SAID 'NO' TO HUSBAND
WHO THOUGHT HE WAS
HITLER

Indefensibly, while on the one hand demanding realism, it reflected the false optimism then prevalent about the progress of the war:

FRANCE'S SIEGFRIED LINE GRIP TIGHTENS

BAYONETS HURL BACK NAZIS IN SAAR

DUCE SHOCK FOR HITLER

The *Mirror* should have known better.

21
THE *MIRROR* IS WARNED

Winston Churchill and the *Mirror* were at this stage on amiable speaking terms. Before the war, in the days when most people except Mr Chamberlain and his principal Cabinet colleagues were aware that the struggle was inevitable, three men had tea together at Chartwell, near Westerham, Kent.

Cecil Harmsworth King, director of the *Mirror* and *Sunday Pictorial,* and Hugh Cudlipp, editor of the *Pictorial,* returned to London with the conviction that the statesman by whom they had been harangued for sixty minutes was the one national personality who was astride events, who grasped the significance of the rising Nazi menace, who could arrest and change the direction of events.

'Nothing can save us,' said Churchill. 'Nothing – except the hammer-blow of circumstance.'

He was enduring his eleven sour years in the political wilderness, the years of the gathering storm. The Tories had cast aside their future leader, and his intimates at that time were few. Beaverbrook, Brendan Bracken, Bob Boothby, Professor Lindemann were among them. And among his admirers and supporters was the *Mirror.*

The result of the visit to Chartwell was that Churchill began his series of articles in that newspaper. 'It is difficult to see,' he wrote in one of them, 'how war can be avoided.' This was his platform, and this was his warning to Britain when the announcement came that the Nazi-Soviet pact had been signed.

Now that the prophet was ensconced in No 10 Downing Street, how long was his relationship with the *Mirror* to continue on terms of amity?

The paper concentrated on the fullest mobilisation. It was clear of panic, defeatism and gloom, for wishful-thinking had been pruned and its columns were full of cheerful vulgar guts; it spoke in the language of the serving men and thus became their mouthpiece.

Dunkirk? The editorial was headed:

BLOODY
MARVELLOUS

There was no complaint of what the *Mirror* had to say in those times of immediate peril or of the ebullience with which it conveyed the message.

Newspapers which had rigorously opposed the entry of Churchill into Chamberlain's Cabinet were now unrestrained in sycophancy. Success has a hundred fathers.

The *Mirror,* however, reverted to its role of constructive critic, for the high promise of Churchill's Premiership was sluggish in fulfilment; the statesman who had flayed the muddlers and the appeasers in the past seemed curiously determined to win the war the hard way with the muddlers and appeasers still in his Government. 'Take from them the supreme direction of the war they have been trying to run as the village vicar's wife runs a gymkhana at a charity fete,' wrote Jennings.

During the lifetime of Churchill's Government a number of conversations, some heated, were to take place in Downing Street between the Prime Minister and Cecil H King representing the newspaper. They occurred often at moments of national crisis, and the purport of the meetings was to enable the Premier to express his views on what he regarded as the reprehensible attitude of the paper to the Cabinet's conduct of affairs. King kept a detailed diary of these conversations, and I am therefore able to quote his version of what was said.

The first meeting was on Friday, June 7 1940, and was the direct outcome of the *Mirror's* criticism of the retention of the appeasers and failures in the Government.

C H King's diary records:

> I was ushered into the presence. Winston was sitting in the Prime Minister's chair in the Cabinet room – in the middle of one of the long sides of the table facing the light and with his back to the fireplace. He was dressed in a very tight-fitting palm beach suit – face bright red with the heat – hair looking scantier than usual – puffing at a cigar. Outside the window paced up and down a man who looked very Civil Service, but might have been a very superior detective. On the walls were two maps; one of the western world, the other of the Low Countries and Northern France.

> I explained that I had come to find out exactly what he did want us to do, as I had had a message through Esmond [Esmond Harmsworth, now Lord Rothermere]. He said he had only been PM a month today (and what a month!) and already the papers were picking on the Government and demanding Chamberlain's head on a charger.

He thought the debate on Tuesday would amount to nothing; if there was any serious criticism he would take it as a vote of censure and no more than 20 would vote against him. I said I thought opinion against Chamberlain was high and rising and would continue to rise. He said there was no one in this Government he had had to accept; that he had heard through a third party that Chamberlain was prepared to take office under him and that he personally was very glad to have him. He was clear-headed, methodical, and hard-working and the best man he had – head and shoulders over the average man in the administration, who were mostly pretty mediocre.

Churchill said not to forget that a year ago last Christmas they were trying to hound him out of his constituency, and by a succession of events that astounded him he was invited by the practically unanimous voice of both Houses of Parliament to be PM. But the men who had supported Chamberlain had got the bigger cheer when they met the House after forming the new administration. A General Election was not possible during a war and so the present House of Commons, however unrepresentative of feeling in the country, had to be reckoned with as the ultimate .source of power for the duration.

If he trampled on these men, as he could trample on them, they would set themselves against him, and in such internecine strife lay the Germans' best chance of victory.

I said I thought his position in the hearts of the people so unassailably strong that he could take stern measures with these people and get away with it. He asked what was the use of being in the position of a dictator if one could not have the governmental personnel one wanted? And after all, though he did have Chamberlain, Kingsley Wood and Inskip, he also had included every single MP who had taken an independent line to Chamberlain – Law, Boothby, Macmillan were all in and Vansittart had been made a Privy Counsellor.

It was all very well to plead for a Government excluding the elements that had led us astray of recent years, but where was one to stop? They were everywhere – not only in the political world, but among the fighting service chiefs and the civil service chiefs. To clear all these out would be a task impossible in the disastrous state in which we found ourselves.

In any case if one were dependent on the people who had been right in the last few years, what a tiny handful one would have to depend on. No, he was not going to run a Government of revenge. If the country did not like his Government they could form another one and God knows where they would get it from – he wouldn't serve on it. After all, Government in these days was no fun – it was listening to a succession of stories of bad news, a heart-breaking job.

He went on to talk about the first eight months of war. He said we didn't attack because we couldn't attack; we lost our air supremacy five

147

years ago and in spite of repeated promises by the Government had never looked like catching up. He supposed that more could have been done in the months from September to April and that he perhaps should have insisted on it. But he was responsible for the Navy, which was going all right, and it was very difficult to step outside one's own department. After all, it was the complete break-down of French generalship that had let us down.

On the future he said he was convinced there would be widespread air raids in this country as soon as the fighting in this offensive died down. He thought the Germans would try an invasion – he doubted whether they could land more than 20,000 men on account of our Navy, and these would – if necessary – be 'choked in their own blood'. At the same time, did I realise how ghastly our position was? We had won last time after four years of defeats and would do so again. Italy might join against us at any time and France might be forced to back out and leave us alone to face Germany.

Was this, asked the Prime Minister, a time for political bickering?

I said the question was not whether this was a time for bickering, but that the feeling against Chamberlain was very strong, and that a popular newspaper had within limits to reflect public opinion.

He said he didn't see the public had any right to take such a line. They had voted for Chamberlain when he was making these blunders: why should they seek Chamberlain's blood when he and they were proved wrong?

Chamberlain, Simon and Hoare remained in the Cabinet. The nation was merely invited to witness a game of political musical chairs.

Six weeks after Churchill's accession to power the paper was seeking a new drive in affairs, a response to the passionate desire of all men young and old to be told what to do.

> Even Churchill's eloquence [wrote Jennings on June 20] will not succeed in stifling all criticism during to-day's secret session of Parliament; any more than he can stifle it outside Parliament... Already here and there, fragments of the old complacency begin to peep out. As when the Petroleum Minister (one of the Dope survivors) can't see why joy-riders shouldn't waste petrol at race meetings.

The Dope survivors were the Ministers still in the Cabinet who had supported the Chamberlain appeasement moves.

There now emerged a series of jibes at the traditions of the Army. Jennings was not in the Forces in World War One, nor had Cassandra yet served in World War Two. But their post-bags were weighted each day with the wailing of citizens conscripted in the national cause. It was this widespread criticism, stifled in the Services, that they were airing in public print; their columns were the safety valve which relieved and therefore subdued mutinous thoughts.

I felt, at the time, that the barrage of niggling was excessive. Some years later, when I sat motionless with four soldiers on a bench in a tent on the fringe of the Western Desert, our feet raised from the ground, I wondered whether Jennings and Cassandra had been right. We were awaiting inspection by the General, and the Adjutant had asked me, an infantry lieutenant, to ensure that the shining black boots of the men were not dimmed by the sand. Rommel's Afrika Korps were a few hundred miles away at El Alamein: the battalion was shortly to move into action.

Right or wrong, the scribes performed their task in a manner which endeared the paper to the rank and file and drove the War Office and the regular officers into a purple rage.

> Suppose we stop talking about ties for the Home Guard. Give them guns, bombs, rifles and clothes for rough wear.
>
> Will Churchill ring up the War Office and ask some of the encrusted barnacles in obsolete brass hats to define Army discipline first, and then to abolish a lot of it?
>
> Discipline appears to be the art of making soldiers so miserable that they are not afraid of dying in intolerably uncomfortable costumes.

Cassandra began his one-man crusade against what he called 'Army foolery' – polished buttons, church parades, saluting drill. It is surprising that he ever recovered from the paroxysm he suffered when he read that serving men were prevented by order from walking arm-in-arm with girls.

Let there be no doubt about the effect of his campaign. Regular officers viewed recruits from Fleet Street newspapers with suspicion. I endured a good deal of this eye-narrowing scrutiny myself, for I knew Cassandra. As for the brutal and savage soldiery, his criticisms of their superiors' more idiotic ideas evoked a state of jubilation rarely manifested in serving men. On the walls of at least one Army billet in Whitstable were stuck *Mirror* cuttings which clearly echoed the unspoken thoughts of its occupants: it was wise, I reckoned, to have them steamed off or camouflaged.

No wonder the Generals were angry.

Cassandra conducted another violent campaign under the heading 'The Dermatologists', an attack upon those who saved their skins in the perilous days of 1940 by fleeing to America.

Symptoms of asperity between Westminster and Fleet Street were now becoming abundant.

The *Mirror* made mistakes, and none more stupid than its brash call just after Dunkirk for *attack, attack, attack*. Where, and with what? It glorified the RAF, but grossly exaggerated the effects of the bombing on Germany. It stormed at Mussolini before Italy came into the war, and called for a stronger line with the Japs.

There was nothing defeatist about this brand of belligerency; here was a demand for a policy more zealous than wise, a policy which showed the right spirit but which that year was demonstrably impracticable.

The paper occasionally asked for the moon. But what did it say that *was* wise and practicable?

It advocated the training of citizen forces and an overhaul at the War Office; repeatedly warned against any desire for a negotiated peace; urged greater effort against the Nazis. At the height of the blitz its message was 'Fight, work, endure – and pray'.

Cassandra conducted a sortie inelegantly entitled a 'Guts-krieg' around the restaurants to expose the excesses of the eaters-out. There was the usual storm of criticism, followed by Government action.

But it was the criticism of strategy and of conduct in high places which chafed Churchill and his colleagues in the Cabinet. The war lords had forgotten they had been elected to Parliament by the vote of the citizens; they were unaware or unwilling to concede that public confidence could be maintained only by an avowal of new principles and by the curt dismissal of those Ministers whom failure, alone, had made conspicuous.

The *Mirror* deflated the notion that criticism in war is cloaked defeatism. It continued its onslaught upon the Municheers, especially upon Hoare, later Lord Templewood, then negotiating a loan of two-and-a-half million pounds to Franco of Spain.

On October 4 1940, the Churchill Cabinet was re-shuffled. 'Another patched Government was suddenly presented to the public yesterday, with the usual puzzling effect,' wrote Jennings. 'The sifting or shunting of mediocrities or reputed successes appears to have been directed by no principle plain to the outsider, unless it be the principle that new blood must rarely be transfused into an old body.'

Churchill considered such criticisms vicious and malignant, and said so in Parliament on October 8.

Behind the scenes at this time there was much activity concerning the policy of the *Mirror* and of its companion newspaper the *Sunday Pictorial.*

Cecil King's war-time diary records important discussions which took place and which have hitherto not been made public:

Tuesday, October 8, 1940.

Churchill spoke in the House of Commons this afternoon. He stood up for Sir John Anderson, described attacks on him as coming from 'ignorant and spiteful quarters' and said there was no better war horse in the Government. (What a back-handed tribute to the Government!)

In relation to Dakar and other and 'more important issues', he described the tone of 'certain organs of the Press' as 'so vicious and malignant' that it would be 'almost indecent if applied to the enemy'. It rather sounds as if this were aimed at two papers...

Friday, October 11, 1940.

Cudlipp learned at dinner last night that Churchill had brought the *Pictorial* article by Cudlipp to the Cabinet, and the phrase in his speech about vicious and malignant criticism was inserted by general agreement.

The drift of the article was that in his recent governmental changes Churchill had shown the same dilatory, short-sighted, party-serving spirit as Chamberlain. Chamberlain, in fact, is dead: long live Chamberlain. And Cudlipp, who signed the article, wound up with a quotation from Churchill's book *World Crisis,* in which Winston says there are good grounds sometimes in peace for a vacillating or cautious policy, but in war decisions must be clear-cut and ruthless, no personal or party considerations must hamper the war effort, and so on.[4]

Cudlipp's concluding words were: 'Churchill, you have warned yourself'. Obviously the article was not likely to please Churchill, but I had no idea a storm was at all likely. It just shows what a guilty conscience the old man must have.

---

[4] Churchill's exact words, quoted from *World Crisis,* were: 'There is no place for compromise in war. In war the clouds never blow over. They gather increasingly and fall in thunderbolts. Clear leadership, violent action, rigid decisions one way or the other form the only path, not only of victory, but of safety and even of mercy. The State cannot afford division or hesitation at the executive centre. To humour a distinguished man, to avoid a fierce dispute, nay, even to preserve the governing instrument itself, cannot, except as an alternative to sheer anarchy, be held to justify half measures. The peace of the Council may for the moment be won, but the price is paid on the battlefield by brave men marching forward against unspeakable terrors in the belief that conviction and coherence have animated their orders.'

I was summoned by Cowley [chairman of the *Mirror*] to the board room late yesterday afternoon and found him in consultation with Roome [*Mirror* director], Bart and Esmond Harmsworth. It appeared that in the course of the morning Esmond, as chairman of the Newspapers Proprietors' Association, had been asked to head a deputation representative of the Press to call on Attlee. He had turned up with Camrose and Southwood and found Attlee and Beaverbrook awaiting them.

Attlee told them that the Cabinet had given attention to the Press at a recent meeting, with particular reference to the *Mirror* and *Pictorial.* He said that if criticism of the 'irresponsible kind' inserted in our papers were to continue the Government would introduce legislation making censorship of news *and* views compulsory. The NPA deputation did not take to this suggestion at all kindly and said that compulsory censorship would wreck the Government, and be most damaging to the country's morale.

Attlee had various cuttings with him – most of them were from Cassandra's column, but one was from the 'Live Letter Box': the point about the latter being the very trivial technical one that it is illegal for a serving soldier to write to the Press without his commanding officer's permission, which had not been obtained. Attlee described the *Mirror* and *Pictorial* policy as 'subversive' and calculated to cause alarm and despondency at a very critical period.

No great stress was laid on the cuttings themselves. The Government had no objection to criticism, said Attlee, but only to irresponsible criticism, and on what constituted irresponsible criticism he was vague or silent.

I think if Attlee had told the deputation that if our papers continued their present line they would be prosecuted, the deputation would have cheered. But to threaten a general compulsory censorship would obviously damage the *Telegraph* and *Times* more than the *Mirror,* and was the one and only way of rallying the other papers to our support. Beaverbrook, incidentally, throughout this interview took the part of the honest broker, the friend of both sides.

After Esmond had told his story it was arranged that Bart and I should call on Attlee this morning and hear the story straight from him.

At 11.30 I repaired to Richmond Terrace, Whitehall, and asked for Major Attlee, but was told he was in the air raid shelter (there were actually some German planes overhead). I was ushered into the waiting room, which was also a passage from the hall to the air raid shelter.

Presently I collected Bart, who had been waiting for me outside. Attlee's secretary led us through a maze of corridors into the basement and into a gasproof room about nine feet square, where Attlee was sitting on a bed reading the *New Statesman*. Though tiny, the room contained three beds, three chairs and a table. The beds were really bunks; they had blankets and sheets and pillows and were made up, but had no coverlets.

We explained that we had come to see him as he had summoned a deputation of the NPA in connection with the policy of our papers; as we were the responsible directors concerned we wished to hear from him direct what the Government had to say.

Attlee said he had been deputed by the Cabinet to deal with the matter and the opinions he would express were not only his own but those of the Government and 'of others'. They felt that our papers showed a subversive influence, which at a critical time like this might endanger the nation's war effort.

I asked him to give an example; he said he couldn't think of one. I said the NPA deputation had seen some cuttings – could we see them? He said he had not brought any cuttings along, that anyway it was not his job to watch the Press and he did not read our papers. There was more discussion on the same lines, but the only specific accusation he would bring was that we criticised the military command.

I said we had never done any such thing and would not do it in wartime. He then said we had quoted H G Wells who, in a review of a Labour Party book, made some contemptuous references to Ironside and Gort. I said we *had* done so – some time after Gort and Ironside had been dismissed by the Government. I said we had certainly criticised the Civil Service and some individual Civil Servants. Was there any objection to that? He said no.

My general line was to pin him down to some specific accusation. Attlee was critical but so vague and evasive as to be quite meaningless. We got the impression that the fuss was really Churchill's, that Attlee had been turned on to do something he was not really interested in, and had not bothered to read his brief. Moreover the Press reaction to Churchill's speech had not been quite what they hoped for. Nor had the NPA deputation's attitude to Attlee, so perhaps we were asking Attlee to fight over again a battle he recognised had been already lost.

I said our policy in general was to win the war at all costs – no personal or party considerations must stand in the way – that our newspapers had contributed largely in my view to the war effort by campaigning for the removal of Chamberlain (from the Premiership). This had not been done by the House of Commons, let alone Churchill, but by public opinion led by the Press, and of all the newspapers we had taken the strongest line and taken it earliest.

Attlee rather naturally said he entirely disagreed with my estimate of the part played by the newspapers in this affair. It was no part of the Government's wish to stop criticism, only irresponsible criticism. Pressed to define irresponsible criticism, he could not do so.

153

He said he would try and give an example. The London gas mains were laid out in Victorian times with no thought, naturally, for air raids. When a bomb hit one it deprived quite a large area of gas for quite a time. If we were to criticise the Government for lack of gas in some areas, that would be irresponsible criticism. I said we had never criticised the Government for the failure of the gas supply in parts of London – to this Attlee said he agreed! I said I thought Churchill had no objection to our kicking poor old Chamberlain, but didn't like being hurt himself. Attlee said he strongly disagreed.

I said we were supporting Churchill, Bevin and Beaverbrook, but I had to confess that our ideas of winning the war and Sir Kingsley Wood's were hardly likely to coincide. He said the Government raised no objection to such difference of opinion. At one point Attlee was doing so badly he was very near breaking off the interview. After about twenty-five minutes we rose and said good-bye; obviously there was nothing to be gained by staying any longer.

As Bart and I walked up Whitehall we agreed that it was the quotation from his own book that really annoyed Winston and caused all the trouble (subsequently Wallace Roome on the telephone volunteered the same opinion). Winston was so right in his book about wartime appointments and has been so wrong since last May that he must be infuriated to be condemned out of his own mouth.

Obviously the Government will do nothing more about it and obviously we shall pipe down for a few weeks until the course of the war alters the whole situation...

There were now heard in the opening month of 1941 the first rumblings of the Parliamentary storm that was to break upon Fleet Street in the third month of 1942.

The Government had suppressed the Communist *Daily Worker* after a warning given six months earlier, and a publication called *The Week* was also torpedoed and sunk without trace.

Mr Herbert Morrison, now Home Secretary and no longer a *Mirror* contributor, explained to the Commons that the suppression of the *Worker* had been conducted with the utmost courtesy on both sides; no animosity had been shown. When the police visited the paper's premises a machine-room employee said to an officer: 'I am just here to earn a living, and do not agree with the politics of those bastards upstairs'.

Mr Morrison went to some pains to explain that he did not like to suppress any newspaper, but that the *Worker* had become a public scandal. He assured the House that he would discharge the great powers with which he was entrusted with restraint and circumspection. Two-hundred-and-seventy-seven Members accepted the assurance and voted their support for the suppression of the *Worker,* eleven were dubious and voted against.

Had the suppression of the Communist paper come as a surprise? Not really. What did astonish the House was a revelation from Mr Aneurin Bevan during the debate. He disclosed that 'only a few months ago the proprietors of two very important papers with large circulations were informed that the Government was worried about the line they were taking. The proprietors said that they would like to discuss the matter with the Government. They saw a member of the War Cabinet who said that in his view the line taken by the papers was subversive.'

Mr Bevan did not tell the House that the papers were the *Mirror* and the *Pictorial,* and that the Cabinet Minister was Mr Attlee.

He went on: 'At that time these newspapers, which both supported the war, were against retaining certain members of the Government. When asked to point out in what way the papers were subversive the Minister failed to do so, but said their general line was subversive.'

Thus, on January 29, 1941, Parliament and public first heard of the threatening interview that had taken place on October 12 1940. There were repercussions which displayed uneasiness among MPs.

Mr Geoffrey Mander, the Liberal, put down a question to the Home Secretary, but Churchill himself entered the controversy on February 6 saying that he was not prepared to give information: the communication to the newspapers, he said, had been confidential.

Mr Bevan: If the Government think newspapers are behaving improperly why do they not prosecute on specific charges so that newspapers may know where they stand, and not use this weapon of secret terror?

Churchill would not accept the version which had been given. So far as he could make out from Mr Bevan's question the Government would only be entitled to prosecute newspapers and would never be entitled 'even unofficially' to have confidential conversations with their owners or controllers. 'Such an idea,' said the Prime Minister, 'is altogether foolish and has no relation whatever to the way in which affairs are conducted in this country.'

Some MPs cheered.

Did they realise, in their enthusiasm for the Churchillian rebuke to the Member for Ebbw Vale, that they were applauding a precept of the British way of life which in modern times was new and ominous? Applause for the odious principle of the Inquisition, the Star Chamber, and the Imprimatur was not a manifestation to which the Mother of Parliaments had been accustomed since the Reformation.

Seven days before the Premier spoke in the House another conversation with Cecil King had taken place at Downing Street. King's diary records:

Thursday, January 30, 1941.

I arrived at Downing Street at 2.55 in the middle of the third or fourth air-raid of the day with all the local guns banging away. I waited ten or fifteen minutes by a big coke fire just outside the Cabinet room. The hat and coat pegs near the Cabinet door were all labelled – that nearest the door being for the Lord Chancellor, followed by the Lord President, Lord Privy Seal and so on in strict order of precedence.

In the course of the morning I had sent the PM a note asking for the interview and to have a letter on the file replying to Churchill's last.

(These letters are published in the succeeding chapter.)

Winston went into the Cabinet room by another door and was standing up by the fire when I came in. He sat me at the table at his right hand and off we started. Outside, German planes came over singly at intervals (it was a cloudy, misty day) and the guns in St James's Park, heavy and Bofors, banged away. When a plane came very near he stopped his talk and listened and twice seemed on the point of retreating to his shelter, but did not do so. Winston himself looked older and more lined than when I saw him last, but if anything tougher.

He started off with a great tirade and returned often to the same theme. The gist of his remarks was that our policy constituted a very clever form of fifth columnism – praising the PM, pressing for an intensification of our war effort, but at the same time magnifying grievances, vilifying Ministers and generally creating a distrust by the nation for its leaders. That this 'rocking of the boat' (his phrase) might well have disastrous results for the nation. What were we doing it for, anyway?

I protested that we supported him as much as we ever had and that we supported many of his Ministers, but others we thought unworthy of high office and said so.

Did this mean, he asked, that we arrogated to ourselves the right of appointing Ministers of the Crown? I said No, but surely loyalty to him as PM did not carry with it loyalty to Attlee as Lord Privy Seal? He conceded this point, more or less. He said our papers had been the subject of much discussion, that much research had been undertaken into the ownership of our shares; some of his colleagues were convinced that there was something or someone behind it all. I said there was nothing – there were five executive directors, of whom I was one. As I was more interested in politics than the others, the politics were largely left to me.

'Well,' he said, 'you look innocent enough!'

He said he didn't mind attacks on the Government; it was the malignancy of the attacks that annoyed him. They had contemplated a prosecution and also denunciation in a speech on the wireless, but had thought these measures out of proportion.

I said there were no personal feelings involved, as hardly any of us knew any of the men we attacked; in a popular paper we were bound to write of politics in terms of persons not of principles. He said other popular papers didn't; that we were different. I said we were proud to be different, and went on to say that I very much regretted he had been disturbed to this extent by our policy. Why had he not got his secretary to ring up and ask us to pipe down? He said he would not ask for favours; I pointed out that a request from the PM in wartime to a paper that had of late always supported him was not a favour, but an order and would of course be obeyed. That since he became PM we had only one request and that was not to attack Chamberlain.

I said we had met his wishes for a month, but I did not see how we could conscientiously do more. Attlee had asked to see a deputation of the NPA, but had not said what for, so our representative was not present. When we subsequently asked for an interview to find out at first hand what exactly was complained of, we saw Attlee who was so vague and evasive that we thought either he had got the wrong end of the stick or that Beaverbrook was up to something.

Churchill said 'No!' Beaverbrook was all for freedom of the Press and for leaving other newspapers alone; that the move was initiated by himself because of three articles in the paper which appeared to strike at the root of Army discipline. I said Attlee never mentioned these articles; that we made it a strict rule not to criticise the conduct of military operations or personnel in any way and that if such matter had been printed it had slipped through, and I personally had never seen it.

This sort of discussion proceeded for a long time; he maintaining that our papers showed malignancy towards the Government and great 'artistry' in undermining the morale of the nation. I said we only showed malignancy to those politicians who had brought us to this plight; as for the rest we were young men naturally anxious to get any and every sort of move on. If, in his opinion, we had gone too far, we would certainly alter our tune.

He said he had never taken back what he had said about the appeasers, but that the MPs who had supported Chamberlain still formed a majority of 150 in the House and that he was not going to fight them as they were too numerous. He had, however, moved away the old bunch bit by bit, keeping Chamberlain on for a time to minimise the shock of the change. Apropos of nothing very much (but presumably reverting to my letter) he said that there was a great dearth of brains, that he had thought of including in his Government some younger men. Hitherto only those above military age had been included, but as this war did not seem to be a blood bath – there were as many civilian casualities as others – he was now thinking of having some Ministers in khaki.

He referred to the lead in the *Daily Herald* yesterday, which forecast an advance on Benghazi by the inland route and said very bitterly that this might well lead to the death of 1,000 Australians. But what did we care, if it made a good newspaper stunt! (A 'D' notice was issued telling us all not to speculate on General Wavell's next move, but this *Herald* story had apparently slipped past the censor.)

He said he thought these journalists would be better occupied working with our national war effort – joining in this great historic and tragic event.

Throughout, Winston was very difficult to talk to – he reminded me strongly of Rothermere – getting up and striding about, shooting remarks at me that often had nothing whatever to do with his last remark or anything I was saying, sitting down again, leaning on the fire-guard or lighting his cigar. Our conversation followed no logical path at all.

I should say he was genuinely optimistic about our prospects of victory. During this discussion, which lasted one hour and ten minutes by the clock, I got a much more definite impression of him than I had before. I should say that politically he is a Victorian parliamentarian and starts from the assumption that the House of Commons (and the present H of C at that) is the only source of political power and that therefore anyone with political capacity or ambition is necessarily there.

Personally (or emotionally) Churchill *is* wartime England – England with all its age, its waning virility, its dogged courage, its natural assumption that instinct is more reliable than intellect. In Churchill the country feels it is personified and for this reason there can be no question of Churchill's departure.

From his point of view he has done, is doing and will continue to do all anyone could to win the war. He feels this, and so attacks on his Government mystify and bewilder him.

After an hour or so I said something about not taking up too much of his time, but he brushed that aside. Eventually, however, he rose saying that I must leave now or I should be attacking him for wasting the country's time!

He still stayed talking when we got to the door, but he eventually saw me outside; asked me not to be offended by all he had said; told me there was an air raid on and asked if I had a car outside. When I said I hadn't, he insisted on sending me back to the office in his own.

22
LETTERS FROM DOWNING STREET

During the months of January and February, 1941 Churchill committed to paper his views on the wartime policy of the *Daily Mirror*. He has agreed that these confidential letters be published for the first time in this book.

From Churchill's Private Secretary, 10 Downing Street, to Cecil H. King.

January 23, 1941.

Dear Sir,

The Prime Minister has had his attention drawn to the enclosed cutting from the *Daily Mirror* of January 1. He desires me to inform you that this offensive story is totally devoid of foundation. No such report was ever made by Mr Eden, nor any such comment by the Prime Minister.

The Prime Minister has also noticed the enclosed cutting marked B. He wishes me to say that it is a pity that so able a writer should show himself so dominated by malevolence. In this case also there is not the slightest truth in the facts underlying the comments. No such changes have yet been considered by the Prime Minister.

Yours truly,

Kathleen Hill

Personal Private Secretary.

These were the cuttings enclosed, both from Cassandra's column:

I am indebted to the magazine *Life* for this apocryphal story of Churchill's continued war on wordiness in official documents.

Shortly after returning from his tour of the Near East, Anthony Eden submitted a long-winded report to the Prime Minister on his experiences and impressions. Churchill returned it to his War Minister with a note saying:

'As far as I can see, you have used every cliché except 'God is Love' and 'Please adjust your dress before leaving'.'

The second cutting, marked B, concerned four Cabinet Ministers:

By the time these words appear in print, Mr R A Butler who is Under-Secretary of State for Foreign Affairs, may be President of the Board of Education, which should not worry you a great deal and doesn't hurt me either.

If this has occurred, it is because Mr Butler has been faithful and loyal and not markedly inept.

If it has not occurred, it may still occur.

If it never occurs, it will be because the system has broken down.

It is a remarkable system because it presumes that the whole of the talent of the British Empire is contained within the number of people who comprise a cricket team.

This cricket team is so good that all the batsmen can bowl and all the bowlers can bat. The wicket keeper is excellent at mid-on and the lads in the slips are grand in the outfield.

Why anybody like Mr Butler, who has been working on Foreign Affairs should be given a job in education as a promotion, beats me. Is a painter a better man when he becomes a plumber?

And more important, is the plumbing improved?

But to return to this remarkable flexibility and versatility of the men who are running the war.

See how they play ball among themselves.

See how the great closed-shop works.

Meet Sir John Anderson, Lord President of the Council, ex-Home Secretary, ex-Minister of Security, ex-Lord Privy Seal, ex-Governor of Bengal, ex-Under-Secretary at the Home Office, ex-Permanent Under-Secretary of State, ex-Secretary to the Ministry of Shipping.

Meet Sir Kingsley Wood, Chancellor of the Exchequer, ex-Secretary of State for Air, ex-Minister of Health, ex-Postmaster-General, ex-Parliamentary Secretary to the Board of Education, ex-Parliamentary Secretary to the Ministry of Health, ex-Parliamentary Private Secretary to the Minister of Health.

Meet Mr Anthony Eden, Secretary for Foreign Affairs, ex-Secretary of State for War, ex-Secretary for Foreign Affairs, ex-Secretary of State for Dominion Affairs, ex-Lord Privy Seal, ex-Minister Without Portfolio for the League of Nations.

And meet all the rest of the gang. Ex-this and ex-that – but never ex a job!

Everybody has done everybody else's business.

Everybody knows everybody.

Keep it in the family!

Scratch my back and I'll scratch yours!

Talk about musical chairs!

The trouble is that this particular game is being played to a funeral march.

Ours.

From Cecil H King to Churchill.

24th *January, 1941.*

Dear Prime Minister,

Thank you for your letter of yesterday's date. The story printed in our issue of January 1st was taken from the very well-known American paper *Life* and was described by Cassandra as 'apochryphal.' The story of impending ministerial changes was originally hinted at fairly circumstantially on the front page of the *Daily Sketch.* It then appeared in the *Evening Standard* in its more detailed form and most of the newspapers reprinted the story, supposing from its appearance in the *Standard* that it was semi-official[5]. I have brought both these cuttings to Cassandra's notice and he is sorry, as we all are, to have given publicity to reports of a change in the Presidency of the Board of Education which prove to be without foundation. Cassandra is a hard-hitting journalist with a vitriolic style, but I can assure you his attitude to neither you personally nor to Mr Eden is in any way 'malevolent'. Quite the contrary.

Lord Beaverbrook, then a member of Mr Churchill's Cabinet, is the proprietor of the London *Evening Standard.* Mr R A Butler did in fact become President of the Board of Education on July 22 1941.

Though we continue to take an unflattering view of some of your colleagues, our criticisms are only directed to the fact that the nation's war effort is less intense than it might be—less intense than it would be if more young men were employed in positions of real authority.

Yours sincerely,

P.S. Cassandra asks me to remind you that he has been for nearly four years in the vanguard of the pro-Churchill mob – and still deems it a privilege to be so!

From Churchill to Cecil H King.

January 25, 1941.

Dear Mr King,

I don't think the mere adding of the word 'apochryphal' is any justification for foisting upon the British public an absolutely untruthful story, which is of course extremely offensive both to me and to Mr Eden. Nothing that appears in the *Evening Standard* or any other paper is

---

[5] Lord Beaverbrook, then a member of Mr Churchill's Cabinet, is the proprietor of the London *Evening Standard.* Mr R A Butler did in fact become President of the Board of Education on July 22 1941.

'semi-official'. Any news about appointments will be given to all the newspapers equally from Downing Street. I thank you, however, for your expressions of regret.

These give me the opportunity of saying one or two things which have struck me very forcibly in reading the *Daily Mirror* and the *Sunday Pictorial*.

First, there is a spirit of hatred and malice against the Government, which after all is not a Party Government but a National Government almost unanimously chosen, which spirit surpasses anything I have ever seen in English journalism. One would have thought in these hard times that some hatred might be kept for the enemy.

The second point is more general. Much the most effective way in which to conduct a Fifth Column movement at the present time would be the method followed by the *Daily Mirror* and the *Sunday Pictorial*. Lip service would no doubt be paid to the Prime Minister, whose position at the moment may be difficult to undermine. A perfervid zeal for intensification of the war effort would be used as a cloak behind which to insult and discredit one Minister after another. Every grievance would be exploited to the full, especially those grievances which lead to class dissension. The Army system and discipline would be attacked. The unity between the Conservative and Labour Parties would be gnawed at. The attempt would be made persistently to represent the Government as feeble, unworthy and incompetent, and to spread a general sense of distrust in the whole system. Thus, large numbers of readers would be brought into a state of despondency and resentment, of bitterness and scorn, which at the proper moment, when perhaps some disaster had occurred or prolonged tribulations had wearied the national spirit, could be suddenly switched over into naked defeatism, arid a demand for a negotiated peace.

I daresay you will be surprised when I tell you that as a regular reader, I feel that this description very accurately fits the attitude of your two newspapers. I am sure this is not your intention, nor the intention of the able writers you employ. It is, none the less, in my judgment, the result. It amounts to the same thing, even though the intention may be the opposite. It has given me much pain to see that newspapers with whom I have had such friendly relations, and from which I have received in the past valuable support, should pursue such a line. It is because of our past relations that I write thus plainly.

Yours sincerely,
Winston S. Churchill.

From Cecil H. King to Churchill.

10th January, 1941.

Dear Prime Minister,

Your letter reached me on Monday just as I was leaving for the north of Scotland, whence I returned this morning.

I can only express my gratitude that at such a crisis as this you should find the time to express so fully and so frankly your view on the policies of these two papers. If you could spare the time to see me I am sure I could convince you that no organisation has more at heart the prosecution of this war to final victory, nor more loyalty to you personally as their leader in this struggle. Differences of method are bound to arise, but if you consider we have gone beyond what should be permissible in wartime, we should, of course, meet your wishes in so far as we conscientiously can.

Yours sincerely,

Mr Churchill saw him that afternoon, and a record of what took place was given in the previous chapter. The correspondence was then resumed.

From Cecil H. King to Churchill.

3rd February, 1941.

Dear Prime Minister,

As I feel our policy has mystified as well as distressed you, I thought I would try to amplify what I said to you when you saw me on Thursday.

Any support we gave you and your policy before the war was not just a newspaper stunt to sell papers. It never did – in fact our readers (and some of my colleagues) wanted to hear that it would be roses, roses, all the way. When I wrote to you on the outbreak of war to congratulate you (or rather the nation) on your going to the Admiralty, I said I hoped that when the inevitable demand came for a more vigorous prosecution of the war that you would step up to a still more exalted office. And when later, in October '39, we 'splashed' a prophecy that you would be the next Prime Minister, this was not idle flattery. It was the realisation by me slightly sooner than by others that you were our inevitable wartime leader – not because of your particular experience or capacity or for any other *reason* but because you ARE wartime England. When you make speeches, yours is the voice of England with all its traditions, its courage, its strength and its limitations. You epitomise our past: you are our present. There can be no question of your replacement during this war. This is not said just on a shrewd view of the political probabilities, but because you and England could not be separated now without both disintegrating.

But loyalty to England means not only loyalty to the past and the present, but to the future. This war is to you the crowning of a lifetime of public service; to us, who are much younger, it is the first step towards a new and better England in which we shall pay our way and not live – as we did in the years 1919-1939 – on the accumulated wealth and prestige

163

of our forefathers. This does not mean that I have some future leader up my sleeve or under the bed: I haven't. I have no idea whom he may eventually prove to be, but I think we shall not find him in any of the existing parties (in which I would include Mosleyites and Communists) and I think he is now much younger than I am (nearly 40).

Loyalty to the future involves not only scanning the horizon for the new ideas and ideals which may shape the world, but also the discrediting of the men who made the period 1919-39 such an ignoble page in English history. This is not done to humiliate them, but to impress on the young people growing up (who read our papers) that that is an era which must not recur.

Perhaps this would be clearer if I gave you an actual example of how it works. We advocate a statement by the Government of the country's war aims. Clearly to do so in any but vague and platitudinous terms would cause dissension among your ministers and between this country and its allies. Therefore you must think that to press such a demand is essentially mischievous. But look at it from the young man's point of view. The Middle East was conquered by the Mahomedans holding a sword in one hand and the Koran in the other – and who will deny that the Koran was the more potent weapon? At this moment we want our Koran and feel its possession would be the decisive factor of the whole war. Perhaps if you have read as far as this, you will see that there is no clear answer to this dilemma. One's loyalty is just divided.

The staff here do not always see clearly what I am driving at. Mistakes occur; but behind everything printed in these two papers is the conviction I have just described expressed in terms of the tabloid newspaper – itself a raw, crude medium but very typical of its day.

Yours sincerely,

From Churchill to Cecil H King.

5 *February,* 1941.

Dear Mr King,

Thank you very much for your letter and I was glad we had a talk. All this fine thought about the rising generation ought not to lead you into using your able writers to try to discredit and hamper the Government in a period of extreme danger and difficulty. Nor ought it to lead you to try to set class against class and generally 'rock the boat' at such a time. Finally I think it is no defence for such activities to say that your papers specialise in 'vitriolic' writing[6]. Indeed throwing vitriol is thought to be one of the worst of crimes. No man who is affected with 'vitriolism' is

---

[6] The Premier was referring to King's letter of January 24, 1941, which mentioned Cassandra as 'a hard-hitting journalist with a vitriolic style'.

worthy to shape the future, or likely to have much chance of doing so in our decent country. There is no reason why you should not advocate a statement of war aims. I wonder that you do not draw one up in detail and see what it looks like. I see that Mr Mander has tabled his war aims which seem to me to bear out what I ventured to say in the House, namely 'that most right-minded people are well aware of what we are fighting for'. Such a task would be well-suited to the present lull.

Yours sincerely,

Winston S Churchill.

From Cecil H King to Churchill.

11 *February,* 1941.

Dear Prime Minister,

Thank you very much for your letter dated February 5th. As I cannot emphasise too strongly, all of us here wish to give you personally all the support possible and it has come as a great shock to learn that you have been so distressed at the line these papers have been pursuing. I am afraid I had assumed that if anything published by us should cause you serious annoyance you would send a message through one of your secretaries asking us to be more moderate.

However, thanks to your very full and frank letters and the talk we had, we now have your point of view clearly before us. The staff have had their instructions and you may have already noticed a marked change of tone. If in the future you have any fault to find with our contribution to the nation's war effort, I hope you will let us know at once.

Yours sincerely,

From Churchill to Cecil H King.

13 *February, 1941.*

Dear Mr King,

Thank you very much for your letter. I take the greatest possible interest in the *Daily Mirror* and *Sunday Pictorial* with which I have been associated since their foundation in 1915. I shall be very glad to see you at any time. Do not hesitate to propose a visit.

Yours sincerely,

Winston S Churchill.

Alas, the rapprochement was short-lived.

23

SECONDS OUT – FINAL ROUND!

How, in Britain, does a newspaper behave when it is warned by the highest authority in the land that it is saying the wrong things? How, at any rate, did the *Mirror* behave in the months between the Attlee Warning and the Churchill Correspondence?

War or no war Harry Guy Bartholomew believed that his writers should express themselves with freedom. He rejected intimidation, for his paper had embarked upon a mission to ensure that the voice of the people was heard in the land.

Jennings had continued to demand total war. 'We must win,' said his editorial on the conscription of women. Then, later: 'A stalemate decision would mean an interval of intensive preparation for a third world war.'

There was little abatement in the waspishness of his critical commentaries. 'It is not 'subversive' to criticise the weaknesses of a Government that is supported by the great majority of the nation. Again and again,' he wrote, 'it has been seen that criticism, at first resented by the Government, is later accepted and acted upon.'

Editorials were sustained and outspoken, and at one time a daily leader appeared for two consecutive weeks criticising the Government or Army leaders in one way or another. Cripps was enthusiastically supported when he spoke of the 'listless' atmosphere in Britain compared with Russia; this was the time when the slogan *Russia bleeds while Britain blancoes* spread among the troops at home. 'You cannot fight a war of to-day with the mentality of yesterday' was the *leit motif.*

The thrashing of the War Office ('Wits and brains will win this war. The Army is starved of both') had continued, for Jennings was convinced that he was conducting a holy crusade against 'War Office minds trying to win a war by losing it'.

What steps, meanwhile, was Cassandra taking to earn the rebuke that was to fall upon him later in Parliament? Let us dip the litmus paper and see how it changes colour. Subversive – or patriotic?

When Whitehall began to probe his work he could look to no friends or sympathisers in the Ministry of Information; their verdict would be 'positively subversive'. For Cassandra had written:

> I see that an MP is to ask why dances are permitted to be held in the premises of the Ministry of Information. What's wrong with dancing in the Ministry of Information? I think the whole place should be turned into one vast dance-hall staffed by scores of red-hot mommas... All play and no work in the Bloomsbury Taj Mahal would be a decisive blow for our cause.

He complained about the official screening of news over the retreat from Benghazi. 'They still treat the British people as a bunch of kids who can't be trusted.'

Nor could the acid columnist, when trouble came, expect protection or mercy from the former *Mirror* contributor who now ruled the Home Office. For in public print he had crossed swords with Mr Morrison on two problems which Mr Morrison, as an orthodox Socialist, had found irksome.

'What is the sense of gagging the *Daily Worker* any longer?' asked Cassandra when the Russians had been obliged by Hitler's betrayal to enter the war on the side of the Western Allies. He continued:

> Mr Morrison has a long memory. He does not forget nor does he forgive.
> That is no reflection on Mr Morrison.
> But he should take care not to forget the record of some of the company with whom he works.

Discussing the administration of 18B, Cassandra called Mr Morrison 'the well-known chief censor and public turnkey'. When a case of mistaken detention was admitted he returned to the attack with a gibe at the Home Secretary's feudal powers.

No. Cassandra could not expect volunteers to go bail for him from the Ministry of Information or the Home Office.

In Westminster and Whitehall anger was rising as it became apparent that the Attlee threat had not diminished courage in Geraldine House. This was a heavyweight contest; it was now 'seconds out, final round'.

The next move lay with Churchill. It was a move difficult to anticipate, for the wily statesman, as in other matters of importance, had indulged himself to the extent of having two views on the freedom of criticism. A few weeks before he became wartime Prime Minister he had declared:

> Criticism in the body politic is like pain in the human body. It is not pleasant, but where would the body be without it? No health or sensibility would be possible without continued correctives and warnings of pain. It is in this fear of criticism that the Dictatorships run their greatest risk.

The Prime Minister who was now insisting on keeping proven failures in his Cabinet said this on May 29, 1936:

> The use of recriminating about the past is to enforce effective action at the present.

24
A MAN ON A BICYCLE

At ten minutes past nine on the morning of March 5 1942, in a flat in Ormond Terrace, Regent's Park, London, a young man announced that he was leaving for the office.

Slim. Thinning hair. Thirty-to-forty. The grinning, Cheerful Charlie type; friendly, energetic; a man with a conscience and talent.

On the top of an upright piano, leaning against the wall, was a piece of cardboard, ten-inches-by-twelve, the fruits of the previous evening's labours.

The young man put the piece of cardboard inside a saddle bag, strapped the saddle bag to his bicycle, and set off along Prince Albert Road. He always reckoned that the journey took him fifteen minutes flat. 'You pass Mornington Crescent – then Crowndale Road to King's Cross. Turn right up Gray's Inn Road, left into Holborn, right into Fetter Lane. On the way back it's advisable to hold on to a lorry; it's all uphill.'

Thus Philip Zec delivered to the offices of the *Mirror* the cartoon which set in motion the events which are now history in Westminster and Fleet Street.

Zec was born on Christmas Day, 1909. He trained at St Martin's School of Art, worked in advertising, and was running his own commercial art agency until Cassandra brought him to the paper in 1939.

The *Mirror* had considered signing up Louis Raemakers, the cartoonist of the Kaiser's war. Would his technique make the same impact on the new generation in Hitler's war? Cassandra and Zec thought not. So Zec must become the Louis Raemakers of 1939.

These were his first cartoons, and they were successful instantaneously. Zec, with his simple technique and sledgehammer draughtsmanship, became the people's cartoonist; he saw the issues of the war in clear terms of right and wrong, shared their irritations over muddle, and hated the enemy as whole-heartedly as they did.

His drawings shocked people, less by what he drew than by the unrestrained way in which he drew. He was in the line of historic British cartoonists in the way he symbolised. He did not create new characters, like Low's Colonel Blimp or Giles's family; his war cartoons are full of apes, snakes, toads, bears, vultures, Death, Mars, and what was fresh was their ferocity. His snakes were more poisonous, his toads more bloated, his Death more horrible and his Mars far hairier than any other artist's. Even when he was compassionate, as in his cartoons about children, he made his point vehemently.

To this he added Cockney street humour. This is seen in the situations, the homely back streets, and above all in the colloquial captions.

See for example his Neville Chamberlain as a lugubrious pianist, with Hitler peeping out from under the lid, and the caption: *Don't shoot the pianist, he's doing his best.* Or the June 1940 cartoon of Hitler as a moth fluttering round a lighted candle with the caption – *Sure, he's getting closer;* the post-atom bomb cartoon (August 8 1945) of two apes with the caption *Crikey! Have we got to start all over again!* And the fine VE cartoon of a wounded soldier holding out a wreath marked Victory and Peace in Europe: *Here you are! Don't lose it again.*

When Hitler announced in 1941 that he was feeling 'fresher than ever, for Spring is coming,' Zec drew a Nazi jackboot crunching a cluster of daffodils into the earth.

He had a turn, too, for prophecy, and at times he was uncannily right. On January 16 1942 he drew a lion stretched over the East with a Japanese hammer crushing down on his tail at Singapore. A month later we lost Singapore.

On April 21 1944, weeks before D. Day, he drew a cartoon – *Sstop ssaying 'ssay when'* – of Hitler and Goebbels among a pile of torn-off calendar pages. Prominent in the background was 'June 6' – D-Day. Readers wrote in later to ask how Zec knew the invasion date.

Cassandra, who worked in the same room as Zec during the early war years, describes how he set about his work:

'Being a cartoonist (like being a columnist) is, of course, a quite impossible mode of life. It is against the laws of nature. Compared with it, the Cat and the Fiddle and the Cow who jumped over the Moon were simply obeying the logical and immutable laws of Sound and Gravity.

'The political artist sees the world unfolding its disconcerting, delightful and deadly panorama, and then is faced with not only recording what he sees, but also explaining and commenting on the daily enigma of events, most of which are beyond human comprehension.

PHILIP ZEC

'With his simple technique and sledgehammer of draughtsmanship he
became the people's cartoonist. He saw the issues of the war in clear terms
of right and wrong, shared their irritations over muddle, and hated the
enemy as whole-heartedly as they did.'

'He must draw conclusions and he must point morals. He must deride and applaud. He must over-emphasise and he must understate. This he has to do, not with the flexible and convenient apparatus of language, but with uncompromising equipment of a large piece of white Bristol board, a brush and a bottle of brutally black ink. Furthermore, his ideas must have a Procrustean quality, in that they have got to be long thin ones or squat broad ones – with an occasional square idea to fill the space allotted to him by the newspaper he adorns. Zec is very good at long thin ideas, but objects strongly to dead square ones.

'Finally, he must perform his work with the regularity of a metronome, and any emotional temperament he feels inclined to display is cowed into submission by the knowledge that newspaper trains don't wait for even the most artistic tantrum.'

Zec was, and is, a Socialist, but his hatred of the Hitlerian creed was motivated by a passion that was deeper than his political convictions. As a Jew he had no doubt of what a Nazi victory would mean.

On Tuesday, March 3 1942, he began a series of cartoons with a single theme: black market activities that were hampering the nation's war effort.

The first portrayed a cynical black marketeer placing flowers on the gravestone of a soldier killed in action. 'Poor fellow,' he was saying, 'now what can I sell his mother?' The second drew attention to the importance of not wasting food. It was the third cartoon in this series which ignited The Great Misunderstanding.

Tankers were being sunk by enemy submarines at an alarming rate, and merchant seamen were dying in appalling circumstances. How could the public be shocked into a realisation of their wastefulness? The Government had authorised an increase of one penny in the price of petrol, but what difference would that make? The public needed to be told that gallant lives were being lost.

Zec usually worked in the office. He would discuss his ideas with Cassandra, produce the finished drawing, and then debate the wording which would most swiftly and potently convey the message. On this occasion he had worked on the drawing at home, producing it from his saddle bag.

'Bloody good. My boy, you're a genius,' said Cassandra.

Zec, as usual, had produced a fine drawing. A torpedoed sailor adrift on a raft in a black, empty, angry sea; a stark scene emphasising the horror of U-boat warfare. And underneath he had written, in pencil:

'Petrol is Dearer Now'

'You're a genius,' said Cassandra. 'But you want a stronger caption. You need to pinpoint and dramatise the extra penny charge.'

Thus:

PETROL IS DEARER NOW

Became

'The price of petrol has been increased by one penny' – Official.

The cartoon was published the following morning, and requests for reproductions reached the editor from garages, savings associations, multiple stores and the organisers of Warship Weeks.

But the man on the bicycle had not only produced a patriotic cartoon: his work was capable of two interpretations. It was also a wicked cartoon. A cruel cartoon. A deplorable cartoon. A horrible cartoon.

25
SUMMONS TO WESTMINSTER

The *Mirror,* not for the first or last time, was unpopular upstairs'. No one was surprised at that; least of all Bartholomew, Cecil Thomas, Jennings, Connor and Zec.

But things were now happening behind the scenes in Westminster not entirely known to the vociferous quintet in Fleet Street. Churchill's patience was exhausted. The newspaper was the favourite with the Forces and was far outstripping its rivals, but Generals were complaining to the War Office that its campaigns were undermining morale among the men. How could a soldier be expected to fight for brass-hats he was told were no good? Here was a caricature of all that officers had been taught in Sandhurst about man-management and morale.

The War Office passed the complaints to a Cabinet already irked by Jennings' satire and Connor's daily bludgeoning.

Who owned the *Mirror?* Churchill demanded an inquiry, and Government investigators examined the list of the shareholders to ascertain whether Goebbels, or Himmier, or Hess, or even Hitler was among them.

Some shares, as in every public company, were held and are held in the name of nominees. That was and is permissible under a law which should perhaps be changed; but a law which the *Mirror* at all events did not enact.

Did the nominees in this case conceal the identity of sinister foreign agents seeking Britain's downfall? Was this unruly newspaper a fifth-column tool of the enemy?

War breeds strange bed-fellows; a Cabinet including Churchill and Morrison demonstrated that. In the post-war years the Tory referred to the Socialist as a caucus boss with a distorted, mischievous and malevolent mind.

War also breeds strange fears.

The Zec cartoon – *The price of petrol has been raised by one penny. (Official)* – was passed around the Cabinet. What was its evil import? Mr

Morrison pronounced the cartoon to be wicked and the Minister of Labour, Mr Ernest Bevin, agreed. They concluded that Zec's intention was not to admonish the public to conserve petrol by portraying its heavy cost in terms of human life; here was a gauche attempt to tell merchant seamen they were endangering their lives so that fatter profits might be made by petrol combines.

The judicial verdict of the Lord Chancellor, Lord Simon, was also sought. He considered the cartoon was cruel, deplorable, horrible.

Thus was chosen the moment to strike.

Fleet Street did not know the inquisition was proceeding; Westminster did not know that the newspaper was receiving requests for reproductions of the cartoon from worthies raising war funds to whom the cartoon conveyed what Zec intended it to convey.

Orders were issued from Downing Street for the compiling of a *dossier;* the files of the newspaper were scrutinised for dubious quotations and on the evening of Wednesday March 19 a summons came by telephone.

Now it happens that a remarkable document has been preserved which describes in merciless detail just what happened when Bartholomew as a director and Cecil Thomas as editor obeyed the command to attend the Home Office to see Herbert Morrison. Thomas wrote a personal letter on April 21 1942 to E F Herbert, a member of the staff then serving as an armourer with an RAF night fighter squadron in Shropshire. He showed me Thomas's letter some years later in Rome. 'Let us type it and each keep a copy. This must be preserved,' I said.

Here is the document, the first account published of how the official warning was conveyed:

> The depth-charge went off without warning... a real Beecham... after a phone call one evening for JC [John Cowley, then chairman] and me to go to our 'Erb at 10.15 next morning. Bart came instead.
>
> We waited in an adjoining room with three or four clerks, or whatever they were.
>
> Behind a vase on the mantelpiece, was a small framed card with names of the current (or recently ex-) murderers. Various columns showed date of sentence, appeal lodged and heard etc, and the last column was headed 'result'. Below the first name was the comment, 'Executed'. A pretty final result, I thought.
>
> A Mr Strutt, in black coat, striped trousers, and wearing a large quiff on his forehead, took us in and in a loud voice said: 'Mr Home Secretary... Mr Bartholomew, Mr Thomas.'
>
> 'Erb was genial and talked of the last time we met at lunch. 'That was a good do,' he said, and he motioned us to the far side of a long mahogany

table. This was in the large room of the Secretary of State, with a beautiful dark brown carpet, a large fire burning in an old-fashioned grate, a big settee in front of it, oil painting of man in wig over mantelpiece, long windows overlooking St James' Park and a pleasant air of dull green and gold over it all. It was there, about a year earlier, Morrison had told me about the *Daily Worker* when he shut that.

Today he was joined by a tall thin man, his Parliamentary Secretary, whose thin long face was creased with extreme pain, except when he smiled as we shook hands.

Mr Strutt came in and was introduced by 'Erb, also Sir Alexander Someone who looked like a Dickensian solicitor, and two more men of the Home Office.

'Well, what I gotta say is going to be rather unpleasant,' said 'Erb in his Cockney voice. He rattled on about the Lor [law]. 'You gentlemen 'ave your own legal advisers. What I have to tell you is the unanimous decision of the Cabinet.'

He kept us waiting a long time for the decision. Half an hour in all. At one time I quite thought we were being shut down that day.

'Criticism is one thing. Unfair criticism is another.' His complaint was that, put in an oblique way, we might well be supposed to be engaged in an attempt to hamper the war effort. He said clearly that all our wish for drive in war production was camouflage to hide our real intent to bring down the Government and Society, to get the people depressed so that we should make peace by agreement.

He didn't say we were Fifth Column, but implied it. He insinuated that we might be playing the enemy's game. 'One might imagine this, could be pardoned for thinking that, etc.'

Produced a dossier. First, Zec cartoon as an instance. 'I my sye, in my opinion very artistically drawn. Worthy of Goebbels at his best.' It was plainly meant to tell seamen not to go to sea to put money in the pockets of petrol owners.

Such an idea hadn't occurred to me or to anyone. He looked at me with his one eye over his glasses: 'Only a very unpatriotic editor could pass that for publication.' He turned to Bart: 'Only a (something I forget) or one with a diseased mind could be responsible for the *Daily Mirror* policy.'

I had half a mind to say; 'Well, I wasn't a Conchy in the last war (as Herbert Morrison was) so I don't know how you look at things.'

Bart and I had agreed to say nothing.

Next he went to an editorial by Jennings which was no more than a ridiculous exaggeration in words about a Blimp. It was only one sentence he quoted. But the full leader showed approval of Grigg's War Office decision. These were both in the issue of March 6, and this was March 19. So no hurry at Downing Street, evidently.

He reminded us he had closed one paper, and said it would be a long time before it was opened. 'And that goes for you, too. You might bear that in mind. If you are closed, it will be for a long time.' No further warning would be given. 'We shall act with a speed that will surprise you.'

Bart said only that the cartoon was one that had proved most popular, that many garages had asked for it, and how about stopping the showing of them.

'You had better get them back,' was the advice.

He concluded by saying: 'Now you can go away and start lobbying your MPs. Nothing said here is secret. I am going to answer a question in the House about it to-day.'

Bart said there was no point in that. We did not do that sort of thing.

By the time we were back at the office the report was coming over the machines. So, had we wished, it gave us no time to inform MPs. A swift move, certainly, by Mr 'Erb, who was, at the close, quite genial. 'Give my kind regards to Mr Cowley,' etc. As we left him he was whistling a little tune to himself.

Later in the day he was lobbying himself in the House and got a surprise in the Press Gallery.

Well, tell me what it was they didn't like. I'm sure I don't know.

Cassandra had quite a lot of letters, one from Augustus John.

The papers gave a very garbled account of the debate, only the *News Chronicle* at all fair. The rest gave all the bits at us and left out our side.

Now the *Sunday Express* is nagging us for not giving the names of all our shareholders. As if we knew them all. Many are held by nominee companies. 'Masked Men' was the leader heading last Sunday. Throw enough mud and some sticks... that's their line.

There is, of course, nothing to hide. These directors have been the same for twenty years. Hope all this does not bore you.

Morrison was stern. Yet, when they departed, not brusque or impolite. The impression Bartholomew and Thomas formed at the interview remains now; they were convinced from Morrison's demeanour that action had been initiated at a higher level. If this impression had not been formed, the personal and political relationship which flourished in post-war years between Bartholomew and Morrison could never have existed.

Ten years after the event, when the characters concerned are no longer impassioned or confused by misguided patriotism, war hysteria or punctured pride, I have re-examined and reassessed the evidence.

Out of hand I reject the theory prevalent in the offices of the *Mirror* in 1942, for the view then held was that the cartoon was deliberately misconstrued by Ministers determined by fair means or foul to put an end to the newspaper's unrelenting exposures of their bungling. A man with the principles and temperament of Simon, to mention no other, would not lend his brain or name to such a plot.

The explanation is simpler. Frayed nerves had led to distorted judgment.

Whatever may be said on either side about the Cabinet's attitude to the daily acidities of Jennings and Cassandra, their misreading and condemnation of the Zec cartoon must go down into newspaper history as the century's most flagrant example of ingenuousness in high places.

Helping the enemy? Nothing exposes the fatuity of the charge more than an order issued by the Nazis that all *Mirror* directors were to be immediately arrested when London was occupied. The existence of the order was disclosed when German High Command papers were examined by the Allies after the war.

26
SILENCE – OR SUPPRESSION

The government's tactics were bold and swift. The newspaper was given no opportunity to ensure that its own case as well as the Cabinet's would be put to the nation, for Morrison went immediately to the House to announce that action had been taken.

Two weapons were at his disposal:

> REGULATION 2C
>
> providing for warning as a preliminary to prosecution, and for no prosecution without the consent of the Attorney General;

> REGULATION 2D
>
> providing for instantaneous suppression of a newspaper on the edict of the Home Secretary.

The weapon had already been chosen: 2D. But with a refinement, for a warning was in fact issued.

The Home Secretary's speech produced a shock in Parliament and stimulated much interest in the Services and in the country. He said:

> The cartoon is only one example, but a particularly evil example, of the policy and methods of a newspaper which, intent on exploiting an appetite for sensation, and with reckless indifference to the national interest and to the prejudicial effect on the war effort, has repeatedly published scurrilous misrepresentations, distorted and exaggerated statements and irresponsible generalizations.
>
> In the same issue the leading article stated: –
>
> *... the accepted tip for Army leadership would, in plain truth, be this: All who aspire to mislead others in war should be brass-buttoned boneheads, socially prejudiced, arrogant and fussy. A tendency to heart disease, apoplexy, diabetes and high blood pressure is desirable in the highest post...*
>
> Reasonable criticism on specific points and persons is one thing; general, violent denunciation, manifestly tending to undermine the Army

and depress the whole population, is quite another... The Government have decided that the right method of dealing with a newspaper which persistently disregards its public responsibility and the national interest is to make use of the powers contained in Defence Regulation 2D.

This authorises the suppression of a newspaper that systematically publishes matter calculated to foment opposition to the successful prosecution of the war...

The fact that those responsible for the publication of such matter may not deliberately and wilfully desire to hinder the success of the Allied cause does not make the publication any less dangerous. A writer's motives and intentions are known only to himself. The test is what effect his words may be expected to produce on the minds of others...

As it is possible that some of the persons responsible for the publication of such matter have not realised that it is within the ambit of Regulation 2D, it has been thought right in the first instance to take action by way of warning. I have seen those responsible for the publication of the *Daily Mirror* and have made clear to them the considerations I have outlined to the House.

It was a blunt warning and it had come unexpectedly to the House. But even in those circumstances the freedom of the Press was an historic Parliamentary cause which did not lack zealous and articulate advocates.

When Mr Emanuel Shinwell saw that Britain was in danger of having the right of public opinion impinged upon – a prospect which 'filled some of those who ventured to criticise the Government with alarm and despondency' – Mr Morrison promised facilities for a debate if any substantial body of opinion in the House required them.

Two Socialists (Mr Shinwell and Mr Seymour Cocks), one member of the Independent Labour Party (Mr James Maxton), one Liberal (Sir Percy Harris) and one Independent (Mr Leslie Hore-Belisha) raised their voices and expressed their fears: their names deserve to be recorded. So does the name of Commander Locker-Lampson, whose sole contribution to the discussion was to spread the lie that the American isolationist William Randolph Hearst was part owner of the London *Mirror*.

A saner, legitimate question came from Lord Trefgarne, then Mr Garro-Jones. He wanted to know who *were* the proprietors and editors.

Mr Morrison replied: 'This is a newspaper which has no wealthy and single owner. It is a mixed proprietorship. It is one of those mixed financial controls in which you cannot trace a single private financial interest.'

That was the deflating conclusion with which Churchill's investigators had returned to Whitehall after their scrutiny of the share lists. No

Goebbels. No Himmler. No Hess. No Hitler. Only people who 'looked innocent enough'.

But Herbert Morrison – or was it Churchill? – was not yet satisfied. For the Home Secretary ended his oration with these hopeful words: '...it is one of those mixed financial controls in which you cannot trace a single private financial interest *so far as I can see at present.*'

The full-dress debate was still to take place, but the following morning Jennings made this first observation on the Morrison threat:

> Mr Morrison was good enough to allow that 'those responsible for the publication of such matter' may not 'deliberately and wilfully' desire to hinder the success of the allied cause.
>
> We must be grateful to him for this small concession.
>
> It will be agreed that no more violent, no more cruel attack has ever been made by a Cabinet Minister upon a daily newspaper since newspapers claimed and secured the right to a relatively free expression of independent opinion. We particularly regret that such violent denunciation should come from a Minister with whom we have had perfectly friendly relations and who was at one time a valued contributor to our columns.
>
> If we are called defeatist, unpatriotic, irresponsible and dangerous it is manifestly useless to defend ourselves against those who have succeeded in convincing themselves that we have the monopoly of a sort of criminality in criticism.
>
> We abstain then from replying to Mr Morrison. We loyally quote his denunciation. The rest we can only leave to our readers – to that part of public opinion which will discuss and judge.
>
> As to that same public opinion we may be allowed to say that it supported us in the days of Munich; that it continued – not, of course, without dissentients – to support us all through the weary months of our endeavour to secure greater efficiency; that it applauded us when reforms we advocated were later adopted, and that it is utterly beyond the power of any reasonable observer to explain why the policies we have supported can have been wrong since most of them have been justified by the event.

One further comment is necessary on the leading article which Mr Morrison quoted from his *dossier* of the newspaper's scurrilous misrepresentations, distorted and exaggerated statements, and irresponsible generalisations.

Jennings was convinced that obsolete trench-war ideas and Passchendaele mentalities among the 'brass-hats' were still hampering the creation of the modern mobile divisions that alone would bring victory. He was determined to express the sense of frustration that a series of military reverses had engendered in the country and in the Services.

His sentences, said the *Daily Herald,* were 'silly, but clearly rhetorical'. Silly they may have been, but it is right to record that in the humourless months of 1942, literary style, at least, was unfettered by Government Regulation.

What still needs explanation is why Herbert Morrison trimmed his quotation in a manner which presented it in the worst possible light. Jennings lampooned the Generals who were mentally bone-headed and physically wrecked. But the Home Secretary omitted to tell the Commons that the subject of the editorial was a new Army Council instruction that all who held positions of authority 'must have an adequate degree of physical fitness and mental alertness as well as purely military efficiency'.

So the Army Council, as well as the *Mirror,* were concerned about the boneheads and the high blood-pressure generals.

Jennings was surprised that such an instruction was necessary in the third year of the second world war, but quoted the Army Council order with approval. That was not mentioned by Mr Morrison in the House.

And what was the subversive sentiment that appeared in the headline above the article? This positive, war-winning advice:

WEED THEM OUT!

Nor was that mentioned by Mr Morrison in the House. The Home Secretary was presenting a black record: a case for suppression. The record had to be black indeed to threaten to suppress a national newspaper in a democratic country which had gone to war to defend the freedoms.

Did Churchill remember, as he read Morrison's denunciation of Jennings, a telephone dialogue which took place in 1939?

Anthony Clarkson, then features editor, was discussing with Winston the article he was writing for the *Mirror* that week.

The initials WM had been missing for a few days from the foot of the editorial column. Churchill, deeply concerned, said:

'Jennings isn't ill, is he? It would be a tragedy if he stopped writing now.'

27
ALARM AND DESPONDENCY

In Fleet Street, headquarters of the national newspaper industry, the *Mirror* was unpopular. Since it had awakened in 1935 from a coma convenient to its competitors it had provoked unceasing controversy. That was its secret.

There were proprietors, editors and journalists who felt the success of the tabloid had lowered the standards of British journalism. Garish, loud-mouthed, unreserved in its selection and presentation of news; plebian in its tastes and outlook; unorthodox in its methods – to them the paper now rapidly winning millions of supporters among the public in and out of uniform was anathema.

Others resented or feared its robust progress and were happy to enjoy its discomforts.

It is interesting, therefore, to examine how Fleet Street reacted to the crisis of 1942. The future of the whole industry was at stake. A vital principle was imperilled. Who put on the gloves? And who, with ill-concealed relish, donned a black tie, smoothed a silk topper, and ordered a wreath for a funeral that was arranged but did not take place?

Few of the national newspapers could resist this Churchill-sent chance to clip the *Mirror's* ear or thump it in the back. Yet, with only two or three dissentients, they did not allow their distaste of the paper's methods or their envy of its expansion to blur the main issue. They were all in the ring the morning after Morrison had sounded the gong.

The *Express*, which in the years to come was to take second place to the *Mirror* in circulation and political influence, deprecated the conduct of its rival and the conduct of the Home Office, advocating that Regulation 2C and not 2D was wholly adequate for Mr Morrison's purposes. In other words, the offending newspaper should have been prosecuted before the courts and thus be given the opportunity to defend itself.

The *News Chronicle* lived up to its traditions of liberalism and fought strongly for its concept of the freedom of the Press though it may have had private thoughts about the brashness of its comrade. The Government's interpretation of the Zec cartoon, they said, was 'not that placed upon it by the majority of those whom we have questioned. The *Mirror*'s leading article from which Mr Morrison quoted is open to evil interpretation, but no one who has followed the *Mirror*'s policy over the war period will doubt that it has been designed – though often expressed in strong and sweeping language – to aid and not hinder the war effort.' The purpose of newspaper criticism was to galvanise both Government and nation to fight harder and work harder.

The Times gave the Government the assurance that 'yesterday's reminder to one newspaper will in no way deter the rest from the discharge of their duty.'

The *Herald,* whose influence on Left Wing movements and politics was to be ignominiously dwarfed by the *Mirror* immediately the war was over, informed its readers that it found the language of its competitor high-pitched and distasteful. But it denounced the Government interpretation of the Zec cartoon and warned Churchill and Morrison that it was amid the twilight of compulsory censorship that Petain and Laval had contrived to do away with legitimate Government in France.

The London *Evening Standard* and *Star* and the Glasgow *Herald* and *Bulletin* all criticised Morrison's action.

The *Manchester Guardian,* swift into battle when freedom is menaced, declared: 'Through Mr Morrison the Government almost seems to say that it does not welcome criticism and is prepared in its dislike to resort to the blackest form of administrative act, suppression of the critic without trial.'

The *Birmingham Post* and the *Yorkshire Post* sympathised with the Home Secretary's misgivings. And from the *Daily Telegraph* alone in Fleet Street fell crumbs of comfort for the suppressors. 'The examples given by Mr Morrison of the sort of publication that has given rise to his warning will be enough for any reasonable mind,' said that newspaper.

It was the *Telegraph* which on June 23 1938 had devoted a complete page to statements by Church leaders applauding the purity of the *Daily Sketch* (at that time its puny, non-starting stable companion), and thus, by implication, denouncing the methods of the vigorous outspoken *Mirror.*

It was Lord Camrose, proprietor of the *Telegraph,* who was to visit the House of Lords within a week to declare that he ventured to think that the warning would be sufficient for Mr Morrison's purpose.

Away from Fleet Street, too, the clouds were gathering. The National Council for Civil Liberties expressed their grave anxiety and organised a public protest meeting in London. The National Union of Journalists condemned arbitrary suppression of a newspaper without trial. Mr

Morrison's threat was also criticised at a private meeting of the Parliamentary Labour Party.

What was happening in these dark days in the offices of the *Mirror* itself? Telephone messages, telegrams and letters brought encouragement. 'We are happy to have received them, and to know that our readers so loyally support us,' said the paper. Nine hundred letters had arrived, of which only thirty-five were pro-Government; nearly all of the latter were anonymous, including one from the Guards' Club.

Cassandra now began his column: 'Trying harder than ever to please, I respectfully draw your attention to the astonishing case of Mr Casey —'

28

IN THE STOCKS

The history of every newspaper is a succession of dominant dates – days of doubt, or defeat, or triumph. When the *Mirror* was arraigned before Parliament it was a day of doubt, defeat *and* triumph.

Champions of freedom were voluble in both Houses, but the newspaper was subjected to a punishment as merciless as any it had delivered in its pages; it could scarcely complain of the ferocity of the language. The thumb-screws were turned to extremity, and near at hand was the executioner, axe poised above the block.

Editors are accustomed in moments of crisis to hearing their handiwork discussed in disparaging terms. God has so made them that it warms the cockles of their hearts when eminent counsel (appearing for their defence) describes their newspaper as a paragon of all the virtues – and then, in a different court case, exorcises them by book, bell and candle. The same eminent counsel, when employed by a plaintiff, will push his wig despairingly to the back of his head, raise an eyebrow, curl a lip, hold the offending sheet between the tips of his fingers lest he contract a contagious disease, and inform M'Lud that 'This, *this* paper, has set itself up as the arbiter of good taste'.

The *Mirror* was juvenile, said Mr A G Walkden. It was a paper written for girls; not for 'gentlewomen', as Northcliffe propounded when he launched it.

Its circulation, said Wing-Commander A W H James, had been built up on the publication of 'deliberately salacious muck to tickle the palates of its public.'

'If the paper depended upon my purchasing it,' said Mr Aneurin Bevan, 'it would never be sold.' Yet – this came later – 'it was the paper of the Armed Forces.' Mr Bevan did not know, for this was 1942, that a prominent article by Mr Aneurin Bevan would appear in that newspaper on February 27 1952.

It was an organ which appealed to baser motives, but unfortunately, said Sir Ralph Glyn, this paper was 'so clever'. It appealed to every sense, 'the sense we all have of a desire to nag those in authority.' It also appealed to 'the "strip-tease" mind, which means an appeal to those feelings which are very prevalent in war and which are absolutely natural'. Sir Ralph conceded that sex was natural.

Was the *Mirror* THE voice of the people, or A voice of the people? And Jane was mentioned. For how could there be a discussion on Britain's wartime morale without a reference to that daily aphrodisiac?

Armed with these epithets, and dozens more, the Members assembled for the grim debate. It was March 1942. 'The Germans are twenty miles from the coast of Kent,' said the Member for Bristol, South. 'They hold the whole of the French coast. The March moon is on; the April moon is coming.'

The Mother of Parliaments was discussing the Freedom of the Press, and the debate was characterised by lofty thinking as much as by personal rancour.

The case for the *Mirror* was put by Liberals and Socialists led by Wilfrid Roberts.

Regulation 2D, they said, was a modern version of the stocks, in which the victim was exposed for all to see. If the crime of the newspaper was against the Government, should the Government judge the crime? The paper's policy had not changed since the Prime Minister had written for it or since the Leader of the Labour Opposition had quoted it with such effect after the occupation of Austria. Did the *Mirror,* when it supported the Leader of the House, Sir Stafford Cripps, want to disrupt and overthrow society? Or did it believe, as the House and the country now believed, that the Government would be strengthened by Cripps' inclusion? Suppression would do far more damage to morale than any of the 'biting, sarcastic, pungent articles which appear in that paper.'

Why did the House always look upon the soldiers in the Army as children? Why did they not treat them like adults? Unfortunately, most of the criticisms made by the *Mirror* about the leadership of the British Army had been confirmed by many military events. Mr Morrison dare not put his case to the courts, said the paper's supporters, because the *Mirror* would then have the right to defend itself by putting the Home Secretary into the box as one of its principal witnesses.

Four members spoke against the *Mirror,* among them Mr A P Herbert. He searched his vocabulary with success for words to express his indignation at the criticism of Army 'brasshats'. 'By God, I say that it is a damned disgusting, blackguardly thing; a disgrace to the honourable craft to which I belong.' He had one remedy for the *Mirror:* he would send the management a large box of liver-pills every morning and stand over them while they swallowed.

Then came Herbert Morrison, to justify the warning he had given and to show that he had acted in the nick of time. He was as cocksure as ever, anticipating another success in his record as a skilled Parliamentarian; but disillusionment was in store for him from his own political party.

Mr Morrison produced new quotations in which, he said, the general implication all the way through was that everything was wrong, that everybody was incompetent – if, indeed, not worse than incompetent. Surely, said he, the logical result of that in any elementary reasoning by an individual was, 'What is the good of going on? Why continue the war? We had better do some sort of deal with the enemy to patch things up.'

To some individuals the debate brought moments of uneasiness or chagrin. But it was Mr Morrison who suffered most sorely, first at the hands of Mr Bevan and then of Mr Bellenger.

When Mr Bevan was entertaining the House to his views on the *Mirror,* he made it clear that he did not like the newspaper at all. 'But the *Mirror* has not been warned because people do not like that kind of journalism. It is not because the Home Secretary is, aesthetically, repelled by it that he warns it.'

After the frankness came the dirty linen.

Mr Bevan: I am sure the Home Secretary does not take that view. He liked the paper. He is taking its money. (This was a reference to the articles Mr Morrison had written before he was a Minister.)

Mr Morrison (springing to his feet): If the Hon. Gentleman wants to be personal, I would say so is somebody closely connected with him.

Mr Bevan: Be as personal as you like. In this matter the harder the hitting the better I like it.

And who was 'somebody closely connected with Mr Bevan' who was 'taking the *Mirror's* money'? Why, the future member for Cannock, alias Miss Jennie Lee, alias Mrs Aneurin Bevan, who for a time worked in the room next to Cassandra.

Mr Bevan read this extract from an article by Mr Morrison which had appeared on February i, 1940, when the country was at war:

> They (the people) want the war to be fought with energy. They want to see every factory and every man at work. They want less muddled advice from on top.

188

Mr Bevan was in a mischievous mood. What was Mr Morrison doing there, he chided – undermining the morale of the country and the confidence of the country in the leaders of the nation and the Army?

For Mr Morrison there was worse in store. There remained Mr Bellenger. And what Mr Bellenger had to say was to make a profound impression upon the House and upon the Home Secretary himself. Said Mr Bellenger:

'If an example of subversion is wanted, I wonder what the House will think of this, which was written in the last war. I will tell my Right Hon Friend (Mr Morrison) why I intend to read it to the House. I was then a young soldier myself, a volunteer and not a conscript, and I presume my morale was something to be considered. Perhaps my Right Hon Friend will be able to say whether he thinks this was subversive:

> Your King and Country need you!
> Ah! Men of the Country, you are remembered.
> Neither the King, nor the Country, nor the picture papers had really forgotten you.
> When your master tried to cut your wages down – did you think he knew of your beautiful brave heart? When you were unemployed – did you think your Country had forgotten you? When the military were used against you in the strike – did you wonder if your King was quite in love with you? Did you?... Ah! foolish one.
> Your King and Country need you.
> Need hundreds of thousands of you to go to hell and to do the work of hell. The Commandment says: 'Thou shalt not kill'. Pooh!
> What does it matter? Commandments, like treaties, were made to be broken. Ask your parson: He will explain.
> Your King and Country need you!
> Go forth, little soldier –

'I was one of those little soldiers,' said Mr Bellenger, and then continued with the quotation:

> Go forth, little soldier. Though you know not what you fight for – go forth. Though you have no grievance against your German brother – go forth and kill him! Though you may know he has a wife and family dependent upon him – go forth and slay him; he is only a German dog. Will he now kill you if he gets the chance? Of course, he will.
> He is being told the same story!
> His King and Country need him.

'I wonder what the House thinks of that quotation,' asked Mr Bellenger. 'I wonder what my Right Hon Friend thinks of it now in this war. He is not unacquainted with the author. I say that a man who could write that stuff in the last war, when many of us were defending our country and he was not, is not the man to be the judge of subversion on this occasion.'

Mr Stokes: 'Who wrote it?'

Mr Bellenger: 'I think the House knows who wrote it. I have not given notice to the Right Hon Gentleman, who is the author, that I was going to quote it. I hope when he reads it he will recognise his effusion in the last war.'

The Right Honourable Herbert Morrison PC, MP, was a pacifist in World War One.

In World War Two he was Minister of Supply, then Home Secretary and Minister of Home Security, and member of the War Cabinet from 1942 to 1945.

The man who had suppressed the *Daily Worker* for saying that the war should not be fought at all. The man who as the Cabinet's mouthpiece was now threatening to suppress the *Mirror* for insisting that the war be fought efficiently.

Thus, so far as the House of Commons was concerned, the tortuous incident closed. For the Government, to the surprise of Churchill and Morrison, the day had not been happy or triumphant: nothing, at all events, was heard again of any attempt to close down the newspaper.

In the Upper House the same day the *Mirror's* hot head was plunged neck-deep into a bucket of judicial ice.

The noble Lords cleared their throats, shuffled into positions of comfort, and prepared themselves to hear The Case for the Government. The Cabinet's illustrious counsel, the Lord Chancellor, Viscount Simon, rose to stage a performance that was impeccable, for he believed in his brief. Indeed, as his speech disclosed, he had had 'the duty of examining the matter pretty closely'.

There was a nod of approbation for all who spoke before him. All. With one of Viscount Trenchard's observations, said Lord Simon, the whole of their Lordships' House would be in agreement in principle and in fact. The speech of the Marquess of Crewe, whose 'devotion to public duties is the admiration of us all', had been interesting. Lord Nathan had presented what he had to say in very moderate terms. His noble friend Lord Vansittart had been very entertaining. Lord Camrose's dignified speech 'impressed us all'. They had reached the conclusion of the debate 'in a very happy spirit of union'.

John Simon quoted John Milton's *Areopagitica;* he also punctuated his oration with two remarks which lightened the heart of the House.

He had always understood that there was a rule in Fleet Street that dog did not eat dog, that there was a strong natural tendency collectively to defend the extremity of their rights. He recalled the lines of Oliver Goldsmith:

> And in that town a dog was found
> As many dogs there be –
> Both mongrel, puppy, whelp and hound
> And curs of low degree.

The Lord Chancellor felt very grateful to Lord Camrose that on this occasion the dignified, well-conducted and benevolent mastiff should have administered a slight nip to the ill-conditioned and ill-bred specimen whose yelpings were the cause of the present debate.

His second remark was prophetic.

'I observe that the articles in the *Daily Mirror* which in some quarters have roused most offence are signed by the *nom de plume* of Cassandra. I do not need to remind those of your Lordships who maintain a memory of the Greek tragedians that Cassandra came to a very sticky end.'

Cassandra, within a few days, joined the Services.

'I cannot and will not change my policy,' he wrote. 'I am still a comparatively young man and I propose to see whether the rifle is a better weapon than the printed word.' He returned to his rostrum five years later and began his column:

'As I was saying when I was interrupted, it is a powerful hard thing to please all the people all the time.'

Two months after the Commons debate, when the annual general meeting of the *Mirror* shareholders took place, only one turned up to make any comment on the newspaper's clash with the Government. He afterwards proposed the vote of thanks to the chairman and directors.

The debate caused no loss in circulation, no drop in the price of the newspaper's shares.

29
A FISHING STORY

There was a curious sequel to the Churchill-*Mirror contretemps* of 1942.

In August the following year the Prime Minister and his entourage travelled to Canada for the Quebec Conference with Franklin Delano Roosevelt. The talks at the Citadel went well; so swiftly was agreement reached that the war leaders had time on their hands – time, suggested FDR, for a little fishing.

Fishing? Winston Churchill is a man of many pursuits, but this for him was something new. The schedule for the remainder of his mission could not be revised, and he was content in any case to spend the available time in amity with the President.

The high-ups got busy with phone calls, and a warning order was sent to two luxurious fishing lodges to expect the visitors. The first lodge was *La Cabane,* on the Montmorency River, and the second was at *Lac de Neige,* in the heart of the Montmorency timber limits thirty-six miles from Quebec's *Chateau Frontenac.*

American, British and Canadian secret service men examined the sites and road approaches to the lodges. Food and liquor were conveyed, and the Canadians camped sentries and posted motor-cycle police to secure the whole area. The Anglo-Canadian Pulp & Paper Company built overnight a fishing boat for Roosevelt, for his paralysis enforced him to sit in a swivel chair.

Then, at the last minute, FDR was obliged to cry off. He had become unwell, and his doctor insisted on cancelling the trip.

Churchill, now boyishly enthusiastic, carried on with the expedition and set off in seventeen Army cars and nine Army trucks for the fishing lodges with his wife, his daughter Mary, and high-ranking British advisers who had accompanied him on the mission.

The Prime Minister was delighted to catch a twenty-inch trout.

But he was unaware that the fishing lodges were owned by the Anglo-Canadian Company, that this company was and is the Canadian subsidiary of the London *Daily Mirror,* and that Colonel Frank Clarke – who was responsible for ministering to the party's needs – was also responsible for selling the company's newsprint in America.

The Prime Minister was enjoying the hospitality, gladly given, of the newspaper he had recently threatened with suppression.

30
HITLER BOMBS THE *MIRROR*

The *Mirror* was the only British newspaper during the war to get into trouble with both sides. Churchill's wrath came as a surprise: Hitler's should have been expected.

The paper had been so busy warning the Government to prepare deep shelters for the public that it neglected to complete a shallow shelter for itself. When the first siren sounded on September 3 1939, the staff retired to a basement stacked high with ill-sorted masonry, buckets of cement and burst sandbags. The equipment consisted of one telephone, no beds, no lavatories, and one exit. A pavement grating which had been removed and not replaced afforded an excellent view of the sky.

The siren was a false alarm.

Can a newspaper show you its operation? The *Mirror,* at any rate, can swap blitz stories with any other cool Londoner, and was on more than a nodding acquaintance with high explosives, fire bombs, flying bombs, rockets and land mines; the paper had more to put up with than its rivals, yet its experiences of hits and 'near misses' are typical of how the whole of Fleet Street carried on. The leading spirit throughout was Guy Bartholomew. There was enough trouble around the place already, but he joined the AFS and tramped the city night and day with photographer George Greenwell recording the blitz in pictures.

Fleet Street knew it was 'for it' when the war was one year old.

On September 7 1940 the ordeal began with a mighty Luftwaffe raid on London docks. On the Sunday night the *Mirror* staff, below ground, felt their stomachs turn over as a 'heavy' fell in the adjacent road, Chancery Lane.

The idea grew that Goebbels was all out for a paper victory. Clustered around one closely built-up street in London are the printing plants of all the national newspapers. Could they be put out of action? Without its daily newspapers, diminished in size but still crammed with war news, Britain could be reduced to a Babel of rumour and propaganda, ripe for the lies Lord Haw-Haw was broadcasting from Germany every night.

The Cabinet called in the Newspaper Proprietors' Association. But the newspapers were already active with their plans for production under siege conditions.

Newsprint was precious. When a portion of the *Mirror's* supply in Manchester was blitzed, and the salvaged remains were moved to London and blitzed again, an elaborate plan of dispersal became urgent. On Government orders the stocks were divided into a hundred units and stored in the oddest of places. To deprive the *Mirror* alone of its raw material Dr Goebbels would have been obliged to request Reichmarshal Goering's air force to score direct hits on –

A pig farm at Potters Bar;

Harringay dog track;

Farms in Essex, Kent, Middlesex and Herts;

The aquarium at London Zoo;

A gardening nursery at Guildford;

Garages in Essex, Herts and Surrey;

A timber shed at Hoddesdon (find that on the map!);

A Croydon studio;

Horse stables at Epsom.

Cameras and similar technical equipment were scattered, and it was arranged that if the Fetter Lane premises were razed a duplicate plant at Back Hill, Clerkenwell, would take its place.

In all departments the staff was depleted by the call-up, but those who remained became skilled in fire-fighting, first-aid, gas-drill, light and heavy rescue; the office ARP consisted of 367 volunteers all eager to go into action to protect the plant around the clock. And, in their spare time, to write, set, print, publish, and deliver the paper in vans to the railway stations. So fine was their example and so important their results that they were exempted from official fire-guard duties. Their fame spread, other offices nearby applied to link up with the *Mirror* Civil Defence, and before the war ended the sector reached a strength of 700 fire watchers, including the heads of firms and office boys.

The roof was never without spotters, two per shift, whose vigilance won the trust of the men at work below. Did they cut it fine in sounding the alarm? Sometimes yes; but they were never once wrong, and work never ceased until the warning of 'bomb-imminent' was given.

By the time The Blitz of Eighty-three Nights began, with raids from early evening until dawn, the organisation was complete, even to a 1913

Packard fire engine they had picked up for a song and pressed into action until two 500 Dennis pumps were available. The strain of travel to and from home during the incessant raids was relieved by a shift system of '48-hours-on-48-hours-off' and during their duties the men slept on iron bunks, ate and washed in the plant; many evacuated their families and made the office their home.

By these devices, and in this spirit, the *Mirror* was brought out without a single issue being missed.

Reporters who were accustomed to journeying far in normal times to seek out and record human stories discovered that Hitler had arranged that for five years the human stories would come into the office to seek out the reporters; all around them were courage, tragedy and grim humour.

...A big bomb hit a public shelter in the street where the paper was produced, killing about twenty people and injuring nearly as many. First on the scene were the *Mirror* ARP men, and by the time the City of London's squads arrived survivors were being treated at the paper's Aid Post.

...Rescuers went out from the office to work on the Holborn public shelter disaster.

...A sub-editor was handed a news-agency flash-message shortly after several heavy bumps had been felt nearby; it announced that a bus had been hit, a church blasted and set on fire. Censorship deleted the locale, but he guessed that the bomb had fallen just outside the Law Courts and that Fleet Street's St Clement Danes was the church. Out to breakfast early next morning the sub-editor found he had guessed rightly. The vicar arrived, silent and sad. 'Oh, look what they have done to our church,' cried his wife. Within a short time the vicar died, for he had given his life to the famous 'Oranges and Lemons' church: his wife, heart-broken, fell to death from a bedroom window.

...No reporters were ordered out to cover stories during the bad spells, but their rivalry was keen to record the people's heroism during the Battle of Britain; they cut the cards to decide who should cover the latest incident. The photographers had an additional difficulty – they were suspected of espionage as soon as they produced a camera. There was one assignment none liked – Christmas in the shelter, with tired little children chanting 'Hark the Herald Angels Sing' as bombs rocked the surface above them. All the Christmas trees, crackers, toys, and forced gaiety in the world could not soften that sombre picture.

...Humour? It was strictly rationed, though there was some. After the 50-lb base of a landmine landed on the office roof the spotters laughed when they heard that the mine itself, lying unexploded in Fleet Street, cordoned off, guarded by police, had been treated with disdain by a mongrel dog.

The *Mirror* office survived, but the fare-fighting team had their fill of excitement and anxiety.

Cecil Thomas and Guy Bartholomew stand outside the *Mirror* office surveying the damage after the fire raid of May 10, 1941.

One night in September 1940 Birkbeck College adjoining the plant was set on fire in the early hours. The yard was full of firemen's hose and the front wall of the blazing building appeared likely to crash at any moment. Flames swept towards Geraldine House, and danger was so imminent that preparations were made to salvage equipment.

In both the big fire raids on London the wind changed at critical moments. In the December blitz it is said that this trick of the weather saved Geraldine House; in the second the fire-fighters were divided in opinion.

On May 11 1941 the ruins of Fetter Lane smoked and smouldered after a nightmare during which at one time alone the spotters reported fifteen fires on and around the office. They saturated the roof with water, for the blaze from Wyman's premises spread rapidly towards the *Mirror* and one incendiary pierced the roof. 'Action stations' was sounded at 11.40 that night, and the raid did not end until 5.30 on Sunday morning.

There were other grim nights, but never did the telephonists abandon their posts, not even when a V1 burst on Breams Buildings. They carried on – like the comps, the foundrymen, the machine room, the publishing, the circulation department, the van drivers, the librarians, the cleaners, the men in the tape room, the dark room and the process engravers, the subeditors, the cashiers, the commissionaires, the copy boys. They carried on, like the rest of London.

Somehow or other newspapers never seem to find time to record their own brave stories. Perhaps that is just as well, for who wants to hear a doctor describe his own symptoms?

FLEET STREET SCENE

This photograph was taken during a flying bomb attack on July 15, 1944.

31
VD DAY

Stories of VE day and VJ Day have been told in a hundred war books. But not the story of VD Day.

We are about to discuss one of the Great Taboos, and describe how the *Mirror,* living well up to its reputation for cocking a snook at convention, strove to distinguish common sense from the hypocrisy which forever befogs this sceptred isle. We are about to wander once more in the history of this gadfly newspaper into realms of 'Tut-tut', 'I say', 'Look here', but it may be recorded that on this occasion the *Daily Sketch* had the good taste to maintain a ladylike silence and avert its eyes.

The problem was venereal disease.

As far back as 1913, when the subject was banned from human conversation, the paper welcomed the appointment of a Royal Commission of Inquiry and devoted space to its work. In 1942 it conducted a public campaign which, stripped of innuendo and euphemism, told the people what they darn well ought to know.

VD had risen by 40 per cent throughout the country, and the reasons were not hard to trace. The war precipitated a break-up of family life; the proximity of sudden death encouraged a devil-may-care attitude to living; foreign troops and factory workers had money to spend, and young English girls were frustrated by the drabness of the black-out cities. Promiscuity was no longer immodest. Prostitution flourished in London and increased in the provincial cities.

Already the problem had been tackled in the Army, where in addition to the efforts of the medicos, virginal one-pippers from Sandhurst found it was their duty to give lectures on prevention and preventatives to platoons which contained many a father of two or three children. The propaganda was partially successful, though at one time in the Central Mediterranean Forces alone the number of men undergoing treatment would have constituted another brigade in the field.

Until the *Mirror* concerned itself in this disease the sole medium by which civilians were warned and informed were the Ministry of Health's chipped enamel placards, furtively plugged into the walls of underground lavatories.

When the Government became alarmed at the rising VD figures the *Mirror* published eight articles by a doctor on recognition and treatment, then made the knowledge available in a threepenny pamphlet. Under the headline *Forbidden Topic* the leader writer hoped that 'nice' people were shocked by the publicity given to the unmentionable subject.

Some were shocked, but nobody for once accused the paper of sensationalism; the Archbishop of York went so far as to applaud the end-the-secrecy campaign in the House of Lords. A committee set up to consider the Women's Services insisted upon fuller instruction on sexual matters and venereal disease. It conceded that standards of behaviour had greatly changed in the past generation, but rejected as a base slander general charges of immorality against women in the Forces.

There was a curious sequel, of which Fleet Street should be heartily ashamed.

When the Ministry of Health, emboldened at last to come into the open and treat the public as adults, issued an advertisement entitled *Ten Plain Facts about VD,* some newspapers were perturbed and insisted that the Ministry tone down its clear and candid statements. This was too much for the *Mirror:* it devoted a whole page to explain what had happened. Fleet Street, said the paper, had displayed a delicacy 'not hitherto considered its predominant characteristic'. The original wording was published in black type with this observation:

> We have on certain occasions shocked the public opinion and will do so again. The truth on ugly subjects is seldom popular. Those who tell the truth are often regarded as having done something scandalous. So it has been with this newspaper when our only offence has been to speak boldly in advance of conventional ideas. On VD we have played a pioneer role in warning young people of its dangers and pressing on the authorities the urgent need for remedial measures. It has not been easy. Nice people are so easily offended, but false modesty won't stop this disease...

Controversy and the *Mirror* were inseparable. It was in the forefront of the campaigns to end 'glasshouse brutality' – the physical abuse of soldiers in Service prisons – to control the activities of black marketeers, reduce the waste of coal and fuel, prevent the premature return of evacuated children to danger areas.

In 1944 the paper found that the old wound of 1942, the threat of suppression, was troubling it still.

Cassandra, in common with other Fleet Street journalists, had been seconded from gunner and tank regiments to units formed to publish Service newspapers. He was minding his own business on *Union Jack* in Italy when he found himself again the centre of a verbal altercation in the Commons. Captain Henry Longhurst, an MP who had gained a reputation as a golfer and sporting journalist, was stupid enough to ask the War Minister 'whether it was not extraordinary that Cassandra, whose writing helped to get the *Mirror* warned, should now be writing the same sort of thing in an Army paper.'

The suggestion was ludicrous. I state this categorically because it happened that I was in charge of the Army newspaper unit concerned and was therefore militarily responsible for the rebel known as Cassandra. During his Service years a hand was tied behind his back, his feet were lashed, a gag was tightly drawn across his mouth; he dipped his pen in honey. Nor did Connor himself consider for one moment that an official publication could be or should be the vehicle for the individualistic and acidulous writing that had brought him notoriety. It was not necessary for General Sir Oliver Leese to protect his troops by banning Connor's articles from *Eighth Army News:* to discourage him from setting foot inside Eighth Army territory (occupying about half of Italy) was a choice example of military hysterics for which General Leese was also responsible.

To Captain Longhurst's question, War Minister Sir James Grigg replied that he had no complaint. He agreed with Fred Bellenger MP, a future War Minister, that the articles by Cassandra and Frank Owen, then editor-in-chief of SEAC, were helping to improve the troops' morale.

The *Mirror* could not let the insult to one of its absent but favourite sons pass without an exclamation of horror. An editorial entitled

WHAT DO THEY FEAR?

pointed out that the attack was not a new one. 'It is taking the form of a vendetta against journalists who in peace and war dared to speak the truth as they saw it. This is not an affair of petty Fleet Street politics, it is a clash of rival political views', said the leader. 'Cassandra became one of the most popular journalists in Britain; the underdog, the exploited, the rack-rented, the unemployed knew they had found in him a champion.

202

'Who is Captain Longhurst? He is a journalist; at least, he writes about golf. He has the temerity to class Cassandra as a 'subversive writer'. Subversive! In 1938 Cassandra was engaged in a campaign – the denunciation of the Fascist-minded at home and abroad. In 1938 Captain Longhurst was winning a golf championship in Germany... The Commons has too many Longhursts, nearly 200 too many. They should stick to the links.'

In Italy, Cassandra read this defence of his reputation. Then continued with the task upon which that day he was engaged – the writing of a waspish, vituperative, subversive article warning the troops of the dangers of excessive drinking or, as he called it, Demon Rum.

32
DEATH – FOR A HEADLINE

Whatever may have happened in wars of the past, the war correspondent's job in the Hitler affair was no dignified away-from-the-front-line sinecure: Fleet Street's roll of honour bears many names.

Two of the *Mirror's* team were killed in the course of duty, Bernard Gray – they called him 'Potato Jones' after the sea captain who defied the Franco blockade – was in Egypt when he decided to fly to Malta to tell the story of George Cross Island during the full fury of Nazi aerial bombardment. A submarine offered him the first opportunity to get back to Cairo with his scoop. The submarine never reached port. Gray, first journalist to fly with the RAF on a bombing raid to Norway, ended his career at thirty-six. Ian Fyfe volunteered to fly in a glider attack on D-Day against a heavy battery on the coast of France: nothing more was heard of Ian Fyfe.

Those who survived – Healy, Archer Brooks, David Walker, George McCarthy – were caught up in a series of fabulous adventures so they could always be near the sharp end of the war. There were no shop stewards, no restrictionist practices and no days off in those parts; their despatches reminded the workers at home of exactly why guns, tanks and planes needed urgent replacement.

T E A Healy, sub-editor turned correspondent, was an Australian and a rolling stone. The war gave him the facilities to roll with some alacrity backwards through France, Burma and the Western Desert and forwards through Italy to Rome.

Healy's first job was to record the military prowess of the French Army, but he took time off to interview the oily Laval; his paper was thus warned of impending treachery long before the French capitulation.

When the French disintegrated, and the roads were choked with the litter of transport and with soldiers and civilians wearing the heavy scowl of defeat, Healy decided that the one way to reach the ports was to drive towards the advancing Nazis, then double south-west to the Mediterranean to grab a place on a ship bound for England.

His plan worked. Then, in 1940, he nearly lost his life when a bomb exploded in a top-floor flat during the London blitz. Rescuers found him unconscious on the roof with bomb splinters in his stomach, and when he left hospital weeks later they told him: 'We had to double you up to keep you in one piece.'

In 1942 Healy was the only correspondent who saw the closing stages of the East Burma battle. He chronicled the Rangoon retreat which ended on the frontiers of India. He was ensnared with the British in Pegu, burst out through Japanese barricades with a tank crew, and drove 800 miles to China in a jeep through bombing and machine-gunning. And he still had with him his dachshund Mattie, a gift from a wounded officer he met on the Rangoon road.

In November 1942 Healy was writing from the Western Desert after the Alamein break-through: 'To-day I have advanced seventy miles in one hop, the first time in my career as a war correspondent I have ever advanced.' Field Marshal Alexander was experiencing, also for the first time, a similar exhilaration.

To David Walker the war brought a brush with the Gestapo, an invitation to be shot by the Serbs, a period as the enforced guest of the Italians, a grim journey through subjugated Europe, and a marking-time session in which he rubbed shoulders and drank cocktails with elegant spies in Lisbon and Barcelona.

He had written much as a foreign correspondent about the intentions of the Nazis before the shooting began, and the knowledge he acquired of Continental geography was useful later on.

In 1940 he was war reporter with the Greeks, sharing their black bread, olives and brandy in the frozen mountains. Then he moved to Rumania, to be seen off by Gestapo agents just before the Germans marched in. 'There was a Nazi censorship', he wrote, 'and we phoned the stuff to Switzerland, whence it went by wireless to New York and then back to the *Mirror*. In Bukarest all the papers were German-controlled and we read of the coming invasion of England. One headline was LONDON A SEA OF FLAME'.

He flew to Sofia, and a fortnight later the Germans caught up with him there. Nazi troops, thinking that his broad shoulders, thick neck, and bullet-shaped head denoted that he was a Bulgarian, slapped him on the back in the streets.

Walker, the last British journalist out of Bulgaria, travelled to Belgrade in time for the blitz on the Yugoslav capital, but there was no back-slapping here. Serbs arrested him as a German spy – the old trouble of the broad shoulders, the thick neck and the bullet-shaped head – and took him out of the town to be shot. He managed to establish his credentials.

On the Dalmatian coast he typed his despatch on thin toilet paper and handed it to the pilot of a Sunderland aircraft – again the last British Press message out of a conquered land. Italian motorised units trapped him, and he was interned for eight weeks in Italy until his repatriation with a party of British diplomats. They travelled home through the 'dead land of France', neutral Spain and Gibraltar.

The *Mirror* announced Invasion Day with two words in massive type:

DESTINY'S HOUR

George McCarthy landed with British troops on the Normandy beachhead soon after D-Day. Walker, with the American Army, saw the might and menace of Germany crumble in confusion before his eyes.

The minds of men began to turn towards their homes, their families, and their future.

33
FORWARD WITH THE PEOPLE

The basic characteristic of a newspaper is what it says, what it stands for. For many years the *Mirror* had been critical of society as it was constituted and had reflected the discontent and cynicism of the Under Forty section of both sexes. It had still to declare its principles: the vague allegiance to a new sense of values which it had displayed since the Tabloid Revolution did not go far enough.

War brought a maturing of outlook, welded the policy, and elevated the newspaper to the status of a power in the land.

Politically, the *Mirror's* history had been chequered. To the uninitiated, or to a Royal Commission, it would seem odd that a newspaper should be launched with no apparent political policy in 1903, support the Liberals on and off for six or seven years, conduct a violent anti-Socialist crusade from 1920 to 1934, support a Conservative 'national' Government in 1935, and help to throw out the Tories and put the Socialists in power in the next election of 1945.

The pattern is eccentric, but the reason is simply a change of proprietorship or control; inflexibility of policy is in any case not necessarily healthy.

A motor car does not drive itself on the wrong side of the road, or dangerously, or under the influence of drink: the licence to be endorsed or withdrawn is the driver's. A newspaper and its controller are in a similar relationship.

So far as the present generation is concerned the point of interest is why, between 1935 and 1945, this particular newspaper reversed its political outlook and turned Left.

During the war, wrote Roy Lewis in *Persuasion,* 'the *Mirror* went after, and told, *the* story of all wars, the story reflected in every individual experience, in the sense of loneliness, frustration and persecution that rises under tightened discipline and lack of channels for self-expression – the story of 'the man at the receiving end', the man whose job it is to do and die and not to reason why, although fifty years of elementary education and popular newspapers have made him into a reasoning animal. That is the real theme of war, whether expressed in the adventures of Sergeant Grisha, the good soldier Schweik, Private Mulvaney, or the man who 'took it' on or behind all Britain's battlefields from 1939 to 1945. The *Mirror* settled down to fight his fight and air his grouse... As everyone now knows, the *Mirror* was in fact an integral part of Service morale. Its circulation showed it. Troops' welfare organisations swore by it. It was in touch with Service feeling as no other paper. It was the paper of armies without political commissars, of fighting men innocent of ideologies.'

There were further grounds for popularity with the Services. It reflected more convincingly and sincerely than other newspapers the atmosphere of life in the Forces, the weariness of waiting as well as the pride in eventual achievement. Staff men in uniform maintained this link in their articles and letters from the theatres of war.

Question Time in the Mess, conducted by Garry Allighan and later by the future Barbara Castle MP, caused some initial consternation in Whitehall. This impertinent newspaper was now explaining court martial procedure to the troops, advising them on their rights, investigating grievances, ensuring that they enjoyed the welfare facilities to which they were entitled. The War Office learned as time went on that the Press was a useful safety valve, and offered its collaboration.

On the civilian front, too, the paper's sympathies were deep and constant with workers and housewives. Hilde Marchant, Mary Ferguson and other writers ensured that no important aspect of the national effort should go off at half-cock through injustice or lack of recognition.

The *Mirror* considered it had a duty to fulfil to the people in uniform or at the factory bench when the war was over.

Time and experience, and the trials of the conflict, had tempered its brashness. It remained and still remains a popular sensational newspaper, but its sense of purpose became highly developed; it regarded itself as a paper with a mission and it was accepted as such.

It sensed that to millions of people the war meant more, much more, than a calamitous waste of time and human energy. Scots who had never crossed the boundary of their native land, Lancastrians who had journeyed no further than Blackpool for the wakes, country lads who had only once or twice ventured into the metropolis, would return when peace came well versed in the social affairs and habits of the Far East, the Middle East and the continent of Europe. They were the diplomats as well as the soldiers of their country. Men of all classes and temperaments were hurled together and devoted their leisure – and even, by permission, the Army's time – to assimilating each other's viewpoint in smoky Nissen huts, seaside billets and desert tents. The routine of their regulated military lives was alleviated by discussions on the future of their race and of its position in the Cabinet of Nations. For the first time many heard educated lecturers and studied the splendid pamphlets of the Army Bureau of Current Affairs.

In *The Last Enemy* Richard Hillary told how the men of Bomber Command picked up a *Mirror* to scan the news. 'Sir William Beveridge on post-war Britain? That has nothing to do with us as we shall not be alive then. We have a discussion on Jane's legs...'

But the valorous fatalism of Bomber Command was not universal. There were not merely thoughts of death in the minds of infantrymen trudging along the roads of the Continent, or of the men and women awaiting the enemy raiders on lonely coastal gun-sites. Danger was not so imminent to them, and the Beveridge Plan gripped their imagination. At home, factory workers and employers were experiencing what could be achieved when mutual suspicion was allayed by common danger; they, too, had their discussion groups.

The *Mirror* stressed that victory must come before reconstruction, but it began to cater for the newly-awakened social conscience of the masses. It published articles on employment, education, agriculture, housing, and warned that the cost of this second world war within a quarter of a century would mean that Britain could no longer afford luxury imports from overseas.

These problems were broached when the first gleam of victory was discernible in 1943. A vision of the future crystallised into practical policy when Bernard Buckham succeeded Jennings as leader-writer, and before many months the constructive thoughts of 'BBB.' became as widely discussed as the acid strictures of 'WM' before him.

> The time must come [wrote BBB] when the present tired obsolete House of Commons is replaced by one which bears some approximation to the country's real feelings, hopes and ambitions. The Labour Party should prepare for that day, not to aggrandise itself, but so serve the community. But if the Labour Party is to go forward its policy must cease to be sectional.

The customers were being prepared for a fundamental development in political outlook. In 1935 the paper supported Stanley Baldwin's 'National' (predominantly Tory) Government for the last time; when the nation voted again in 1945 the policy was reversed. In 1935 the *Mirror* expected little from the 'Old Gang' and even less from the Socialists: in 1945 it expected *nothing* from the 'Old Gang' and *too much* from the Socialists.

Women were bluntly told they were no longer entitled to dismiss post-war problems from their minds with an 'I-don't-understand-politics' attitude. And on May 11 1945, ten days after the death of Hitler, the *Mirror* erected as its maxim the four words

FORWARD WITH THE PEOPLE

'There are shining victories to be won in the cause of peace and social justice,' said the editorial. 'We shall reach the new freedom not by submitting to economic slavery but by doing our duty faithfully while we lead a full, enjoyable life. The bill has to be paid, but we shall work and we shall play. Happy indeed shall we be if we can feel that our system is fair to all, that a real attempt is being made to bridge the gap between rich and poor. To weld the nation into a contented, busy, prosperous whole is a noble cause. Forward with the People.'

There could be no paradise without work, no security without service. The paper demonstrated its realism the very next day by advocating the most unwelcome of all causes. 'Conscription', it said, 'is a military necessity. It can also be a social virtue; it can make the Army and the nation truly democratic.'

Yet there was some anxiety to point out that a policy of reality did not mean a policy of misery. A second declaration of faith appeared a year later in a discourse upon optimism and the better life, all adding up to a philosophy that struck a note in the hearts of the multitude:

> We believe in ordinary people. So we find in Britain to-day more reasons for being happy than for being miserable. Millions of men and women are sustained in the battle of life by love and good fellowship. For us their adventures are more exciting and inspiring than any story of folly or failure. We rejoice in the good humour, the fine spirit and the success with which the British people are tackling the problems of modern life.
>
> Social evils exist; the *Mirror* exposes them. There is sloth in some high places; the *Mirror* attacks it. But we produce no daily doctrine of misery. We do not play politics with the vital interests of the nation...
>
> We stand for equal opportunities for all children, good homes and robust health for everyone, a high standard of living for all. And we challenge every vested interest, whatever its political colour, that obstructs the realisation of that ideal. We believe that industry must serve

man so that man may better serve mankind. So we strive to smash every artificial barrier to full expression of the moral qualities of the British people at home and in the Commonwealth. That is the faith that defines our daily purpose.

The cat was out of the bag. With this inspiriting mission the *Mirror* was soon to sweep past the *Daily Express* to the world's record daily sale.

Unlike the *Daily Herald,* which is financially controlled by Odhams Press but politically by the Labour Party, it was unencumbered by any obligation to deaden its columns with extravagant publicity for the orations of Transport House masters. Nor was it impelled like the *Herald* to defend the Labour Party right or wrong. The influence of the official and sycophantic Socialist newspaper was therefore swiftly dwarfed.

Here for the first time in British political history was a flourishing, independent, national newspaper of the Left – without the straightjacket of Party overlordship or the enforced insincerities of Party affiliation.

The indignity which the *Herald* endured in 1953, when the National Executive of the Labour movement instructed one of its functionaries to rebuke the editor officially, would never afflict the *Mirror.* It could tell Arthur Greenwood to go to blazes – and would.

34
HOW POWERFUL IS THE PRESS?

Mischievous or otherwise, the part played by popular newspapers in the historic General Election of 1945 cannot be truly assessed until we examine the question of Press power or Press impotence.

Butchers rarely recommend vegetarian restaurants. Politicians seldom expose their own false promises. But, happily, newspaper proprietors and editors are not always reticent. Some are ready to state their claims with a rational regard for the facts; one, at least, is willing to prick the myth.

Witness Lord Beaverbrook.

He informed the Royal Commission on the Press, roguishly, that he conducts his newspapers for the purpose of propaganda, for 'The Cause'. For three decades or more he has preached the gospel of Empire in the columns of the *Daily Express,* the *Sunday Express* and the London *Evening Standard* with all the fervour and ferocity his battery of indoctrinated leader-writers can command. Famous men of the stature of Leo Amery have gloried in the same crusade, and have thus enjoyed his approbation in common with obscure MPs who have said the right thing, accidentally or by design, and have been rewarded with front-page notoriety. Statesmen like Baldwin and Anthony Eden who wandered from the path, or worse still betrayed the faith and turned to Europe, have been subjected to a ceaseless vendetta.

But the Empire campaign failed, and Lord Beaverbrook confessed his failure to his readers. The symbol of his remorse is the chain which shackles the figure of the Crusader on the front page of his daily newspaper.

The first Lord Rothermere dedicated the *Daily Mail* to many causes, some noble, some repellant. Did he exult in a success which evaded Beaverbrook? Rothermere for nearly twenty years pressed for creation of a mighty Air Force, yet Britain went to war in 1939 with a handful of obsolete planes; when he contrived to cajole the nation into accepting Hitler and his unholy clique as a group of energetic Right-wingers, his allegiance to the Germans was viewed in Britain with suspicion; his admiration for Oswald Mosley was received by the public at large with the contempt it deserved.

The catalogue of Press campaigns that failed is not a short one.

The Times enjoys a standing as the world's most influential newspaper, but when it urged appeasement towards the European dictators its reputation withered to the same degree as that of the Chamberlainite politicians it applauded. On a different scale there is the example of agriculture. Both the *Mail* and the *Express* advocated the case for the British farmer between the two world wars, but neither could ever claim that Parliamentary action was effectively influenced or that urban sympathy was truly aroused.

In *War Begins at Home* Tom Harrisson discussed in 1940 the attitude of a section of the Press to war-time rationing: 'When the plan to ration butter and bacon was announced, *Daily Express* posters all over the country demanded 'Stop Rationing!' The Beaverbrook Press launched thereafter an immense campaign against rationing. By selecting reports and by headline emphasis, they gave a highly inaccurate impression both of the facts of food supplies and of people's feelings on the subject. They were largely instrumental in stimulating several bewildering (for the mass) delays in rationing. But a large majority of the people, in all classes, was decidedly in favour of rationing'. A subsequent investigation showed that the proportion was larger after the *Express* campaign than before it.

Mass Observation, a fine research team whose value is its independence, gives further examples of the extent and limits of editorial influence in *The Press – and its Readers*.

When a 'small-sized sample of people distributed all over the country' were asked in 1942 what they thought of the official Government warning to the *Mirror,* this interesting result emerged:

Percentage of readers of these papers in favour of the *Daily Mirror* warning:

	%
The Times	53
Daily Express	45
Daily Telegraph	38
News Chronicle	25
Daily Mirror	12

NB – Although *Daily Herald* readers were very few, *none* was in favour of the warning, the research team reported.

'It is interesting to relate these results to the editorial policy of each paper with regard to the warning', said Mass Observation. 'The *Daily Telegraph* was the only paper wholeheartedly to support the warning, and against it were *The Times, Daily Express, News Chronicle* and, naturally, the *Daily Mirror* itself. Yet only a third of all *Daily Telegraph* readers were in favour of the warning, fewer than amongst the readers of either *The Times* or the *Daily Express.* It seems fairly clear that the immediate editorial attitude of the papers had very little influence on their readers; but the position of the *Daily Telegraph* and of *The Times* is difficult to understand. The majority *of Daily Telegraph* readers were Conservative, their paper was whole-heartedly in favour of the *Daily Mirror* warning – yet nearly half of them held opinions differing from their paper's editorial. Of *Times* readers, on the other hand, only two out of five were Conservative, their paper did not agree with the warning – and yet more than half of them approved of it themselves... Results make it clear that resistance, political as well as more purely emotional, may play havoc with a paper's editorial influence on its readers' opinions.'

Mass Observation conducted a series of tests over the years on the British public attitude to the Russians. 'Repeated check-ups from 1938 onwards have indicated a deep-seated desire to think well of them, even at times when Press opinion of that country (Russia) was at its lowest,' they report. 'Since the end of the war unfavourable feeling about the Russians has been slowly mounting, but always reluctantly.'

This gulf between Press Opinion and Public Opinion is not a British phenomenon; in no country is it more apparent than in the USA. Until the election of Eisenhower as Republican President in November 1952 the Democratic Party was in power for twenty years in spite of the vehement and often venomous opposition of nearly the whole of the American Press.

The truth about the efficacy of editorial opinion is not always understood or acknowledged in Fleet Street, but is not hard to assess.

However profoundly Lord Beaverbrook and Lord Rothermere may have felt about their Causes, the economic benefits and fallacies of Empire Free Trade are beyond most readers' grasp. It was the duty of Mr Baldwin and Mr Chamberlain to provide the planes, and not the responsibility of the public to demand them. The ordinary people of Britain sensed the menace of the Nazi regime long before most of the newspapers and politicians; to tell them that 'There will be no war', as the *Express* did, convinced

214

nobody and merely made that newspaper look foolish. The public knew, once war had come, that rationing was not only fair but inevitable. In just the same way the majority of Americans had the prescience to understand why the newspaper proprietors preferred Republicanism but, thank them very much, voted for the Roosevelt New Deal themselves.

The assumption that newspapers form and control public opinion cannot be substantiated: newspapers sell as much in spite of their policies as because of them.

However brilliantly or subtly it may be conducted, a Press campaign will fail

if it flies in the face of public opinion;
if it advocates a course of action which the average reader instinctively rejects as unfair or imprudent, or
if it deals with an aspect of life beyond the readers' daily experience or interest.

The newspaper with integrity and a ripened sense of responsibility may advocate lines of national action whether its public are interested or not. But a campaign will flourish only

if it is in tune with public opinion which already exists;
if it stimulates with new ideas and information a process of thought which has formed in the mind of the masses;
if it advocates a solution to a problem or scandal which is angering the average reader.

A newspaper may successfully accelerate but never reverse the popular attitude which commonsense has commended to the public. Where there is evidence of wrath over a political or social issue it may effectively direct that feeling against an individual, but the newspaper which lightly or wrongfully apportions blame will find that public contempt will boomerang against itself.

There is, finally, the matter of timing. During a month of ceaseless November rain the British nation is not interested in measures to avert an August drought. Its concern over a potential coal shortage is equally difficult to arouse during a heatwave

Funny people, the British.
Even during elections.

215

'Here you are! Don't lose it again!'

35
VOTE FOR HIM!

The role of the *Mirror* in the social revolution of 1945 will always be much discussed. On the most conservative estimate, a new force emerged in British political affairs.

The Labour Party had twice been in office before, but for brief periods and with no working majority. 1945 was without precedent in its result. Labour, with a majority of 146 over all other parties and factions, decisively attained power and the Conservatives were decisively defeated. Twice only – in 1906 and 1832, after the Reform Bill – were the Tories humiliated to a greater degree.

Let us re-create the political battlefield upon which statesmen and the Press were called to array their forces.

Ten years had passed since the last election, a decade with three Premiers, of whom two were disastrous. Stanley Baldwin had concealed the need for rearmament, and then in November 1936 cynically confessed his motive; the need had become apparent in 1933, but he felt he could not have won an election and retained personal power on such a programme. In 1937 came Neville Chamberlain the appeaser, who occupied No 10 Downing Street until a surge of public disillusion swept him from the pinnacle in 1940 and put Winston. Churchill at the head of the Coalition which won the war.

War disfranchised the people and rendered Parliament comatose. The nation was willing to forego the luxury of democratic disputation in order to save democracy itself, but those who supposed that war also reduced the people to political unconsciousness were soon to see their misjudgment exposed.

There was the sounding board of the 1942 by-elections.

The twin springs of public discontent were disgust over the progress of the war and a suspicion that social reform was being side-stepped; if there had been no electoral truce between the main parties the Socialists would have gained the by-election seats and brought the House more into line with feeling in the country and the Services.

The major stumbling block was the Beveridge Report early in 1943, promising freedom from want. The Report was produced at the instigation of the Coalition Government and became the cause of the only revolt staged by the Parliamentary Labour party during the war-time regime. To them the statement of the Chancellor of the Exchequer was inadequate, and in spite of attempts by Labour Ministers to quell their misgivings all Labour MPs except two recorded dissatisfaction in a vote against the Government.

Towards the end of 1944 Churchill urged that the Coalition should not be broken 'before Nazidom is broken', but he acknowledged that the Parliament of 1945 was unlikely to last the full year. The 'odour of dissolution' was in the air, and the Prime Minister's critics began to hint impolitely that Churchill the war-leader and Churchill the Tory party boss were manifestations of a schizophrenic personality.

The political atmosphere was filled again with the vinegary exchanges of party combat: the war-time marriage was sundered with the rancour which accompanies divorce.

Soon the nation was to hear Churchill expressing the suspicion that Labour Ministers might divulge Cabinet secrets; Attlee castigating such a suggestion as disgraceful; Bevin resenting the claim that it had been a one-man war and accusing Churchill of exploiting VE celebrations for party advantage; Churchill denouncing a statement by Morrison as cowardly and un-British, uncharacteristic of British pluck and good taste but thoroughly characteristic of Mr Herbert Morrison himself; Morrison describing Churchill's rejoinder as spiteful and petty.

Churchill took the initiative and presented his colleagues with an ultimatum on May 18:

1. Stay in the Government and postpone the election until the Japs are beaten; or
2. Resign now and fight the election in July.

Rush tactics? Mr Attlee and Sir Archibald Sinclair wanted an election in the autumn, the Labour leader urging that the delay would not only make it possible to use the new electoral register but would enable the men overseas to study the issues. The Premier resented Mr Attlee's implication that he had abused his position as leader of the Coalition to seek party advantage and rejected forthwith the demand for postponement.

On May 23, twenty-two days after Hitler perished in the ruins of the Berlin Chancellery and fifteen days after the unconditional surrender of Germany's armed forces, Churchill tendered to the King his resignation as Prime Minister and Minister of Defence and requested dissolution. Never had his personal prestige and authority stood higher, for the exultation of VE-Day still thrilled the nation that had been so near, so very near, to disaster only five years before.

Such was the immediate political background of the first post-war election battle in which Fleet Street now joined with enthusiasm.

An examination of the behaviour of the two national dailies with the biggest circulations is rewarding – the *Express* (3,300,006 at that time) and the *Mirror* (then 2,400,000). Neither was officially attached to a political party; the *Mirror* described itself as 'a paper of the Left', the *Express* claimed to be 'independent' but was a paper of the Right. Both campaigned ferociously, but only one successfully.

In their election speeches Mr Bevin and Mr Attlee spoke with some frankness about Lord Beaverbrook's activities. 'I object to this country being ruled from Fleet Street, however big the circulation, instead of from Parliament', said Mr Bevin. Mr Attlee was equally specific, proclaiming that 'the power of great wealth exercised by irresponsible men of no principle, through newspapers with enormous circulations, is a danger to democracy and a menace to public life'.

Neither placed on record his debt to, or distaste for, the *Daily Mirror,* but Mr Morrison, who three years before had threatened to close it down, now praised its 'fine work' and enrolled Philip Zec, whose work he denounced in 1942, to draw propaganda cartoons for the Labour Party.

The *Express,* judging by its election policy, considered that it could best assist its hero Churchill by staging a succession of eccentric and uproarious stunts; never has Beaverbrook been more prolific in drawing red herrings across the trail.

When Churchill in his first broadcast said that the Socialist system could not be established without a political police, a Gestapo, the *Express* magnified his blunder instead of burying it. GESTAPO IN BRITAIN IF SOCIALISTS WIN dominated the front page. The 'Opinion' column asked its readers: 'After ripping the Gestapo out of the still bleeding heart of Germany, will you stand for a Gestapo under another name at home?'

Then followed the Laski affair, a demand for high wages, an appeal to trade unionists to vote Tory, a series of stories designed to show that Labour was torn by internecine strife. And then the campaign against 'controls'; the *Express* could not know in 1945 that when the Tories were to come to power in 1951 the first control to be lifted, somewhat tardily, would be on the importation of parrots – a decision later reversed.

'Hit the cymbal, bang the drum! Walk up, walk up, to the greatest sales circus of all time, the biggest most important General Election in the history of mankind, or the British nation', wrote William Barkley. The *Express* announced that July 5, the day of the voting, was a GLORIOUS DATE; on the day itself the public were informed by that exuberant newspaper that 'We are winning'.

The *Mirror* said what it had to say with sincerity, eschewing the buffoonery which characterised its rivals and speaking with a moderation that was new to itself.

When the news pages announced that 'Labour will build 5,000,000 houses quickly – Bevin tells his plan', the leading article suggested: 'Shall we let him try?' The high-jinks of Beaverbrook were tackled in the same quiescent manner. 'What does it matter what Beaverbrook says?' asked the *Mirror;* his function was to draw the fire of the Labour party.

It did not condemn out of hand all politicians who did not support its policy; on the contrary it commended certain candidates regardless of their affiliation as 'People above Parties'.

The Forces, said the paper, were 'dead against' a rush election, and letters from servicemen and from correspondents supported the point. When a serving man who was also a Liberal candidate advocated the forming of 'The League of Angry Men', mentioning in passing that they expected little or nothing from a Conservative Government, an editorial declared:

ANGRY! AREN'T WE ALL?

The keynote was set by a war correspondent with the Army of Occupation in Germany who announced that soldiers had decided to write home to their wives and mothers to tell them to 'vote the soldiers' way'. The ingenious slogan

I'LL VOTE FOR *HIM!*

appeared for the first time on the front page on June 25, accompanied by this letter from a woman:

> To the Editor,
> *Daily Mirror*

Dear Sir,

My husband won't be home to vote. He is in the CMF. He has fought against the Fascist enemy in Italy and North Africa for a better Britain – now he is denied the chance of hearing candidates give their views for a better Britain.

I shall vote for him. I know what he wants.

He wants a good house with a bit of garden. He wants a job at a fair wage, however hard the work may be. He wants a good education for the children. He wants to feel they won't have to go through what he has gone through in this war. So he wants a Parliament that will be faithful to our alliance with Russia and America.

How my husband would despise these politicians who are trying to scare us and stir up our fears. I can hear him laughing at those who think the world holds no promise for Great Britain unless we return to the bad old pre-war days.

If he and all his pals had not had the courage to laugh and have faith in each other after Dunkirk where would we be now?

My husband would say, 'Vote for Courage'. I shall. I shall vote for him.

(Mrs) C. Gardiner, Ilford, Essex.

The *Mirror* stated that it believed this letter expressed something more than the intention of one woman; it offered advice to all women. 'Is your husband in the Forces, your son, your brother, your sweetheart? Then vote for HIM. Look at his letters again. Make up your mind what, in the circumstances of a General Election, he would have been likely to do if he had been at home. And vote for HIM!'

The campaign reached its climax a few days before the election when the aid even of the Churches was invoked. Reporters discovered that the clergy, or some of the clergy, were also concerned over the plight of absent soldiers, and headlines announced;

CHURCHES CALL ON THE PEOPLE OF BRITAIN

THE FIGHTING MEN DEPEND ON YOU
VOTE FOR THEM

MORE THAN 200,000 BRITISH FIGHTING MEN
DIED TO MAKE THIS FREEDOM AND THIS
ELECTION POSSIBLE

'SURELY THE DEAD AS MUCH AS THE
LIVING SHOULD HAVE THEIR SAY' WAS
ONE PULPIT CRY YESTERDAY

A clergyman was quoted as saying: *'I'll vote for them* – the cry of a woman – is a challenge in the spirit of a Mother Mary dreaming of the world her child would help to create. It is not the cry of a political adherent but the cry of Mother England, tired of the meanness, the pettiness and squalor of partisan politics'.

No hint was given in the 'Vote for Him' campaign as to which way the soldier would like his womenfolk to vote. But the clergyman's ideal of politics without partisanship was not shared by the *Mirror* in other pages. It was loaded down to the Plimsoll line with the case for the Labour Party, and five points were stressed: 1, This was a trick election; 2, Many voters would be disfranchised; 3, The Tory stunts were obscuring the real issues of housing, full employment, social security and international co-operation; 4, The Tory party was not fit to rule; it wanted to go back to the 'good old days'; 5, Controls might be tiresome, but there was no other way in which the public could be sheltered from 'the avarice of profiteers and monopolists'.

One final bludgeon the *Mirror* brought out from its armoury. It had long known the power of the cartoon, and on its staff was the most potent political cartoonist of the day.

Philip Zec worked overtime. Churchill was portrayed looking at two empty picture frames, both headed 'Our Great Prime Minister'. One said: 'who led us back to the good old days of Tory domination, money-grabbing, etc'. The other: 'who led us to victory in the cause of a brave new world'. Churchill appeared in another cartoon as a ship's prow on a pier, with Beaverbrook as Crusader and Brendan Bracken as admiral. The caption: 'We've got a figure-head, we've got an admiral – and if nobody notices we haven't got a ship we shall be OK.'

On July 4 the paper front-paged its last message to the voters from the editor:

> To-morrow the future of Britain and of yourselves is at stake, your hearths and homes, your families, your jobs, your dreams.
> Vote for them!
> For five long years the lusty youth of this great land has bled and died.
> Vote for Them!
> You women must think of your men. For five years you have depended on them. To-morrow they depend on you. The choice is plain: to march forward to a better and happier Britain or turn back to the dangers that led us to the brink of disaster.
> You know which way your men would march.

Vote for Them!

On July 5, it repeated a cartoon by Zec which had originally appeared on VE-Day. A war-scarred soldier, depicted against a background of blasted houses, dead citizens, and the ruination of modern warfare, held in his hand a laurel wreath labelled 'Victory and peace in Europe'. The cartoon was entitled: 'Here you are – don't lose it again!'

Lest the message had still not penetrated, the news pages carried these headlines:

SAYS THEY MUST GIVE UP UNBORN BABY
THEY CAN'T FIND A HOME

WIFE AND DCM. HUSBAND
ROOM TWO MILES APART –
GRANDMA HAS REST OF FAMILY

It was polling day.

36
WHY THE *MIRROR* WAS RIGHT

A Tory cabinet minister has expressed in private the view that the *Mirror* won a hundred seats for the Socialists. The opinion of *The Economist* was that it was one of the decisive influences in the campaign: 'the *Mirror* was perhaps the only popular paper to reach an unconverted public and may have won a lot of new votes for Labour, especially among Service people.'

A third view of much value comes from two Oxford observers who conducted a social study of the election, its machinery, its issues, candidates, contests, Press propaganda, forecasts and results.

Mr R B McCallum, Fellow of Pembroke College and Faculty Fellow of Nuffield College, and Miss Alison Readman, research assistant at Nuffield College, deal extensively with newspaper influence in their survey *The British General Election of 1945*. An interesting comparison, they state, may be drawn between the *Express* and the *Mirror*, 'the two most widely read papers during the election... the papers which may claim to have had the most extensive influence by reason of their huge circulations'. Here are the conclusions Mr McCallum and Miss Readman reached:

THE *MIRROR*

The 'Vote for Him' campaign may well have won more votes for the Labour Party than any other journalistic enterprise. It was calculated to give political expression to the discontent of serving soldiers, who had been deprived of their votes owing to the confusion in the Service Register, and to the more widespread discontent of those soldiers who looked forward to demobilisation without a home to return to. Furthermore it gave an object to large numbers of women who had never before voted, nor taken any interest in politics.

The *Express* and the *Mirror* came to the same conclusion about the wants of the electorate, but they differed in their interpretation of its mood... The verdict of the electorate shows that the *Daily Mirror* was right. The *Daily Express* had misinterpreted the mood of the electorate.

The tone... was elatedly optimistic. It greeted the elector with unbounded enthusiasm and took up all the so-called stunts.

This note of flamboyant tomfoolery was not in harmony with any other elements of election propaganda. The various opposition newspapers, not the least the *Daily Mirror,* had warned politicians that the electorate was in a sober, serious mood, that it was seeking sincerity above all things, and was quick to detect its absence. Lord Beaverbrook disregarded these warnings and aimed at the spectacular... (His) campaign succeeded in achieving notoriety, but it failed to inspire confidence.

The truth is that nothing said or done during the election by politicians or newspapers affected the *nature* of the result, only its landslide proportions. If Churchill had suppressed the *Mirror* in 1942 instead of threatening to do so, there would still have been a Labour victory.

Last-minute machinations of party leaders during the dissolution, the recriminations, the Gestapo and the Laski tricks had little or no effect. It did not matter one whit whether the election took place in July or in the autumn: the issue was resolved beforehand.

The nation was in a radical mood and the *Mirror* campaign succeeded because it was a radical campaign in tune with public opinion. The intriguing point is not that the newspaper was accurate but why it was accurate.

It was not the decision of one man that the *Mirror* should discard its previous Conservative fealty and support a Socialist policy. Harry Guy Bartholomew was never a political visionary, nor did he issue a holy writ which his subordinates must obey or disregard at their peril. Indeed, among his younger directors and editorial executives were men better versed in political affairs; radicals are not born at three-score-years-and-three, which was Bartholomew's age when the paper first urged the Labour Party to prepare itself for office.

The Tabloid Revolution had attracted a new school of young journalists with an unorthodox outlook upon life and affairs in general as well as upon newspaper technique. What the situation required of Bartholomew was not that he should imbue his followers with the vision of a new society but that he should have the courage of their convictions. And Bart had courage. He enjoyed the cut and thrust of the battle and was elated at the victory, but he was not always positively cognisant of the cause in which the battle was joined.

New methods drew millions of new working-class readers who were encouraged to express their views to their newspaper; they did so, and still do so. In fact the *Mirror* became an immense, permanent Gallup Poll Survey of changing mass opinion. Whatever nonsense might be purveyed by politicians in Westminster, the staff of that newspaper were guided by the mood of the public and by their own faith.

Minutes of board meetings at Geraldine House may be searched in vain for a decision officially recording a change of political view. The Labour Party enjoyed the support of the *Mirror* in the 1945 election because it incorporated or appeared to incorporate in its programme more of the aspirations of the *Mirror's* readers and writers than any other political group.

The public demanded a change in the direction of affairs, and the Tory party which Churchill now chose to lead had ignominiously failed. By what right, or folly, did that party or its Press assume that public disapproval was so ephemeral? The war had dimmed but not dismissed the memories of pre-1939 ineptitudes. It was the *Mirror's* frankness since 1936 about these shortcomings that was responsible in part for the bond of understanding with its readers.

There had been Conservative majorities in Parliament since 1918 with the brief exceptions of 1923-1924 and 1929-1931. The Tories might fairly gibe at the pacifist tendencies of the Socialists between the two wars, and therefore saddle the Labour Party with a modicum of liability for Britain's un-preparedness, but the Socialists were never in power in the crucial years. Churchill himself, on October 5 1938, had used the words: 'They (the Tories) left us in the hour of trial without adequate national defence or effective international security.'

They had been fearful of the Russians, yet it was the help of the Russians which proved indispensable in crushing the Germans. They had been courteous to Hitler, obsequious to Mussolini, magnanimous to General Franco: how could they defend such a record of misplaced confidence and downright delusion?

The new generation of voters who were to go to the polls on July 5 1945 for the first time, had lived for the greater part of their lives in a period of national humiliation under the recurring threat of war; they had no reason for gratitude to the Tories and no grounds for confidence in a post-war revival of their regime.

Domestic issues meant even more. There were the records in unemployment and housing. Forgotten in the exigencies of battle? Why should they have been forgotten by the people who had suffered?

These were the subjects on which *Mirror* readers had complained to their newspaper over the years of the gathering storm. No one in Geraldine House was surprised that the same fears were expressed for the future when victory was in sight.

Against this record the Tories had little to offer in the way of a new distinctive policy. Anti-nationalisation, anti-bureaucracy. A better standard of living conditions. Protection of the freedom of the individual. Free enterprise. Plus a dose of unspecified proportions from the Beveridge medicine bottle to be taken only after hard work.

Their one trump card was Churchill, the man whose counsel they had rejected before the war, the giant from whom Conservative Cabinets of pygmies had withheld office until public opinion could no longer be resisted. His beaming countenance now lit up the Tory Central Office placards: 'Vote National. Help him to finish the job.' The old job; not the new job of rebuilding Britain. The electorate were regularly nudged in the ribs to remind them that Churchill more fittingly and effectively than any other statesman could fill Britain's shoes at the peace-making confabs of the Big Three Alliance; no reference was made to the Conservative Party's record over Russia during the negotiations which preceded the Hitler-Stalin Pact.

Churchill journeyed through the land, and what a noble reception the people gave him. This buoyant, tenacious war-horse who had held aloft their spirits through the grimmest days and nights of war deserved and possessed a permanent place of affection in their hearts. They remembered his cocky gait, the pictures and newsreels of his boyish 'V' sign as he walked on chin-up tours through London's ruins. They recalled the sprightly, defiant phrases of his speeches and fireside broadcasts as they awaited the drone of enemy bombers above with diminishing anxiety as he spoke to them. *This is our finest hour... Hitler and his Nazi gang have sown the wind, let them reap the whirlwind... We are waiting for the long-promised invasion – so are the fishes... Never in the field of human conflict was so much owed by so many to so few... I have not become the Kings First Minister to preside over the liquidation of the British Empire... Some chicken, some neck!*

Cheers and tears came spontaneously from the mobs as the triumphal tour proceeded through the land, and there were flags and bunting and wild delight.

Alone among the ecstatic newspaper reports the *Manchester Guardian* struck a sombre note: would those who lined the streets to acclaim The War Leader record their vote for The Party? 'It would indeed be a brave man who would profess to find in their happy faces a reliable index to their political opinions,' wrote a *Guardian* correspondent. 'Had they possessed tails they would have wagged them all together, and still concealed from Churchill and everybody else the secret of their vote.'

At the opening of the Northern tour the same paper had expressed this opinion:

> When Winston Churchill calls up the nation's vast reserves of affection towards him for the benefit of a reactionary party which only lately despised and rejected him, when he divides the candidates at the election into his friends and opponents, when, in short, he asks for a personal plebiscite he is straining loyalty too far.

A survey conducted for the *News Chronicle* between June 6 and 13 revealed that 84 per cent of those questioned claimed to have made up their minds already on how to vote.

Said Churchill of his tour:

> I have been profoundly moved by the kindness and confidence with which I was everywhere received – what can I say to you of the girls and women, whose beauty charmed the eye, or of the old ladies who were brought out in chairs, or waved encouraging flags from high-perched windows?

There could be nothing more genuine than the magnificent reception accorded him, but Churchill forgot that women whose beauty charms the eye are also fickle. He awaited the answer of the nation – 'not with pride or thirst for power; for what have I to gain after all that has happened and all you have done for me?'

The answer was No, No, fifteen million times No[7].

Churchill was as dumbfounded at his defeat as he was on May 10 1940, when by a surge of public faith the fate or future of Britain was placed in his sure hands. Ingratitude? If so, this was the basest single act of ingratitude in the history of mankind. Stunned by the result, Churchill may

---

[7] The Labour Party polled 11,992,292 votes, but just over 15,000,000 votes were recorded against the 'Caretaker Government' which had taken office between the dissolution and the election.

have been pardoned for misreading the significance of his peremptory dismissal: does he understand it in retrospect?

There were unquestionably those whose trust in him as war leader was matched by mistrust in him as politician, and who therefore voted against. But the election of 1945 was a mass censure on the record of the Conservative party and an overwhelming vote of no confidence in its ability to lead post-war Britain.

The debate on the threat to suppress the newspaper in 1942, and the correspondence between Winston Churchill and Cecil H King which preceded that act of precipitous imprudence, now emerge in a new light.

The *Mirror* had advocated the shedding of pre-war Tory Ministers who had failed, a declaration of war aims, a plan for the reconstruction of post-war Britain, a rapid democratisation of the Services, the elevation of younger men in command of affairs. Churchill summarily rejected the advice, rebuking the advocates in private and impeaching them in public.

The passing years established that Churchill was wrong and the *Mirror* right.

In these times of austerity, when humour is at a premium, the following jape should not go unrecorded.

The Tory Central Office became concerned shortly after the war about the paper's new political line. So what did the Central Office do? They confidentially advised their officials in the constituencies to buy not the *Mirror* but the *Daily Sketch*.

The insolent tabloid unearthed this example of wholesome fun and could not resist sharing the laugh with its customers. It 'felt honoured' that it should be regarded as a menace in such quarters. 'As to the *Daily Sketch*', it said, 'we shall be happy if our readers will take a look at the paper. They will then discover what the Tory party really stands for.'

37
TALKING DOGS, FALSIES, AND QUINS

Sir George Waters, member of the Press Commission, was discussing the Mirror *with Mr E R Thompson, Parliamentary Correspondent of the BBC.*

WATERS: The Mirror *is attaching more importance to politics, but there is still a great deal of matter that is not very serious there.*

THOMPSON: *Yes, but there is a good deal of matter in life that is not very serious.*

Noel Whitcomb exercised his talents on a farm and in a bank, for the Government and the film industry, for an engineering firm and a publishing house – with no significant success. Then The Talking Dog met him.

Now it happens that this newspaper we are taking a penetrating peek at is not solely occupied in avoiding suppression and in winning elections. That sort of escapism is all very well. It grips one's attention for the fleeting moment, and gives rise to a certain amount of chit-chat in the places where the famous foregather.

But there are other things that matter in life – record-breaking exhibitionists and daffy animals, for instance; pole-squatters, Siamese twins, teetotallers who die aged 102, the Dionne quintuplets, Nancy Lady Astor, phoney mediums, beer-drinking cats, marathon dancers, Jack Solomons, brides in glass coffins, GIs who change their sex, parsons who hold church services for circus clowns and bless children's roller skates.

And The Talking Dog. The only difference between *The Times* and the *Mirror* is that when the *Mirror* meets a talking dog it believes what it says.

Since Noel Whitcomb, a breezy young man with a boyish face, curly hair, a grin and a carnation met Ben of Royston he has never looked back. Gone for him are the back-breaking days of the harvesting, the temptations of working in a bank and the sluggish progress of the Burnham scale. This story in the *Mirror* changed everything:

> I have just had a conversation with a dog – Ben, smooth-haired fox terrier pet of Mr and Mrs Brissenden, of Green Street, Royston, Herts. Several times he said to me 'I want one'.
>
> My conversation with Ben happened this way. I was sitting in Mrs Brissenden's kitchen sipping a cup of tea when Ben came in. He looked at my cup, then at me, then he sat up and remarked in a rich baritone 'I want one'. I took no notice. I have had many dogs in my time and I know their limitations. Dogs don't talk. Then – and honestly not a drop have I touched this day – Ben strolled right up to me and said it again, clearly, in a low-pitched authoritative tone: 'I want one'.

Ben's photograph appeared in the paper, tests were conducted, and the animal became a nine-day wonder. Scientists had never seen anything like it.

The end of this simple Success Story is that Noel Whitcomb is a success; a man who could make a dog talk could make anybody talk. Whitcomb now writes a jaunty energetic gossip column, which has the essential quality that it is not like anyone else's; he is one of a band of new writers with new ideas who have become prominent in the post-war set-up.

Columnist Whitcomb was introduced as

> 27, an ex-gunner, widely travelled (particularly in London at night). Likes theatres, cricket, people, horses, good food, beer. Cigarettes: ninety a day.

Mirror readers prefer to know the qualifications of their entertainers.

Originality and *joie de vivre* are rated as highly in a newcomer as hard experience.

Joan Reeder, chosen to cover the goings-on at Buckingham Palace during Coronation year, had already enjoyed several Big Moments in covering Royal occasions. When the Queen as Princess Elizabeth visited Paris with the Duke of Edinburgh at Whitsun, 1948 Joan was called to the assignment at short notice. She had no evening gown. So she went to the Opera in her nightdress.

The *Mirror* gleefully announced

A NIGHTIE AT THE OPERA

'Reporter Joan Reeder, rushed to Paris to assist the news coverage of the Royal visit, arrived without an evening frock. Then she got an unexpected chance to be in on the Princess's visit to the Opera – perhaps the most glamorous theatre in Europe. What to do? The allowance of francs available under the exchange restrictions would not stretch to a new evening gown. But Joan's resourcefulness did. Here she tells how she covered herself—and the news.'

In her story she said:

> A girl's best friend is her nightdress... There was a heat wave, but after I had changed into my black and pink silk nightie I didn't feel so darned hot. ...There were New Looks everywhere, though the looks I got were the most old-fashioned in the world... The Princess had her tiara, her jewels, her crinoline to take *off* when she got home. I didn't even have to change. And, you know, I couldn't help thinking that for £2 worth of five-year-old black and pink silk that was a good nightie. And as far as good nighties go – it went.

Audrey Whiting, a bright spark who later took over the paper's New York bureau, and who now writes from Paris, was in a similar predicament at Deauville, but she mentioned her no-evening-dress problem to the Aga Khan. 'By all means borrow one from the Begum's wardrobe, my dear,' he said.

As newspapers gradually grew bigger alter the war the features which rocketed the paper to its top-sale pedestal returned.

Mary Brown became known to the millions with the same rapidity as Noel Whitcomb but in a different sphere. She was a widow who had worked hard on low pay to bring up an only child. Writing with the experience she had acquired as a factory worker and welfare officer, she pleaded for a new sense of personal responsibility and a 'Christian approach to the shaping of the new world'.

One day an article appeared from an unhappy sailor, the story of his wife's unfaithfulness; they called it *So Died my Dreams,* and its note of sincerity encouraged others to send in letters about their own problems.

> For years I have been thinking: If only my husband would say something nice – even call me 'Dear' – I'd faint with shock. He hasn't called me 'Dear' once since the day I married him.
>
> For some time past my chief has been inviting me out to dinner and theatre or cinema occasionally. He is a middle-aged, married man with a grown-up family, and apparently happily married. I am 24.
>
> I am 20 years old and my girl's 18. I am not too confident about her cooking. Sometimes I feel qualms about how my girl will make out. Do you think if I really loved her such things would bother me?

Mary Brown was asked to reply to them and thus began her personal service feature.

The Brave New World still had its love-starved wives, philandering bosses, hesitant swains, roving husbands and jilted fiancées, and they could not be neglected, not at any rate by the *Mirror*. Solving the problems of perplexed humanity was as much its line of business as explaining the dollar crisis or being sued for libel by the Prime Minister.

There were pictures of a charwoman who was given a beauty treatment with startling results. 'If it's glamour you're seeking, search at home', said the story; 'there's real loveliness in our own little homes, but it is hidden under dust-caps, mops and scrubbing brushes.'

The leader-writer occasionally turned from the riddles of war and peace, from Mr Attlee's shortcomings and Mr Bevan's excesses, to discuss such pressing matters as falsies:

> A British actress criticises Hollywood stars on the ground of their artificiality. It seems that they have committed the enormity of wearing false bosoms. Well, what of it?
>
> Where does reality end and make-up begin? How much is padding and how much is girl is surely nobody's business so long as the effect is all right!

A Live Letters correspondent philosophised: 'One good point – they can't ration love.' There was a campaign to get justice for tall women whose need of longer stockings and bigger knick-knacks was ignored by the rag trade. At his eve-of-the-wedding party Prince Philip borrowed a camera from photographer Phil Jackson, saying 'Now it's my turn'; he snapped the Pressmen and his picture was reproduced next morning. Cassandra received a gift from a reader – twenty-two tin whistles; eleven black, seven mauve and four buff. 'Psychiatrists, fetishists and symbolists should enjoy themselves explaining this shrill present', he said. *'I find in the incident a note of gentle madness pleasantly reminiscent of old times.'*

On a cheerless Monday morning a headline informed the waiting world that –

NUDIST COLONY ON TROOPSHIP SHOCKED
SKIPPER 40 YEARS AT SEA

The gentle madness was infectious. It spread in a virulent form to the sports pages where there emerged a new personality in the form of Tom Phillips. He had been one of the backroom boys of whom the public never hears; he was among the team of top executives – Jack Nener, Cyril

Morton, Alex Little, James Eilbeck, Jack Miller – who re-shaped the paper after the war.

Phillips' anonymity was short-lived. To him the limelight of provocative sports-writing was irresistible, and he embarked upon a one-man exhibition of tight-rope walking which engaged his readers' attention. Inseparable from this young man's literary style was his family's underwear: sometimes it became difficult to tell whether he was writing a column or running a laundry.

He chose boxing as his subject, for he had written a lively pre-war novel on the ring, *Cheap Glory*. On the morning of the second Woodcock-Savold fight he wrote: 'I hate sitting on the fence, and if I wagered on boxing I would put my shirt on Bruce Woodcock; I'd put the house, furniture, car, everything down to my wife's second set of undies on the Doncaster lad'.

Savold stopped Woodcock in four rounds, and readers sent in dozens of shirts to cover the tipster's nakedness. Unabashed, Phillips began a feature called Shirt Tales.

When he put his shirt on Randolph Turpin to beat Sugar Ray Robinson he was one of the two – the other was John Macadam of the *Express* – who forecast correctly. But it was the Turf which brought him his greatest exhilaration. He gave Nimbus 7-1 as winner on his first venture as a racing tipster, following it up in 1952 with the Derby first and second, Tulyar 11-2 and Gay Time 25-1. His wife supplied the third, Faubourg II at 100-6. No tips were needed from his son and six daughters: they were no doubt willing to help, but it wasn't strictly necessary.

The tipster Phillips could not emulate was George Kreiner, who began his racing advice a few months after the paper's first number and continued until 1948. As 'Bouverie', Kreiner named five Derby winners in ten years, then added two more; he gave a glittering Lincoln-National double and selected five winning tote doubles in four days. One woman reader won £720 and wrote in to say so.

The wisdom of forty-four years on the Turf was distilled into this twenty-five word caution to punters: *'Never back a horse unless you know it is fit and fancied, and never bet in doubles, trebles or accumulators. They'*, said George Kreiner, *'are the bookmakers' delight'*.

Thus the *Mirror* re-affirmed the tenets of the 1935 Tabloid Revolution and regained the gaiety, originality and effervescence which had been dimmed or doused during the war years. It did not forget that the only certain way in which a newspaper may avoid having its head in the clouds is to keep its ear to the ground.

Miss C A Lejeune could look after the intellectuals in the *Observer:* when Reg Whitley went to the cinema for the *Mirror,* he went, as he had done for nearly thirty years, as an ordinary man-in-the-street, seeking a laugh, a cry, and above all 'a good story'. And Donald Zec knew that millions of fans were still interested in their favourite stars' views on love, divorce and crimson toe-nail polish.

Nor did the paper forget the efficacy of shock tactics on matters of importance.

Instead of dutifully printing the honeyed bulletins from General MacArthur's HQ, like the rest of the newspapers, David Walker blew the nonsense sky-high with an article headed:

FAIRY TALES FROM KOREA: THE WORLD
IS NOT GETTING THE TRUTH

Every year the *Express* publishes acres of words about the Empire, but nothing more effective than the dash made by John Walters and Trevor Williams to the West Indies to expose strong-arm rule in Trinidad; their reports led to questions in the Commons and action by Parliament. Sydney Elliott's visit to South Africa produced an early warning of the true significance of Malan's accession to power.

The Government were startled when photographs were front-paged of Greek police and soldiers riding through Greek towns with the severed heads of rebels swinging alongside their saddles. 'The British soldier stationed in Greece,' said the story, 'objects to being forced to witness brutalities that outrage his conscience as a citizen and his traditions as a soldier.'

The shock was effective. The Foreign Office demanded an assurance from the Greek Government that these savageries would cease.

38
SENSATIONALISM

The fault of the *Mirror* in the eyes of its critics is sensationalism. But instead of denying the charge or disguising its deportment with some tactful euphemism, this newspaper, damn it, admits that it is sensational, just like that. Sure it is sensational, and is proud of being sensational.

Some of the top men associated with it over the years have been engagingly candid. Kennedy Jones was a newspaper doctor whom Northcliffe called to the bedside during the *Mirror*'s sickly first year. 'There's nothing to beat a good meaty crime for increasing circulation', said Dr Jones in his best bedside manner; he prescribed politics and sport in that order, as other efficacious medicines.

Cecil Thomas, editor from 1934 until 1948, was equally unreserved in the reply to *World's Press News* already quoted in full in Chapter Eleven:

> What is a newspaper? Does it or does it not exist to provide news for its readers? Are news editors to be asked to say that this or that is not 'nice' news? Are they to be constantly acting as nursery censors?
>
> The truth is that the London Press is already too niminy-piminy.
>
> A newspaper that wishes to retain the confidence of its readers should be ruthless and remorseless in revealing all the news it can get.

Thomas practised what he preached. When in the early stages of the war there was heavy criticism about the defences of Singapore I asked him if it was true that the Governor, Sir Shenton Thomas, was his brother. 'Yes', he said, 'but if he is in any way entitled to a share of the blame let him have it.'

In evidence to the Royal Commission on the Press the frankness about sensationalism became positively brutal. Cecil Thomas and I, representing the *Mirror* and *Pictorial,* accompanied Bartholomew to the session held on February 19 1948. The volcano did not take lightly to being kept waiting in the corridor. 'Why don't we go?' asked Bart. 'It's not a court of law.' We were also a little concerned at how he would react to the solemnity of the proceedings inside, for he was notoriously not susceptible to schoolmasterly cross-examination.

What happened? Bart charmed them all with his bluntness. When Mr Hubert Hull CBE endeavoured to ascertain how and why the *Mirror* allocated its space in the way it did he was treated instead to a homily on sensationalism.

Said Bartholomew: 'If you will look at the *Daily Mirror* every day next week you will find we will be more sensational than we have ever been for six days running. You will think we have gone mad. We are going to do something in a very sensational way.' The Commission smiled, but Bart was referring to the *Mirror*'s bold plan to teach the economic facts of life to the public at large; the campaign received much praise.

However generous the critics might be in ladling out their alarm and dismay at such a policy, none can say that the paper is equivocal or pharisaical in declaring its intentions. Any doubts, if they still existed, were dispelled by Silvester Bolam who succeeded Thomas in the editorship from 1948 until February, 1953. Bolam expressed himself thus in a front-page manifesto:

> The *Mirror* is a sensational newspaper. We make no apology for that. We believe in the sensational presentation of news and views, especially important news and views, as a necessary and valuable public service in these days of mass readership and democratic responsibility.
>
> We shall go on being sensational to the best of our ability...
>
> Sensationalism does not mean distorting the truth. It means the vivid and dramatic presentation of events so as to give them a forceful impact on the mind of the reader. It means big headlines, vigorous writing, simplification into familiar everyday language, and the wide use of illustration by cartoon and photograph.
>
> To give two examples. We used it during the war to launch a VD campaign which was vitally necessary for the welfare of the Forces when a too-timid Government Department had the facts and dare not use them. We used it again when the national economic crisis demanded an explanation to the public which the Government, not expert in these matters, was leaving bewildered and ill-informed.
>
> In both cases we were widely praised for our enterprise, and our methods were at once followed by the Government. Today the needs for sensational journalism are even more apparent. Every great problem facing us – the world economic crisis, diminishing food supplies, the population puzzle, the Iron Curtain and a host of others – will only be understood by the ordinary man busy with his daily tasks if he is hit hard and hit often with the facts.

Sensational treatment is the answer, whatever the sober and 'superior' readers of some other journals may prefer.

As in larger, so in smaller and more personal affairs, the *Mirror* and its millions of readers prefer the vivid to the dull and the vigorous to the timid.

No doubt we make mistakes, but we are at least alive.

Bolam's contribution to the paper's technique was this presentation of heavy subjects in digestible form. During his editorship no paper did more to bring home the realities of life to the multitude.

Except for ten months with the *News-Chronicle*. Bolam had been with the *Mirror* since 1936; he came south from the sturdy school of journalism which flourished on Tyneside, and had worked there during the boisterous but brief 'battle of the evenings' provoked by Rothermere's intervention in provincial journalism.

He was a friendly, wiry bird with a dozen interests – books, art, music, the countryside – outside the immediate problem of newspaper production; to him came the honour of occupying the editorial chair at the exciting moment when the *Express* was outdistanced in the race for the world's biggest daily sale.

Bolam graduated in economics at Durham University in 1926, and was under no misapprehension about the difficulties of bringing the economic facts of life within the understanding of his readers. 'It's not simply what happens and what people think about it – it's what they *feel* about it, too,' he would tell his staff. 'If we can get that into the page, well, we've got something that counts.'

What did the *Mirror* do when travellers came back to Britain with tales of 'juicy steaks' across the Channel at a time when food in Britain was at its scarcest? It invited four workers and their wives – men in mining, farming, steel and textiles – to put on their best suits and bonnets and accompany a member of the staff on a tour of Holland and Belgium to see for themselves.

When Lord Boyd Orr warned of the gravity of the world food situation Bolam again demonstrated his method of mass-education. He asked a member of his staff to produce a nostalgic article on bacon and eggs, a delightful piece of writing which really sizzled; you could smell 'em being cooked. Next day the main feature article carried a picture of the bacon-and-eggs epistle with the reproving headline:

TO THIS GREEDY FOOL
– AN ANSWER

The reasons for the bacon-and-eggs shortage were hammered home and it was hoped that every reader who had smacked his lips the day before now felt a downright cad.

Similar methods were used to explain the dollar crisis, with the moral that only harder work, increased production and less money spent on inessentials would improve Britain's position. The *Guardian* recorded this pat on the back: 'This is an admirable enterprise on the part of a popular paper and contrasts strongly with the attitude of some of its rivals towards the crisis. The idea of giving exceptional space to a major subject is a healthy development of post-war journalism'.

A woman in Watford cancelled her order for the paper, not because the *Mirror* was wrong, she explained, but because she and her husband could not do more than one day's work at a time or go without any more food or goods. 'Your articles no doubt make clear exactly how things are', she wrote, 'but what the hell can anyone do about it?'

An excursion into sensationalism in a different direction in 1949 deprived the editorial staff of Silvester Bolam's company for three months. If a newspaper is inaccurate or unjust it is the editor's duty and privilege to accept responsibility; in certain circumstances the editor may go to gaol.

The case concerned the arrest of John George Haigh, acid bath murderer. Without directly linking Haigh's name, the *Mirror* published details of 'vampire' murders in London and indicated that the police held a man in custody.

At 9.42pm on March 3 a confidential memorandum was issued by Scotland Yard saying that any statement about the matter might be held to prejudice a fair trial. Three editions of the paper of March 4 were already on their way to the North when the editor was summoned to the office by telephone. The story was amended and mention of a confession deleted; later it was admitted that an error of judgment had been made in not excluding the whole of the 'vampire' material.

Proceedings were taken before a Divisional Court presided over by the Lord Chief Justice, Lord Goddard, for contempt of court. They rejected the explanation and expressed the view that there had been a deliberate pandering to sensationalism. Bolam spent three months in Brixton and the paper was fined £10,000.

Frank Owen, a newspaperman of wide experience and a former editor of the *Daily Mail,* referred to the case at Oxford in a discussion on the general difficulties that beset editors. Said Owen: 'When Fleet Street

239

editors talk of the case they could say with sincerity: 'There, but for the grace of God, go I.'

The truth is that the *Mirror* had perpetrated a blunder.

The law of England is that once a man is charged with a crime anything published in a newspaper which may tend to prejudice his fair trial constitutes a contempt of court; the veto holds good until the expiry of the period during which the accused may appeal against his sentence.

That law is a good law. The editor took his punishment and did not complain.

When Bolam was in gaol a large black Rolls-Royce drew up outside the forbidding gates of Brixton. Chairman Guy Bartholomew, Philip Zec and I stepped out and rang the bell. Said Bart to the chauffeur: 'We will be out in twenty minutes.' Zec added: 'I hope.'

We filled in a form with the name of the occupant we wished to see, and were led by a warder with a ring of keys past 'trusties' with swill-bins and prisoners exercising in the yard.

In the distance we saw Bolam talking to an official through a grill. Then he was brought by a husky but pleasant warder to a chair in the corner of a small room set apart for interviews.

It was necessary for him to see a letter concerning *Mirror-Pictorial* business of urgency, but first it had to be read and examined by his 'keeper' and then by a uniformed censor in the corridor. They weren't accustomed to editors at Brixton – might be dangerous people. Bolam eventually studied the document, signified his agreement, and the dialogue ended with an awkward exchange of small-talk.

Outside the gates Bartholomew said:

'I bet that's the first and last meeting of newspaper directors ever held in gaol.'

Bolam some years later philosophised on his experience. 'The point about Brixton is that most executive journalists never get time to think,' he said. 'If you have eighteen hours a day by yourself with yourself for three months you have a valuable opportunity for reading objectively – for clearing your mind, for setting your sights. It was a most valuable experience.'

SILVESTER BOLAM (Editor, 1948-1953)

'The *Mirror* is a sensation newspaper. We make no apology for that.'

39
MIRROR VERSUS *EXPRESS*

In one particular newspaper building the resurrection of Northcliffe's 'newspaper for gentlewomen' was followed with the same keenness as in the *Mirror* itself. The palace of black glass which is the headquarters of Beaverbrook's *Express* was filled with ambitious and astute executives who had experienced too much of savage rivalry not to recognise the emergence of a competitor on the horizon.

They had snatched the blue riband of the 'world's largest daily sale' from the *Daily Mail* by building up a news service which outstripped Northcliffe's own creation, by pitching their product on a note of human appeal not previously attempted in British journalism, and by embarking upon enterprises which made other papers look moribund in comparison. They deserved their success and regularly told their readers that they were proud of themselves.

They understood, too, the infidelity of public support. The pace in Fleet Street is set by the strongest; the multitude follow the band.

Arthur Christiansen, editor of the *Express,* was producing a brilliant 'sub-editors' newspaper' in which style and rewriting were everything. Information and opinion were served piping hot and pre-digested, a form which might not stimulate the brain but was pleasing to the palate. The paper was respectability itself. There were certain things in the *Express* code of morality which were not and still are not mentioned.

People were divorced in their columns in the same droves as in other newspapers, but it was hard to discern just why they had parted. For the darker offences the sentences were duly recorded, but no evidence was published which might embarrass or intrigue the most innocent member of the family.

Political and financial brigandry were lavishly and exultantly reported; national disasters, particularly adventures or rescues at sea, enjoyed 'saturation coverage' in crisp, shampooed English. But the subtler and baser foibles of human nature did not, so far as the *Express* was concerned, exist.

The policy was energetically pursued. The paper was aiming at the man with a car in a garage. Or with a car without a garage. Or with a garage without a car. At any rate, their target was the chap who *wanted* a car *and* a garage.

Those bright young men with their rubber gloves and white coats in the glass-house news clinic knew the *Mirror* was a menace. Here was a newspaper pitching its appeal on a broader human basis to the millions who made cars and built garages rather than owned them. They divined the folly of the *Daily Sketch* campaign against the *Mirror* – 'All the News and Pictures Fit to Print'; it had merely driven the public to the paper they hoped was publishing the news and pictures not fit to print. Their own reply of 'no salacity' was negative, inadequate humbug.

It was not the supposed salacity that worried them so much as the whole tempo of the lusty tabloid. Calling a spade a spade was likely to appeal to the British; here was a paper with the nerve to splash on its front page a story of the rise in price of cups of tea from 2d to 2½d, a paper more concerned with the aspirations of the humble than with the triumphs of the great. There was the irresistible appeal of the tabloid's gaiety and frankness to young readers.

The dilemma of the *Express* was complete. It could not become less sophisticated or it would lose its special ranking with advertisers: it could not become more sophisticated or it would lose its sale. Could it stand still?

The circulation battle between the two papers was the most stimulating the country has seen.

The *Express* became concerned about the pulling and holding power of its rival's strip-cartoons. Several national newspapers had plagiarised the presentation of the *Express*. The trouble about the new tabloid was that it aped nobody's style, it copied nothing; nor did it seem to care if it was scooped on an item of news which did not fit in with its general approach.

'*Express?* I never read it,' said Bartholomew. Nor did he.

There was room for both papers: there had to be. But with the *Express* in second place. The public were invited to witness a heavyweight contest, with two interventions by the Government as newsprint referee, and with the fight finally stopped at the end of the fifth round.

ROUND ONE, JANUARY, 1934:
  Express 1,709,904 *Mirror* 732,448
(In 1934 the *Mirror* reached the bottom of its circulation curve.)

ROUND TWO, JANUARY, 1941:

243

Express 2,511,333 *Mirror* 1,685,821
(In 1940 the Government had 'pegged' circulations to conserve newsprint.)

ROUND THREE, MARCH 1947:
  Express 3,706,669 *Mirror* 3,446,856
  (In September 1946, for the first time in six years, publishers were allowed sufficient newsprint to issue all the copies they could sell.)

ROUND FOUR, JULY, 1947:
  Express 3,879,938 *Mirror* 3,741,971
  (In this month circulations were again 'pegged', the *Mirror* returning to 3,700,954.)

ROUND FIVE, JANUARY, 1949:
  Express 3,985,336 *Mirror* 4,187,403
  (Newsprint was again released and the sale of the *Express* passed, though later that paper topped 4,000,000.)

In June, 1949 the *Mirror's* sale topped four-and-a-half-million, and in the first six months of 1951 averaged 4,514,339 daily. It seemed possible at that date to reach the five million target, but rising production costs enforced an increase in the selling price from one penny to three halfpence on May 7 1951. All newspapers lost circulation, but the *Mirror's* sale of 4,381,395 in July-December 1951 kept it in the lead of the race. G W Budden, circulation manager for twenty-two years, died before the battle for supremacy between the two most popular British newspapers ended; he was cheated out of the moment of exhilaration only by one month. Had there been no reduction in sizes or restriction of sales he would have been in at the final count.

The system by which paper-rationing was based on pre-war circulation figures was unjust. It benefited stick-in-the-mud newspapers and imposed a penalty on enterprise and success.

A *Mirror* editorial pointed out that all over the world men in the Forces had been able to read the paper – 'though stupid attempts were made by officers in some places to ban us'. Now, when these men were coming home, they could not get the paper they wanted; it was sold out everywhere by 8am. 'We could sell half-a-million extra, but our potential readers have to put up with the second-best', said the paper.

This was not a boast. For when restriction on sale was temporarily lifted in September, 1946 circulation instantly mounted by more than a million.

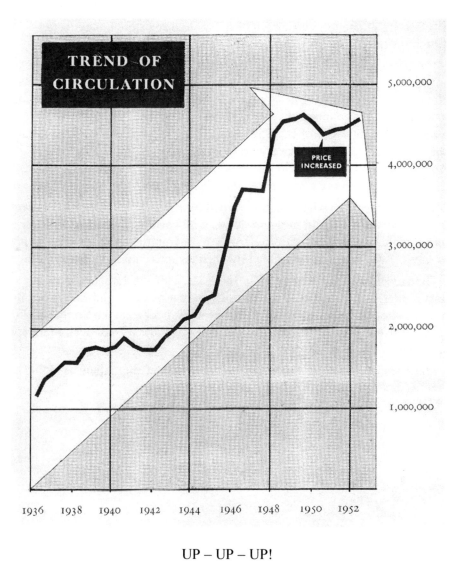

TREND OF CIRCULATION

PRICE INCREASED

5,000,000

4,000,000

3,000,000

2,000,000

1,000,000

1936 1938 1940 1942 1944 1946 1948 1950 1952

UP – UP – UP!

'An immense power for good lies within its grasp.
Can it increase its popularity and at the same time raise its prestige?'

In Fleet Street itself the influence of the tabloid registered in expected directions but in curious ways.

The *Daily Sketch* sought to change its fortune just after the war by changing its title to *Daily Graphic;* it began to use more liberally the bold black type which the public now associated with the *Mirror.* But nothing, said loudly, is even more obviously nothing. The ruse failed. A rose by any other name... In December 1952, Lord Kemsley threw in the towel and sold his unhappy paper to a combination formed by the present Lord Rothermere and Mr W Emsley Carr's *News of the World.* It again changed its title and once more became the *Daily Sketch.*

Serial strip-cartoons had been regarded by the *Express, Mail* and *Herald* before the war with mild derision. Now, with varying success, they entered into nimble competition with each other to buy up the artists who remained or new ones who could be cajoled by cheques into entering a fresh field.

The *Herald* did not stop at this. In 1952, with the Labour Party out of power, it felt it could at last relax its pretentiousness and cease for the nonce to be the *Telegraph* of the Left; besides, it was uncommonly short of readers. It resolved to purloin, as far as it dare, the *Mirror* technique and spread it over a larger page.

The latest report from the bedside indicates that the patient is doing as well as can be expected.

40
CHURCHILL SUES FOR LIBEL

There was some concern among politicians, and a certain amount of interest among combatant newspapers, over the course the *Mirror* would take in the 1950 and 1951 General Elections. It would have been discomfiting to the Socialists if the readers of the paper with the greatest sale had been disillusioned by Labour's record in power; there could be no alibis, for the Party enjoyed a mammoth majority.

The line-up of the rest of the Press was prescribed, but the *Mirror* had been at some pains to remind the Socialists of its independence. A communion of thought and principle existed and still exists, but the paper had been curtly critical during the Government's period of office.

In 1947 it viewed with dismay the lack of fire in Clement Attlee's leadership and complained the Government had failed to devise a general wages policy. Morcover – a view which would have been heresy at the *Herald* – it attributed this omission to intimidation by the Trades Union Congress.

'The *Mirror* is not and never has been a blind supporter of any Government', said a leading article. 'We are of the Left and so is the majority of the nation. But the time has come for everyone to turn to work of national importance'. A timidity had been detected in the imposition of essential measures; there was a campaign against restrictive practices by workers and employers.

In 1949 public patience reached breaking-point over recurring trouble at London's docks and the effect on food supplies. Harold Hutchinson, son of a trade union leader, had gained a reputation as writer and broadcaster on industrial affairs. He was the paper's expert in trade disputes, recognised as an objective observer with the tenacity and integrity to ferret out the facts.

Hutchinson concluded that among the strike's causes was the failure of the Labour movement to bestir itself sufficiently to give men a spirit of social purpose that would drive out old sournesses and discontents. Sir

Richard Acland, MP for Gravesend, advocated in the House a 'thorough-going inquiry, not by people whom the dockers will feel are tame stooges, but manned by people like the industrial correspondent of such a paper as the *Mirror*".

When the election came the paper re-emphasised its independence but commended Labour to the electorate as the party which had kept its promises and carried out a fair policy.

'We believe that the ideas of social justice which Labour-led Britain has shown the world are the only effective answer to Communism', said the *Mirror*. So far as the cold war was concerned, its belief was that Britain's future was safest in Labour's hands.

Labour had been in office five years during a period in which honest government demanded austerity and other unpopular measures. The pre-war Tory record, so important a factor in 1945, was now fading from public memory. A swing of the political pendulum was inevitable, and the man to convince was the marginal voter, the floating vote which was not pledged.

The principal page was placed at the disposal of Maxwell Fyfe for the Tories, Megan Lloyd George for the Liberals, and Herbert Morrison for the Socialists. In text and pictures the two centre pages underlined the contrast between full employment and the mass unemployment of the between-war years.

The Ruggles strip-cartoon became a 'discussion group', educational and informative, impartial to both sides until polling day was near: this was the first time a strip had been used extensively in an election.

When Tories made promises about petrol a front-page splash told THE TRUTH ABOUT PETROL and the leader of that day exposed THE STUNT.

The election of 1950 resulted in a photo-finish and the Parliament of the long nights: so small was Labour's majority that a three-line whip was practically a permanent necessity.

Interesting verdicts on Press activities came from two impartial observers, one British, one American. Following the pioneering example of R B McCallum and Alison Readman in 1945, H G Nicholas, Fellow of Exeter College Oxford, probed the campaign in *British Election of 1950*. He spoke of the *Mirror*'s 'skill and calculated thunder', and of how it held its fire.

'If any paper directed its policy to cornering the marginal vote, that paper was the *Mirror*", wrote Nicholas. 'The short editorials were admirable at reducing the issue to the lowest level of pungent comprehensibility. There was no time or space wasted on exploratory argument or exposition of the other side's case before knocking it down. At the same time the pro-Labour or anti-Tory statements were unattached to any official or party line. Finally, towards the end of the campaign, there was a most effective blending of text and photographs designed to add pictorial weight to the political arguments.'

Nicholas found that most British national dailies were avowedly partisan in their politics and their election reporting was frankly coloured by their sympathies, but that since these were rarely concealed any intelligent reader knew what to expect from the paper of his choice. The *Mirror* was not alone in practising the black art of bias.

The second observer was Charles Higbie, Assistant Professor of Journalism in the University of Wisconsin. In an American quarterly he wrote that the *Mirror* was Labour's most valuable asset in the mass-communication field – 'it was the only huge circulation newspaper whose policy was likely to convince the independent or undecided voter'.

In power for the second time since the war, the Labour Party began to show symptoms of the same indisposition which afflicted the pre-war Tories – a reluctance to jettison proven failures before they tarnished the Government's reputation as a whole.

In British political life this protection of flops and hacks has reached the proportions of a restrictionist practice exercised by all Cabinets. Under the precept of collective Cabinet responsibility the most astounding duffers are kept at their Ministerial posts regardless of the country's interests or of public censure They are paid handsome salaries for doing nothing, or worse still for doing the wrong thing, and nobody seems to care except the taxpayers. The Old Gang who in the past have shown themselves ineffective but amenable lock out the New Gang who might be vigorous and productive.

Now that the Socialists were clearly up to the same old caper, the *Mirror* bluntly told Mr Attlee early in 1951 that the Cabinet should be reconstructed to make way for back-benchers who had displayed ability: 'there are at least half-a-dozen Ministers who have made no mark'. The paper sensed that public confidence was waning, and said so. It was right, for within a year the Tories were in power.

The *Mirror* was on the losing side, but it again conducted its campaign in the oblique manner first evolved in the 1945 election. Attlee visited America to discuss the atom bomb, and eight months before the Election the paper asked:

WHOSE FINGER DO YOU WANT ON THE TRIGGER WHEN THE WORLD SITUATION IS SO DELICATE?

When it repeated the question dramatically on its front page on polling day, that was too much for Churchill. Here was this paper in his hair once more. Was the implication behind this wretched idea that he relished war, that he was a 'warmonger'?

Churchill immediately issued a writ for libel, and for months after his victory at the polls there was much speculation as to whether the new Prime Minister would go into the witness box to be cross-examined by Sir Hartley Shawcross, whom the *Mirror* had briefed for its defence.

But the case did not go before the courts. There were negotiations and a settlement, and the paper, expressing its regrets, said that its statements and pictures were never intended to suggest that Churchill did not dislike war and the possibility of war as much as the *Mirror* itself disliked them. It was agreed to pay the Prime Minister a sum to cover his costs and a contribution to the Church Army Churchill Homes for Elderly People, a charity named by the distinguished plaintiff.

Rumours in Westminster and Fleet Street that an immense amount of money changed hands were not correct. The total sum was £1,250, and at Churchill's request the whole was sent to the Homes.

41
LIVE LETTERS, ALIVE O!

Congreve wrote, in *The Way of the World:*

> *O' Ay, letters.*
> *I am persecuted with letters.*

He would have made a very poor editor, for the newspaper which is not persecuted with letters is failing to hold the lively and active interest of its readers. What would Congreve, for instance, have had to say to the young lady who presented the editor of the *Mirror* with this problem:

> I have read your advert stating that you will help us girls. Well it's like this. I am 30 years of age but people tell me I look 18 and although, not wishing to be conceited, I have got a pretty face, I have not got a young man as my nerves are rather bad and I am always trembling. There is a man I am very fond of in fact I would do anything on this earth for him in fact I have, but unfortunately he is a bachelor twice my age. The other day he said he had heard something about me and insulted me with vile insinuations and would not give me any reasons and having a bit of a temper slapped his face and then he promised me he would kill me in fact he was going to strangle me and afterwards thought better of it so went and found a knife. You see I have not got anybody to tell these things to and it is a relief to tell someone. I still love him in spite of all this what is your opinion of the case if I had another man to take his place I should be OK but I haven't.
> Hoping you will help me.
>
> P.S. He has not said in so many words that he loves me but the way he used to kiss me and hold me spoke more than words to me. He doesn't believe in marriage.

They tell me that Miss H. (whose signature was on the letter) was not accorded the dignity of public print, but hers was among the 3,758,441 letters to reach the newspaper in the past ten years. Just under a million-

and-a-half of them were sent to Live Letter Box and more than a quarter-of-a-million to 'Viewpoint'.

The idea, gentlemen, is this: *If you want to blow off steam you can do it right here.* And a glance at the *Mirror* any day will indicate the sort of steam the public is pining to blow off.

Mrs G L Pritchard wants to know why people aren't fined for indiscriminate coughing and sneezing in public. 'DMV.' is concerned because women have much larger mouths than they used to have, asks is it due to smoking? 'Worried', of Ashton-under-Lyne, has heard that eating salt makes one look old, and she loves salt. 'Wondering', of Sheffield, wants to know the origin of the phrase 'He died in the odour of sanctity'. Mr R H Knight wants to know what right anyone has to condemn or patronise youth when all we have given them are social, commercial and political morals of a descending order and an increasing fear of atomic annihilation. Mr R Gardiner wishes to point out that the 'explanation of the fact that women hate each other is a classic example of familiarity breeding contempt'. And then comes Miss A M of Hammersmith, to inform the waiting world that she wears four-inch heels to work and four-and-a-half heels in the evening; her friends, she says, think she's crazy, but 'Oh, boy! have I plenty of boy-friends!'

One man who knows what makes the *Mirror* readers tick is Edwin Radford, who varies his journalism by writing detective fiction and compiling dictionaries of fact and fable. The 'Old Codgers', who reply to the readers who write to Live Letter Box, are intimate friends of his. Their identity has never been disclosed, but their experience of life, it seems, is varied.

One day their postbag contained these two letters:

> Sir: – I have to give a lecture at a working men's club next month. Would you please send me a detailed explanation of Einstein's Theory of Relativity? The lecture will last about half an hour.

The second came from a woman reader who related how, on the first night of her seaside holiday, she went up to bed some time after her husband and undressed in the dark. As she was about to slip into bed she whispered: 'Isn't it lovely, Charley, being here and listening to the sea?' A strange voice answered her: 'Yeah, honey. But I reckon it wouldn't be so lovely if that husband of yours happened along!' She had climbed one flight of stairs instead of two and undressed in the room of an American visitor.

252

It is, nevertheless, the humanity rather than the humour of the *Mirror*'s letters which is their chief characteristic. The paper makes friends. No letter is left unacknowledged. Every reply begins with 'Dear Mrs So-and-So', never with 'Dear Madam' or 'Dear Sir'. No reply to a woman reader is ever sent out typed: women, say the Old Codgers, do not like typed letters – they are too impersonal.

A message reached Live Letter Box from a widow. All she had in the world was her son, aged twelve, and the doctors had told her that he was dying. She had been a reader of the paper, she said, for many years. Could she please ask other readers to pray for his recovery?

The plea was published, and the next week letters arrived from other readers with the same request. From that simple beginning grew the present Saturday feature...

YOUR PRAYERS ARE ASKED:

For a father with cancer... For 'Little Lady... For a brother... For Derrick, aged ten... For Enid, aged twelve...For a darling mother... For Bob... For a mother critically ill... For Linda, aged five, with TB meningiti ... For Germaine, going blind... For Gilbert... For a dear sister and mother... For Jessie, given only a few weeks to live... For the Rev G Davies, of Tredegar... For the mother of four children.

When the prayers had appeared for some months Dr Temple, then the Archbishop of Canterbury, wrote to the editor: 'I had never expected to see in a lay newspaper a corner devoted to the asking for prayers. Nothing but good can come from so noble a gesture.'

Today the *Mirror's* list of names for whom prayers are asked is placed each Sunday on the altars of more than a hundred places of worship in the country.

The achievements of Live Letters have been quite remarkable, and anyone who believes that the Helping Hand is rarely extended by the public in these days of economic stress should have a word with Edwin Radford.

During the war six women readers offered their wedding dresses and two hundred Service brides, beaten by the clothing coupon shortage, borrowed them in turn.

A woman in hospital pleaded for a lemon. The answer was – 507 lemons.

When the war began readers were asked to build up a blood bank for air raid victims; 4,000 immediately volunteered.

A letter came from 'Margaret's mother' as a tribute to her young daughter. It said that the family had hired a radio set; unfortunately illness had descended on them and the child had heard her parents stating that they could no longer afford the rent of the set. On the following Saturday Margaret, who had been out of the house each day for an hour or two, handed over the sum of £1 – earned by running errands and scrubbing – with the remark: 'If daddy can put a bit more to it, mummy you can keep the set.'

A wealthy reader telephoned on the morning the letter was published asking for the address of the family and the amount of the rental; he would, he said, pay a year's subscription. He found that the mother had TB, that her case was considered hopeless and that her death was only a matter of time. He called in the TB officer – the verdict was the same.

The mother was convinced that if she could go to Switzerland she would be better, but the doctors said she was too ill to travel. The reader chartered an aeroplane and nurses and flew the mother to Switzerland to a German doctor using a new method of treatment. Her English doctors said that a cure would be 'a miracle'.

Two years later the woman came home, completely cured, and now she is enjoying a normal life.

The gesture cost the reader £2,000, and the *Mirror* never fails to hear from the woman each month.

A missionary wrote that after he had read his *Overseas Mirror* he stuck the pages on a large wooden frame outside his church. His flock of natives could not read but they liked the pictures.

The trouble was that the paper was in rags almost within minutes. Were there any readers who would post on their copies of the paper?

In went the letter with a 'thank you' in advance from the Old Codgers.

Eight weeks passed by. Then came an SOS from the missionary. *Mirrors* had been arriving at the rate of six sacks a day for the last month, and as they had to be carried by bearers for some miles the Post Office people were playing the deuce.

Before the supply could be stopped two hundred sacks had been carried home by the native population.

The same big-heartedness plagued a war-bride in Canada. 'Why is it?' she asked 'that when I left England all my friends said 'be sure to write and we'll send you all the news'? I have written regularly, but not a single letter has come in reply.'

Her address was published as a reminder to her friends. There came an air mail letter a month later: she had not as yet heard from all her old friends but she had received 3,000 letters from *Mirror* readers giving her news from practically the whole of Britain.

Is it any wonder that the GPO know where to deliver an envelope addressed to 'The Old Codgers', with no further detail?

One, from Brompton, London, bore a drawing of two old men with beards – nothing else.

It arrived safely.

42

WHO OWNS THE *MIRROR?*

'Nothing in the newspaper world has intrigued the public so much as the ownership of the *Daily Mirror.*'

The words came from Lord Camrose. He was not attempting to magnify the enigma; indeed, no personality in the newspaper industry has done more than Lord Camrose to explode the financial myths.

'The ownership of the paper,' he continued, 'has been discussed in Parliament and made the subject of conversation in political and other circles on innumerable occasions. The so-called mystery developed first of all when the paper was being attacked before the war for the nature of its contents. It arose again when the *Mirror* took a violent anti-Government line during the war. In my booklet *Newspapers: Their Owners and Controllers,* printed first in June 1939, I showed that there was no mystery of any kind about the ownership, and I repeated the statement when speaking in the House of Lords in the Debate on Censorship.'

Lord Camrose brought the facts up-to-date in his post-war book *British Newspapers and their Controllers,* where the remarks just quoted appear.

Lord Beaverbrook has not been so altruistic in his attitude; in fact, he created the mystery. He has always regarded the subject as ripe for Machiavellian merriment. The *Mirror* was challenging and thrashing his *Express* before a joint audience of more than eight million onlookers; it was to his advantage to impute veiled ownership.

Beaverbrook's newspapers are not anti-Jewish. They have made a public declaration to this effect. Furthermore, they have recently recorded their distaste over the terms of the *Observer* Trust, which rigidly exclude a Jew or a Catholic from the editorship of that newspaper. Nonetheless, the Londoner's Diary of the *Evening Standard* has regularly insinuated that the *Mirror* is controlled by Mr Israel Sieff, of Marks and Spencer: the frequency with which the paragraph appears, usually prior to the shareholders' annual meeting, suggests that it is kept in type and feather-dusted at the appropriate times.

There were frequently large dealings in *Mirror* shares on the Stock Exchange, and in 1943 there were rumours in the City and in the Press that a syndicate was busily buying shares in a bid for control on behalf of Sir Hugo Cunliffe-Owen, Philip Hill and J Arthur Rank.

Foolishly, the *Mirror* never told the public the facts. Two references only to its ownership and control appeared in that newspaper since the death of Northcliffe.

The first was in 1936, briefly stating the severing of Lord Rothermere's connection, though not disclosing the reason for his action: he was, quite simply, appalled at its new racy policy and outraged in particular at its attitude to sex. The second appeared as an editorial on March 24, 1942, when the paper was arraigned before Parliament:

HEARST AND OURSELVES

On the day following the Home Secretary's statement about the *Daily Mirror,* we published by a fortunate coincidence an article from our New York correspondent, John Walters.

In that article our correspondent said that the American newspaper proprietor Hearst – famed for his hatred of England – had been 'debunked too often and too effectively to be taken seriously by any but moronic nitwits'.

He added that Hearst is 'an embittered old man whose mind still lingers in an age that is long past'.

These blunt descriptions should be enough to refute the suggestion made by an MP on Thursday to the effect that Hearst is part owner of the *Daily Mirror.*

We are resolved not to reply to criticism, but we feel free to state – if the above quotations are not sufficient evidence – that at no time in our history has this evil man Hearst had any financial or other interest in our newspaper.

The grim joke was that at that very moment the interests of William Randolph Hearst were in debt to an alarming degree for newsprint acquired from the Anglo-Canadian Mills, Quebec, the *Mirror* group subsidiary.

He was not the rich uncle; he was the impecunious nephew.

When the present *Mirror* company was formed in 1920 it was controlled by the first Lord Rothermere. He was not a director but he held the largest block of shares, and it was agreed that due regard was to be accorded to any instruction he might send.

This situation was terminated in 1931 by an exchange of letters between Lord Rothermere and John Cowley, then *Mirror* chairman:

The *Daily Mail,*
Editorial Department,
Northcliffe House, E.C.4
16 March, 1931

Dear Cowley,

Referring to our conversation this morning, I wish you to understand most clearly that, in future, the *Mirror* and *Sunday Pictorial* businesses are entirely under your and your colleagues' control.

As my responsibility, I am reserving for myself the Associated Newspaper Company, Northcliffe Newspaper Company and the *Daily Mail* Trust. This is sufficient for a man of my age.

Yours very faithfully,

R.

P.S. Of course, all vacancies on the Boards of the two companies will be filled by you.

17 March, 1931.

Dear Lord Rothermere,

I have to acknowledge your letter of yesterday's date, and I quite understand and appreciate what you say. You may rely upon me and my colleagues to carry out to the best of our ability the affairs of our two Companies as thoughtfully and carefully and as satisfactorily in the future, as we have always endeavoured to do in the past. You pay me a very great compliment, which I very much appreciate.

Yours sincerely,

John Cowley.

Five years after this congenial exchange of confidence Cowley was not so appreciative of the very great compliment. On Lord Rothermere's instructions 80,000 out of 80,450 *Mirror* shares held by the *Daily Mail* Trust were sold. John Cowley left a note saying that he regarded this sale as a reflection on himself and on the directors of the paper. He was at that time a director of the *Daily Mail* Trust, but refused to attend the relevant meeting.

Rothermere, believing that the paper was going 'broke',' realised his personal holding sporadically on the Stock Exchange; the shares thus passed into the hands of a large number of investors, many of whose identities changed year by year. In a few instances only were the holdings of considerable size.

In 1939 the *Mirror* Chairman was able to inform the shareholders that no individual shareholding was sufficient to constitute a controlling interest.

During 1947 a significant readjustment took place involving the *Mirror*, the *Pictorial* and Associated Newspapers Ltd, which controls the *Daily Mail* group of newspapers.

Rothermere died in 1940, but what remained of his financial empire survived him. One of the incongruities was that the companies publishing the Left wing *Mirror* and *Pictorial* were in a position to exercise influence over the Right wing *Daily Mail*. The companies had extensive shareholdings in the *Daily Mail* and General Trust, which was heavily invested in Associated Newspapers; they also had large shareholdings directly in Associated Newspapers.

This financial interlocking was undesirable, particularly for the new Lord Rothermere. To strengthen his group's independence it was necessary for him to manoeuvre into a position where an exchange deal would be possible; he therefore made large purchases of *Mirror* shares over several years.

The rearrangement was the result of direct negotiation between Rothermere and Harry Guy Bartholomew, representing the *Mirror-Pictorial* boards. On March i, 1947 it was announced that:

> 1. The block of shares held by *Mirror-Pictorial* in the *Daily Mail* and General Trust had been sold to Lord Rothermere.
> 2. The Trust itself had acquired the large share-holdings which the *Mirror* companies owned in Associated Newspapers.
> 3. At the same time the *Pictorial* largely increased its holding in *Daily Mirror* Newspapers Ltd.
>
> The *Pictorial* company had bought from Rothermere the block *of Mirror* shares he had been building up.

The result of the rearrangement was of consequence to all parties. Rothermere became one of the biggest shareholders in the *Daily Mail* Trust, which by the same deal increased its holding to 50 per cent of the share capital of Associated Newspapers and thus obtained control of the *Daily Mail* group. So far as Geraldine House was concerned, the *Pictorial's* holding in the *Mirror* expanded to such a degree that it became beyond question the owner of the largest block of shares, approaching 20 per cent of the Ordinary capital.

In 1949 the Press Commission reported that there were over 9,000 Ordinary Stockholders; apart from the mutual holdings of the two companies there was no single *Mirror* holding larger than four per cent.

To-day there are 10,300 Ordinary Stockholders, with the largest single holding apart from the *Pictorial*'s standing at under 3 per cent of the issued Ordinary capital. Holders of Ordinary Stock at 3ist December, 1952 were split as to: –

7772	Stockholders holding	up to		£100 Stock			
1822	..	..	between	£101	..	and	£250 Stock
496	..	..	..	£251	..	..	£500 ..
95	..	..	..	£501	..	.	£750 ..
40	..	..	..	£751	..	.	£1,000 ..
26	..	..	..	£1,001	..	.	£1,250 ..
25	..	..	..	£1,251	..	.	£2,000 ..
4	..	..	..	£2,001	..	.	£2,499 ..
20	..	..	..	£2,500	..	and	over.

Holders in excess of £2,500 collectively represented ten per cent of the Ordinary capital of £1,400,000. Bank Nominee and Trustee Companies hold a total of nearly £113,000 Stock.

In spite of the danger point reached in circulation in 1934, the financial record of the company has always been impressive, and often a source of delight to its stockholders.

Between 1927 and 1935 it paid over £2,000,000 in bonuses, and before the recent war regularly returned a dividend of 30 per cent on the initial Ordinary capital. During the First World War it paid 60 per cent; during the second, in spite of the heavy Excess Profits Tax, it maintained 10 per cent on a much larger capital.

The immensely strong position of the *Daily Mirror* to-day as the world's biggest-sale daily newspaper ensures the future financial success of the company.

43
YOUNGER MEN

In the closing week of December 1951 the paper's affairs were again the subject of speculation. Bartholomew had just returned from a visit to Australia and there were reports of directors' meetings and top-level changes.

On December 21 this announcement appeared in *World's Press News:*

> A resignation which has occasioned surprise in Fleet Street by reason of its unexpected nature took place last weekend when H Guy Bartholomew relinquished his chairmanship of the *Mirror* and *Pictorial* companies.
>
> In an official statement issued by the respective companies it was said that the resignation had been accepted with regret. Mr Bartholomew, aged 67, wrote that his advancing years and an earnest desire to promote the advancement of younger men had moved him to this decision. He would, however, remain as a director until the end of the financial year.
>
> Cecil Harmsworth King has been elected chairman of both companies in his stead.

Thus ended The Bart Legend. Those who knew the qualities of the personalities involved expected the succession of Cecil King; he became at fifty the head of the greatest mass-circulation daily newspaper – 'an exciting and terrifying prospect', said the *New Statesman,* 'even for the nephew of the great Northcliffe'.

The *Guardian,* which for years had taken an interest in the progress of its rambunctious contemporary, the *Mirror,* commented: 'Mr King prides himself on his ability to take the long view and to choose the right men. He has great financial shrewdness. He is a strange man to find at the head of a tabloid newspaper. But he is a nephew of Northcliffe and has inherited the famous forelock and perhaps something of his uncanny flair for knowing what interests the common man and – more important – the common woman'.

Over the years Cecil King had a certain influence upon his predecessor which the older man resented. It was this resentment which clouded their association and occasionally led the volatile Bart to plan petty discomfitures he would later regret and reverse.

King wholly admired Bart's gifts and knew that the eruptive nature was a corollary of his genius. There were therefore no false courtesies or insincerities on the occasion when he was first able to pay public tribute; he acclaimed the great services of the retiring chairman, his decisive influence on the paper's development, his organising zest and inspirational leadership. King's respect and affection were profound for the active volcano on whose slopes he had resided, sometimes uneasily, during the two rousing decades in which the *Mirror* had been transformed.

The public are entitled now to know something about the new man.

When King turned up at 10 Downing Street on January 30 1941 to try to persuade the Prime Minister that the Cabinet could not claim a monopoly in patriotism, Churchill scrutinised his austere, reticent visitor with some surprise. A Wykehamist ('Manners Makyth Man'). A student of constitutional history who took honours at Christ Church in the same vintage period as Anthony Eden. A quietly-spoken man whose greatest sin was a voracious appetite for the books Churchill himself relished.

Outside the Cabinet Room the Bofors were banging away in the third or fourth air raid of the day. 'Well', said Winston, *'you* look innocent enough!'

Beaverbrook, at a hush-hush conference held to discuss what the Press should say, or should not say, about the curious materialisation of Rudolph Hess in Scotland, mistook Cecil King for the equally tall Gordon Beckles. 'Speak up, Gordon,' he shouted.

The forbidding factor in King's relationship with the rest of the human race is his aloofness, and few have vaulted the stile. Once over, old hikers report, the going is harder. His demands on his colleagues are exacting, but his trust, once placed, is complete.

A sycophantic biographer would be hard put to it to explain away the more ascetic aspects of his emotional make-up. The aloofness could be accounted for by the shyness which afflicts other men of unusual tallness, but there can be no such pleasing vindication of the imperious gusts which on occasion cause trepidation in those around him. The world at large rarely experiences the warmer, friendlier facets of his personality, and his occasional joyous guffaw betrays a sense of humour unsuspected by new acquaintances.

CECIL HARMSWORTH KING (Chairman, 1951-1968)

At fifty he became the head of the greatest mass-circulation daily
newspaper – 'an exciting and terrifying prospect,' said the *New Statesman*,
'even for the nephew of the great Northcliffe.'

Cecil King is essentially a Harmsworth, scion of a family which has enjoyed genius, wealth and power, and more than its share of tragedy.

His uncle Lord Northcliffe, creator of popular magazines and important newspapers, a diviner of future events, was unsurpassed in his time as patriot or as pioneer in a dozen fields. His ability, not his desire or avarice, attracted millions of money. But Northcliffe died insane at the age of fifty-seven. The twilight of his life was clouded by Napoleonic fulminations about his 'great armies' and by warnings that his approach would have the effect of an earthquake. He informed the stationmaster at Boulogne that an attempt had been made to assassinate him. He issued orders that editor Henry Wickham Steed be turned out of his office at *The Times* by the police. He ordered that a commissionaire at Carmelite House be appointed to supervise the 'coarse, abominable and offensive' advertisements of the *Daily Mail*. He demanded on his deathbed that *The Times* should record his passing with 'A full page and a leader by the best available writer on the *night.*' The wish was granted, but – a final bitterness – Northcliffe died at 10.15 in the morning and a rival newspaper, not his own *Evening News,* scooped the world with the announcement. He was the greatest figure, said Lord Beaverbrook, who ever strode down Fleet Street.

In the 1914 war another uncle of King's, the first Lord Rothermere, lost two sons, and King himself lost two brothers, the first in action, the second while returning to school in a mail boat torpedoed in the Irish Sea. He has four children of his own, but a year ago adopted the three children of a nephew who with his wife was killed in an air crash.

It is not surprising that newspapers are in his blood, for his mother, who came between Northcliffe and Rothermere in age, was quite a factor in the Harmsworth business in the pioneering days of that money-spinner *Answers;* she ferreted out material for feature articles from the archives of the British Museum.

After leaving Oxford, King worked for a year on the *Glasgow Record.* Three years in the advertisement department of the *Mail* under Grimaldi preceded a transfer in 1926 to the *Mirror* – the result of a peremptory and unexplained order from Lord Rothermere. He became a director in 1929 and eventually advertisement and financial director.

These experiences, together with his association with editorial reforms in the *Mirror* and *Pictorial,* gave him a deep knowledge of the newspaper industry. But his patience and diplomacy did not spring from the rough and tumble of the Press game. There was another influence in his life, the academic education planned by his father, Sir Lucas King, a civil servant in India who became Professor of Oriental Languages at Trinity College,

Dublin. There King spent his early years until the austerities of Winchester led to Oxford. While at Christ Church he met Agnes Margaret Cooke, daughter of Canon G A Cooke, Regius Professor of Greek; she became his wife in 1923.

From this admixture of scholarship and Harmsworthian tenacity there emerged a personality of ambition, tempered by an impassive exterior which some find disconcerting.

After the effervescent, headstrong Bartholomew, those working for the first time in close contact with the new chairman of the tabloid papers are puzzled. I have seen hardened debaters emerge from their first conference bearing the demeanour of men who have failed to penetrate the sound barrier; small comfort to them to hear of other pilots killed in the attempt.

Bartholomew could play Macbeth, Iago or King Lear at a moment's notice – singly or simultaneously – and frequently did; but there is nothing theatrical about his successor. Black type and sensationalism seem alien to Cecil King's make-up, but closer inspection reveals a twinkle in the eye and an impish desire inherited from Northcliffe to put the cat among the pigeons.

The first quality which emerges is his talent for organisation. He abhors untidiness and unpunctuality; he likes 'to get things done'. His is the scientific approach, for he thinks in the realm of facts and figures, cause and effect; once he has found out for himself and drawn his own conclusions, nothing short of aerial reconnaissance, artillery bombardment and infantry attacks with close fighter support will entice him to change his mind. His verdict, as a rule, is immutable: few can persuade him to conduct a re-trial.

His second quality is judgment. While his shyness makes it difficult for him to establish any very satisfactory relationship with anyone, the sense of 'being apart' is an aid to reaching a cool and correct assessment of men and situations. In the maelstrom of journalism the long view is a steadying influence.

In his closest colleagues he seeks the qualities he lacks himself.

On the production, labour relations, and advertising sides he values the easy affability of his deputy chairman John Coope, a man whose practical shrewdness has won him many friends in the industry. In his editorial staff he prizes flair.

King was associated with Bartholomew in the Tabloid Revolution from the beginning. When John Cowley and Wallace Roome applied the brakes, King's diplomacy and if necessary his vote were in favour of the new methods. This attitude shocked Uncle Rothermere, for the later years of

Harold Harmsworth's life, which had been fully enjoyed in all its aspects, were conducted in an atmosphere of prudery and self-righteousness often apparent when a rich man is about to enter the gates of heaven. In speaking of the new *Daily Mirror* he used the same rude epithets which had been used against Northcliffe and him by critics of their new *Daily Mail* in 1896.

King's first opportunity to apply his experience in a more or less unfettered manner came with his appointment as editorial director of the *Pictorial* in 1937. That paper was still suffering from the malaise from which the *Mirror* had escaped in 1935; during ten years its circulation had declined by one million to 1,200,000 or less. He took the writer of this book from the feature editorship of the *Mirror* to the editorship of the *Pictorial,* and under the new regime the sale of the paper rose above five million – the swiftest expansion in British newspaper history. *Operation Pictorial* was the final testing of Cecil King for the responsibilities he now holds.

In his laconic, candid opinions of other people lie the clues to his own character and aspirations.

'That goose will never be a swan.'

'Dishonest.'

'A catalogue of his shortcomings would be tedious.'

'No fire in his belly.'

'Not ruthless enough.'

'You can see he is the boss of the department as soon as you walk into the room.'

'He is not the sort of man you would hand your hat and coat to.'

'Yes' – and this is the highest accolade of all – 'he *could* set the Thames on fire'.

It is now known in Geraldine House that when the new chairman sets out on a business mission overseas and asks an executive or a writer to accompany him, the travelling companions are under surveillance, their characters are being weighed, their knowledge probed.

They return with stories of how the tall man fought his way through a mob of four hundred excited gibbering Indians to buy a ticket for a native cinema in Bombay, of how he stopped his car in the Australian bush to pick a wild flower; of his request to a pagan tribesman in Nigeria to demonstrate his prowess with a bow and arrow in return for a handsome tip; of the loud guffaw that astonished a group of nude African villagers when King discovered that the total equipment of their mud hut consisted of a sleeping mat, an eating bowl – and a selection of Hollywood pin-ups stuck to the wall.

By these methods, and by a lifetime of reading, King has built up a vast fund of knowledge on almost every subject – except music. It was this knowledge which made him a successful chairman of the British Film Institute, a position he held for four years.

In the first year of his newspaper chairmanship he travelled to Australia, Nigeria, the Gold Coast, Germany, America twice and Canada once. He understands in detail the operations of the *Mirror-Pictorial* subsidiary, the Anglo-Canadian Pulp and Paper Mills Ltd, Quebec, for he has been a director of that concern since 1944 and helped to reconstruct its financial affairs; for several years before he became chairman he was responsible for the firm's newspapers in West Africa; he made two journeys to Australia to study the potentialities of the Melbourne *Argus,* its allied publications, and an extensive radio network. In all these operations the parent companies have interests; for the project whose headquarters is in Geraldine House is now world-wide.

What effect will King have on the *Mirror?* It is early yet to tell how large his name will be written when the history of that paper's next fifty years comes to be recorded. All that Fleet Street knows is that there are signs of great activity.

Other newspapers expected a period of consolidation; more developments have in fact been considered during the past eighteen months than ever before in the company's story. It was also speculated that there would be a deviation in the *Mirror's* political allegiance, a move to the Right: this was based on the erroneous assumption that one man and one man alone had turned the paper Left.

The politicians watched with interest when King took over.

Mr Aneurin Bevan was pained when the *Mirror,* which had often in the past applauded his vigour and his work for the masses, turned upon him with wrath in 1952 when the machinations of the Bevanite Group threatened to tear the Labour Party wide open. The *Mirror* and its sister paper the *Sunday Pictorial* questioned Bevan's motives and suspected a bid for personal power. But a man of action strongly appeals to a newspaper of action, and it was doubtful whether the breach would exist for long.

Mr R A Butler, Tory Chancellor of the Exchequer, was delighted at the spectacle of the *Mirror*-Bevan split. 'As for the *Mirror,* it is constant to Jane and unfaithful to Nye', he told his constituents; 'I suppose it is a very healthy state for it to be in and long may it continue'. Mr Butler's pleasure was short-lived, for a few months later the paper was lambasting his unhappy colleague, Mr Oliver Lyttelton, for his mishandling of the Mau Mau disturbances.

In 1953 the paper was urging the Labour Party to cease internecine warfare and declare its new objectives. It even praised a Tory Budget.

It was by then apparent that under the new chairmanship the *Mirror* would not only remain an independent paper of the Left, but would be free of influence by individual politicians. King privately exchanges ideas with all factions of all parties, and thus ensures that his top executives are inoculated against pressure from any one source. A personal collaboration of the type which existed between Harry Guy Bartholomew and Herbert Morrison is therefore unlikely to emerge.

There is evidence that the paper is becoming more, and not less, political; that it is striving for new methods of presenting serious news as well as light and human items. With a circulation of more than 4,500,000 the *Mirror* claims to be read every day by 11,000,000 people. An immense power for good lies within its grasp.

Can it increase its popularity and at the same time raise its prestige? If this goal is achieved Cecil King's name will be fourth on the list of the men who have decisively influenced the *Mirror's* history.

The first was Lord Northcliffe, who founded it and built up its circulation to over a million. The second was the first Lord Rothermere, who killed its reputation as a newspaper but created the company's financial structure with a genius unequalled since his death. The third was Bartholomew – brilliant, truculent, mercurial – whose own pulse beat in unison with the pulse of the masses and who drove the paper so far and so fast that for the second time in its fifty exciting years it carries under its title the magic words –

THE BIGGEST DAILY SALE ON EARTH
FORWARD WITH THE PEOPLE

CORONATION ISSUE

Circulation director Alfred Ashwell was able to announce in June that
the Mirror had broken a new world record by publishing more than
7,000,000 copies of its Coronation issue.

CASSANDRA

At His Finest And Funniest

For thirty-two years – with time off to go to war – William Neil Connor wrote his famous column in the London *Daily Mirror* using the nom-de-plume of Cassandra.

Its crisp and trenchant sentences set a new standard for columnists, copied everywhere but never bettered. Cassandra's rivals envied him many things but, most of all, the cut and thrust of his style, so devastating in chopping opponents down to size.

Three decades was a long time to occupy a pulpit in public print.

Cassandra did it brilliantly, with never a yawn from his daily congregation of fifteen million. But he observed in his first column after four years away on active service: 'As I was saying when I was interrupted, it is a powerful hard thing to please all of the people all of the time...'

To satisfy Cassandra's fans – and the more literate of his enemies – in one book is a powerful problem indeed. These pages can only skim the cream of his genius. Included is some of his finest and best remembered writing side by side with certain jocular items (much relished by *Mirror* readers) such as the saga of the Goose-Egg Man, the Fourteen Day Soup, and Cassandra's private collection of Square-Wheel English.

This is a book for all occasions and all moods, a delight for those who love to see their own language used stylishly, a primer for young writers who are willing to learn from a master of words.

Published by Revel Barker Publishing
ISBN: 978-0-9558238-2-4

CRYING ALL THE WAY TO THE BANK

Liberace v Cassandra and the Daily Mirror

By Revel Barker

It's the Liberace Show...! – *Time* magazine

'bizarre and hilarious... Nothing shorter than a paperback could achieve a balanced report of the brilliance of the advocacy and summing-up.' – *Hugh Cudlipp*

CASSANDRA: 'a literary assassin who dips his pen in vitriol, hired by this sensational newspaper to murder reputations and hand out sensational articles on which its circulation is built.' ... 'as vicious and violent a writer as has ever been in the profession of journalism in this city of London.' – *Gilbert Beyfus QC*

CASSANDRA...On Liberace: They all say that this deadly, winking, sniggering, snuggling, chromium plated, scent-impregnated, luminous, quivering, giggling, fruit-flavoured, mincing, ice-covered heap of mother-love has had the biggest reception and impact on London since Charlie Chaplin arrived at the same station, Waterloo, on September 12, 1921...He reeks with emetic language that can only make grown men long for a quiet corner, an aspidistra, a handkerchief and the old heave-ho. Without doubt he is the biggest sentimental vomit of all time. Slobbering over his mother, winking at his brother, and counting the cash at every second, this superb piece of calculating candy-floss has an answer for every situation.

Hugh Cudlipp wrote of the trial in *British Journalism Review*: bizarre and hilarious... Nothing shorter than a paperback could achieve a balanced report of the brilliance of the advocacy and summing-up

Published by Revel Barker Publishing

ISBN: 978-0-9558238-7-9

A CROOKED SIXPENCE

By Murray Sayle

It has taken 47 years for Murray Sayle's classic book about popular newspapers to become readily available.

A CROOKED SIXPENCE tells the tale of a young Australian reporter, fresh off the boat, brimming with excitement, enthusiasm and ambition, securing casual shifts on a mass-circulation Fleet Street Sunday scandal-sheet... and the disillusion that set in very shortly afterwards.

> 'A classic' – Peter Stothard, editor, *Times Literary Supplement*...
>
> 'The best novel about journalism – ever' – Phillip Knightley...
>
> 'Effectively a documentary, lightly disguised as a novel' – Neville Stack...
>
> 'Wonderful – the best book about British popular journalism. Every journalist should read it' – Roy Greenslade...
>
> And 'the best novel never published' – Anthony Delano.

In fact the book was published in London and New York, in 1961. It became an instant hit, and sold to Hollywood for a movie, but it lasted in print only for a number of days.

This was because a near-penniless London aristocrat believed that he was identifiable in the story and wanted to sue.

Incredibly, the would-be litigant was actually a friend of Sayle's; he had no real beef but thought that, since he'd heard that all publishers had libel insurance, he could collect a load of cash without anybody being seriously harmed.

But his get-rich-quick plan backfired because instead of paying up, or bothering their insurers, the publishers simply recalled the book and pulped it. And the Hollywood project was abandoned.

The book had lain dormant, then, until being revived in this edition.

Published by Revel Barker Publishing

ISBN: 978-0-9558238-4-8

SLIP-UP:

How Fleet Street found Ronnie Biggs and Scotland Yard Lost Him

The story behind the scoop

By Anthony Delano

Perhaps the best analysis of Fleet Street at work ever written. – Keith Waterhouse

No journalist can afford to miss this cautionary tale... the story of the in-fighting and downfall of all concerned has one rolling in the aisles. Mr Delano's eye is astute, his ear a credit to his profession at any level; and his wit is accompanied by the ability to write clear English. – *The Times*

Marvellously funny and told with ease and wit... The best stories are sometimes the ones behind the news. There never was a more hilarious tale. – *Daily Mirror*

Anthony Delano, a reporter of much experience, has written the most useful, intellectually coherent and – yes – serious action-study of the British Press that anyone has given us for years... and hysterically funny... A beautifully articulated case-study of the Code of the Street in action. –*New Statesman*

Delano mercilessly exposes the savage Fleet Street competition that underlay the Biggs scoop, and the tale is pacey, absorbing, humorous. – *New Society*

Has an authentic ring. For anyone interested in the inner workings of a popular newspaper, it is enlightening and amusing. – *Listener*

I'd say it's the funniest book about Fleet Street since Evelyn Waugh's *Scoop*. I stayed up half the night to finish it. It's one of those you-can't-put-it-down books. SLIP-UP includes some devastating portraits of Fleet Street characters. Delano's wicked pen spares no one. – Phillip Knightley, *Press Gazette*

Published by Revel Barker Publishing

ISBN: 978-0-9558238-3-1

LADIES OF THE STREET

By Liz Hodgkinson

It is now more than 100 years since the first woman became editor of a national newspaper.

She lasted in the job only a few weeks... before being replaced by a man.

Since then, scores of determined and ambitious women journalists have stormed the newspaper offices of Fleet Street, gradually beating down all the barriers that tried to keep them firmly out.

Who were these extraordinary pioneering women? Their stories are all here, from the superstars such as Marje Proops, Claire Rayner, Jean Rook, Anne Robinson, Katharine Whitehorn, Jilly Cooper, Felicity Green, Nancy Banks Smith, Doreen Spooner, Julia Langdon, Sheila Black and Mary Stott, to the supporting cast who largely toiled without any recognition.

Many of these women blasted their way into jobs previously reserved exclusively for men and they dared to write about things that had never been written about before in the public prints, for a large and grateful readership.

Here is the story of Fleet Street in its bold, brash, powerful, influential – and often alcohol-soaked – heyday, and of the women who, by their courage, persistence and sheer talent, feminised and humanised national newspaper journalism.

An entertaining historical overview – Roy Greenslade, *Media Guardian*

Published by Revel Barker Publishing

ISBN: 978-0-9558238-5-5

Lightning Source UK Ltd.
Milton Keynes UK
16 October 2009

145054UK00001B/69/P